WITHDRAWN
UTSA LIBRARIES

PEACE NOW
PEACE FOR THE FUTURE

Selected
Speeches and Writings
Second Edition

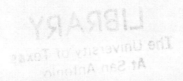

Related titles of interest

BREZHNEV: Selected Speeches and Writings

LEBEDEV: Great October and Today's World

PONOMAREV: Selected Speeches and Writings

PONOMAREV: Marxism-Leninism in Today's World

SUSLOV: Selected Speeches and Writings

LIBRARY
The University of Texas
At San Antonio

A. A. Gromyko

PEACE NOW
PEACE FOR THE FUTURE

Selected
Speeches and Writings

Second Edition

by

A. A. GROMYKO

Translated by

Y. S. Shirokov

PERGAMON PRESS

OXFORD · NEW YORK · TORONTO · SYDNEY · PARIS · FRANKFURT

U.K.	Pergamon Press Ltd., Headington Hill Hall, Oxford OX3 0BW, England
U.S.A.	Pergamon Press Inc., Maxwell House, Fairview Park, Elmsford, New York 10523, U.S.A.
CANADA	Pergamon Press Canada Ltd., Suite 104, 150 Consumers Rd., Willowdale, Ontario M2J 1P9, Canada
AUSTRALIA	Pergamon Press (Aust.) Pty. Ltd., P.O. Box 544, Potts Point, N.S.W. 2011, Australia
FRANCE	Pergamon Press SARL, 24 rue des Ecoles, 75240 Paris, Cedex 05, France
FEDERAL REPUBLIC OF GERMANY	Pergamon Press GmbH, Hammerweg 6, D-242 Kronberg-Taunus, Federal Republic of Germany

Selection, management and translation copyright
© 1984 VAAP, Moscow

All Rights Reserved. No part of this publication may be reproduced, stored in a retrieval system or transmitted in any form or by any means: electronic, electrostatic, magnetic tape, mechanical, photocopying, recording or otherwise, without permission in writing from the copyright holders.

First edition 1979
Second edition 1984

Library of Congress Cataloging in Publication Data
Gromyko, Andrei Andreevich, 1909–
Peace now, peace for the future.
Rev. ed. of: Only for peace. 1979.
Includes index.
1. Soviet Union   Foreign relations—1975–
—Addresses, essays, lectures. 2. Peace—Addresses, essays, lectures. 3. Arms race—Addresses, essays, lectures. 4. World politics—1975–1985—Addresses, essays, lectures.
I. Gromyko, Andrei Andreevich, 1909–   . Only for peace. II. Title.
DK275.G76A5 1984   327.47   84-2806
British Library Cataloguing in Publication Data
Gromyko, A. A.
Peace now, peace for the future.—2nd ed.
1. Soviet Union—Foreign relations—1975–
I. Title   II. Gromyko, A. A. Only for peace
327.47   Dk274
ISBN 0-08-0313213

Typeset by A.U.P. Typesetters (Glasgow) Ltd., Scotland
Printed in Great Britain by A. Wheaton & Co. Ltd., Exeter

Contents

AUTOBIOGRAPHICAL INTRODUCTION

In my view it is no easy task to write an introduction, especially for a book that is to be published in a foreign country. Tradition demands at least some autobiographical data. But this is, of course, not the main thing. The main purpose of any book about the milestones in the diplomatic work and views of any political personality is to bring into focus the basic international problems confronting mankind and affecting the destinies of the world, to show the difficulties involved in surmounting various barriers to the consolidation of international security, and to expose the broad possibilities that do in fact exist for transcending these barriers.

In other words, when the story is about a political personality, it must necessarily touch upon the main political events with which he has been associated. In my case they are international developments in which I have been and still am a participant. I feel that this is mirrored best in my articles and speeches over a period of over four decades, beginning with the Second World War, when the Soviet people crushed Nazism, and ending with the present day, when the CPSU and the Soviet Government are, in fulfilment of the will of the Soviet people, firmly pursuing a policy of *détente* and peace. Some of these speeches and articles, appearing in the last six years, are preserved in this volume.

I should like to emphasize that in this difficult job I am only one of many Soviet statesmen carrying out the will of the Soviet people, the will of the Leninist Communist Party. It is this in particular which explains the simple fact that Soviet foreign policy is not so strongly susceptible to subjective factors, as is so frequently the case with the policy of some major powers belonging to the other social system. Indeed, dishonesty and sudden shifts in foreign policy are alien to us. Our policy is consistent and peaceful, and safeguards the interests of

1

the Soviet people and of our allies and friends. It is a Leninist foreign policy, a policy of the people. In this lies its strength and the reason for the manifest impotence of those who oppose it, of those who often go so far as to calumniate it.

The 1960s and 1970s brought Soviet foreign policy particularly striking successes. Peace on earth was made more secure, socialism's strength grew immeasurably, and the proponents of cold war suffered telling setbacks. Nonetheless, the efforts to undermine *détente* continue to this day. In many cases they are dressed up with propagandistic fireworks. But these fireworks cannot be an alternative to foreign policy.

All the anti-Soviet propaganda campaigns of the past have sunk into oblivion, and the same fate will overcome all who are today following that inglorious path. It is a labour of Sisyphus to fight peaceful coexistence and *détente*, to endeavour to impose upon other nations one's views and sometimes even way of life, to teach them how to conduct their affairs. The experience of history shows the futility of this approach to international affairs. If we look at it closely, the anti-Sovietism of some foreign politicians and their yesmen, evident at the close of the 1970s and beginning of the 1980s, has many points of similarity with the propaganda that emanated from the German Third Reich of the 1930s and 1940s. It is, therefore, heading for the same fate—namely, the scrap-heap of history. Some readers may perhaps find my words much too harsh, but, frankly, I can find no others for those who are trying to destroy the structure of peace and plunge nations into the abyss of a thermonuclear war.

Led by the CPSU, the Soviet people clearly see this danger. But we also know our influence and potentialities. That explains why the Soviet leadership is conducting its international affairs so calmly and confidently, counterposing political myopia with competence, composure, and purpose in defence of *détente* in the world. An especially hard worker for peace is the leader of the Soviet Communists and head of the Soviet state, Leonid Brezhnev. He often repeats, quite justifiably, the wise dictum that one cannot take peace for granted, as something that goes without saying, but that one must constantly fight for it. This is borne out by my own experience of international politics, an experience that covers a period of nearly forty-five years.

Briefly, about myself. I was born in 1909 into the family of a semi-

2

peasant, semi-worker. This population category existed in pre-revolutionary Russia. It consisted of people who had neither sufficient land to feed themselves and their families, nor steady employment in industry. In short, ours was a poor man's household. There were days when there was not even enough bread in the family. On top of that, my father's 'allotment' of land was infertile. When I was still a juvenile, from the age of 14, I joined him in looking for work on the side—in industry or in cutting timber.

The region of Gomel, where I was born, is situated in the south-western part of the East European plain, approximately halfway between Moscow and Kiev. It has always been richly forested, but there is also no lack of swamps alternating with stretches of sand. The winters are usually relatively mild, and the summers are quite warm. The people there are always kind and responsive, but not to those who come with sword in hand. During the Great Patriotic War, when the USSR was attacked by the fascists, all of Soviet Byelorussia, the young and the old, fought them with supreme valour. But the Nazis brought great, very great grief and sorrow to that land and its people. One in four perished.

I spent my childhood in the environs of Gomel. The town of Gomel is first mentioned in ancient chronicles of the mid-twelfth century. In the fourteenth century it was part of the Grand Principality of Lithuania; in the sixteenth century it was seized by Poland; in 1772 it was incorporated into Russia. The Gomel of my childhood remains in my mind as a large railway junction with a small amount of industry, the largest enterprise being the big Vesuvius Match Factory. Reduced to ruin during the war, the town has not only been restored but turned into one of the industrial and cultural centres of Byelorussia. In 1970 Gomel was decorated with the Order of the Red Banner of Labour.

In 1931 I married Lydia Dmitrievna Grinevich, daughter of a Byelorussian peasant. We have two children, Anatoly and Emilia. Today Anatoly is a professor and doctor of historical sciences, and heads the African Institute of the USSR Academy of Sciences. My daughter is a candidate of historical sciences, equivalent to an English Ph.D. My wife and I are pleased with our children. Moreover, we have three grandsons, Igor, Andrei, Alexei, and granddaughter Lidia. My two brothers died in the war.

In 1930 I joined the All-Union Communist Party (Bolsheviks), as the Communist Party of the Soviet Union was called at that time.

I must admit that as long as I can remember I had an irrepressible passion for study. My parents did all they could to enable me to study regularly. Usually I only had to stop in the summer, when I had to go to work in order to help the family. I finished a rural elementary school, then a seven-year school, a technical college, then an institute and a post-graduate course. The institute where I did my post-graduate work was headed by Professor Borisevich, who gave all of us his closest attention.

An event occurred during this period which unquestionably determined my further career. During my second post-graduate year a group of six, including myself, was transferred from Minsk to Moscow. I completed my post-graduate studies in Moscow with the relevant academic degree in economics. In 1936, soon after I had defended my dissertation, I joined the Institute of Economics of the USSR Academy of Sciences as a senior scientific associate. Academician G. M. Savelyev was director of the institute at the time.

I felt that I had started seriously on a long-term scientific career. I doubled as a lecturer at Moscow's Municipal Construction Engineering Institute. Incidentally, one of my students was Victor Vasilyevich Grishin, who is today a member of the Politburo of the CPSU Central Committee. Sometimes we recall the days when students were often almost the same age as their lecturers, a circumstance that made me, at any rate, feel awkward on occasions.

With the passing of the years the Soviet Union developed and gained strength. The people were building socialism, turning the Russia of the tsars, a downtrodden country on the outskirts of capitalism, into a flourishing state of workers, peasants, and a working intelligentsia. However, already then, at the close of the 1930s, there was an unmistakable smell of gunpowder in the air. All the indications were that the stern test of war was closing in on the Soviet Union. Of course, nobody wanted to believe it, but it was true nonetheless. All of us felt it in our hearts.

At the close of 1938 I was appointed Academic Secretary at the Institute of Economics. I decided to enrol in a flying school without discontinuing my work. In those days this was the dream of many.

But here disappointment awaited me—I had come too late. I was told that 25 was the age limit for enrolment.

I was sorely disappointed; I was so eager to fly. But, I repeat, there were many who wanted to be fliers. In the Soviet Union, as in other countries, there was in those years a veritable cult of aviation, that rapidly advancing area of human endeavour. It was the time when aircraft were being used for the development of the Arctic. There was nothing I could do but resign myself and say: 'Goodbye, flying, evidently you weren't for me.'

I had only just begun to get into the routine of scientific work when unexpectedly I was summoned by Vladimir Komarov, President of the USSR Academy of Sciences, and offered the post of Academic Secretary of the Academy's Far Eastern Division. I did not turn the offer down out of hand, but felt very strongly that this important scientific and organizational job required a scientist with much more experience than I had—in fact, it required an eminent scholar. I believe Komarov agreed with my view and appreciated why I was reluctant to take the job. However, I was not destined to work much longer at the Institute of Economics. True, later, when I was Ambassador in Washington, I began, and then during my tenure as Ambassador in London, I completed and published the book *Export of US Capital* (under the pen-name of G. Andreyev), for which the Academic Council of Moscow State University conferred upon me the academic degree of Doctor of Economic Sciences. Still later, under the same pen-name, I published my second book *US Dollar Expansion*. My third book *External Expansion of Capital* was published at the end of 1982, and continues on the same theme.

In early 1939 I was suddenly notified that I was to present myself to a commission set up by the CPSU Central Committee to select new, trained personnel for foreign policy and diplomatic work. The commission sat in the Foreign Ministry's old building on Kuznetsky Most. When, at the appointed time, I reported to the commission I recognized among its members Vyacheslav Molotov and other leading Party and government officials. I was informed that I was being considered for a foreign policy post, most likely in the diplomatic service. With me on that day were three other candidates.

Today it is, of course, hard to say what exactly motivated the commission when they chose me. I think what decided them was that ever since my early days in the Komsomol I was involved in political education, delivering lectures and reports, and conducting seminars and study groups at offices and factories: in short, I was an activist. Also in my favour was, I believe, the fact that as a post-graduate student I had mastered English, although I was far from being perfect. When I was asked what I had read in English, I named some books, including *Rich Land, Poor Land* by the American economist Stuart Chase. Within a few days I was again summoned to the CPSU Central Committee and informed that I would be transferred to diplomatic work.

Thus, in the spring of 1939 I was appointed head of the American Department of the People's Commissariat for Foreign Affairs. My tenure in that office was short, about six months. I was soon immersed in diplomatic work, meeting officials of the US Embassy. Laurence A. Steinhardt was the US Ambassador at the time, and I must say he left no perceptible trace in Soviet–US relations. In fact, I often wondered why President Roosevelt, with his breadth of views, including those on Soviet–US relations, had chosen the man. Life, however, corrects decisions of this kind. Steinhardt did not stay long in Moscow, apparently to the satisfaction of both sides.

One day I received a summons from Stalin. Until then I had only seen him at a distance, in Red Square, where he took the salute at parades or waved back to anniversary processions. Of course, within minutes of receiving the summons I was in the waiting room of Stalin's office in the Kremlin. I introduced myself to his assistant and secretary Poskrebyshev. He reported my arrival. I soon found myself in Stalin's office. He was sitting not at his desk but at the head of the long table usually used at meetings of the Politburo. With him was Molotov, who was People's Commissar for Foreign Affairs at the time and with whom I had often discussed questions concerning relations with the USA.

I was courteously greeted by Stalin and Molotov. Stalin spoke first. He said that they proposed to post me to the Soviet Embassy in the USA as the number 2, as counsellor. Frankly, this took me somewhat by surprise, although I had already come to the belief that, like soldiers, diplomats had to be prepared for unexpected transfers.

Sparing of words, as was his custom, Stalin named the areas of priority in Soviet–US relations. He noted that the USSR could maintain good relations with a major power like the USA, especially in view of the mounting fascist menace in Europe. German fascism, he said, was marching towards war, and this was obvious to any observant person. Molotov put in a few remarks in support of what Stalin was saying. From what was said I realized that I was not being sent to the USA for a month or a year, particularly as the Soviet Ambassador in the USA, Umansky, who evidently did not impress Stalin or Molotov very much, had been recalled to Moscow. Although Umansky returned to the USA it was felt that his work there was coming to an end. Indeed, he did not stay long. He was replaced by Maxim Litvinov, who likewise held the post of Ambassador for a short time. After Nazi Germany had attacked the USSR it was believed that Roosevelt would perhaps like to see as Soviet Ambassador to the USA a diplomat who had won a name for himself in the League of Nations and was associated with the League. But developments made it plain that Stalin, and Molotov for that matter, regarded this as a purely temporary step.

Thus the author of this book soon replaced Litvinov as Ambassador in the USA.

Incidentally, Stalin asked me how well I knew English. I replied that I was struggling with it and seemed to be gradually mastering it, although the process was very difficult, especially when there was little or no opportunity to speak the language. Here Stalin gave a piece of advice that was both puzzling and enlivening. It helped me to shed some of my constraint. Stalin said: 'I don't see why you shouldn't go to American churches and cathedrals and listen to the sermons from time to time. They usually speak good English. And their diction is excellent. You know, when Russian revolutionaries lived abroad they used this method to improve their knowledge of a foreign language.' I remember, I was confused at first that Stalin, an atheist, should suddenly recommend that I, also an atheist, should go to foreign churches. I almost blurted out: 'Did you, Comrade Stalin, use this method?' But I resisted the temptation to put that question, for I knew that Stalin spoke no foreign language, and my question would obviously have not been quite proper. I held my tongue, so to speak. Although I am sure Stalin would have made a jest of it, as I often saw him do in later years in similar circumstances.

This was perhaps the only instance of a Soviet Ambassador not carrying out Stalin's instructions. I can just imagine the impression my visits to American churches would have made on hustling reporters. Unquestionably, they would have been puzzled, nonplussed, lost in conjecture over the reason why the atheist Soviet Ambassador was regularly visiting American churches and cathedrals and whether there was some threat to the USA in this.

In the autumn of 1939 my family and I were aboard the Italian luxury liner *Rex* en route to the USA. We had had to change trains several times on the way from Moscow to Genoa.

We had a curious experience in the Atlantic on 7 November when the ship's master invited Ambassador Umansky and me to his cabin out of considerations of etiquette. Treating us in private to excellent Italian wine, he proposed the toast: 'To the Great October Revolution in Russia, to Lenin.' We seconded him enthusiastically, of course. It must be remembered that fascism ruled Italy in those years. Umansky and I later recalled that toast, saying that had the Duce learned of it our captain would most certainly have been in trouble. But there obviously were decent Italians among the captains of the Italian merchant marine, who held fascism and the fascist order in contempt.

A few days after encountering our first-ever real storm in the Atlantic we arrived in Washington, where I soon made the necessary contacts with officials of the US government, mainly of the State Department, and later with President Franklin D. Roosevelt. I saw him for the first time at the opening of the National Art Gallery in Washington towards the end of 1939.

The first period of my stay in the USA bore the imprint of the military clash between the USSR and Finland. The nation's press was mostly hostile to the USSR. In those days very few Americans gave much thought to fascism's intention in the south and north of Europe. Subsequently an ever-growing number of them began to see the actual objectives of the fascist military plans. The mood changed, of course, when Nazi Germany attacked the Soviet Union and the USA's own existence was in peril.

However, the complexity of international processes made itself felt. Even the tragedy of Pearl Harbor, inflicted by the perfidy of Germany's accomplice, militarist Japan, failed to open the eyes of all Americans to the designs of German fascism. Moreover, even after the Nazis attacked the Soviet Union, there were American politicians who wanted to see the USSR and Germany bleed each other and thereby, in their view, increase the chances of the USA having the last say in the war. It was during the first days of the war that Harry S. Truman, who was later to be the US President, declared that the Germans and Russians should be allowed to bleed each other as much as possible. It is not surprising that on this man's orders atomic bombs were needlessly dropped on the Japanese.

A new phase commenced. The Soviet people rose to a man to fight for their independence and freedom. The Soviet Union and its allies, one of whom was the USA, began a life-and-death struggle against mankind's most sinister enemy—Nazi Germany and its accomplices.

Together with Britain, the USA became our ally. In some European countries a Resistance movement sprang up that was to play a major part in the great anti-fascist struggle.

In a short introduction it is not possible to write in detail of wartime events. I must, however, note that from 1943 onwards I was a direct participant in the political events that developed on the crest of the wave of the heroic military struggle waged by the Soviet Union and its allies against fascism.

I took part in the Crimea (Yalta) Conference in early 1945, and some of the intermediate Allied conferences, for instance, in Atlantic City.

The Potsdam Conference was held in May 1945. It passed historic decisions on the denazification, demilitarization, and reintroduction of democracy in Germany. At both the Yalta and Potsdam Conferences, I was a member of the Soviet delegation in my capacity as Soviet Ambassador to the USA.

Towards the end of the war, after Molotov's departure, I led the Soviet delegation at the San Francisco Conference that drew up the UN Charter, and prior to that I led the Soviet delegation at Dumbarton Oaks.

Much water has flowed under the bridge since then. The world has changed perceptibly for the better. But this change has not, of course, taken place by itself. It is a result of the persevering efforts of the anti-fascist and progressive forces to end the terrible world war and then the cold war. There passed before my eyes, to speak only of American Presidents, Franklin Roosevelt, Harry Truman, Dwight Eisenhower,

John Kennedy, Lyndon Johnson, Richard Nixon, Gerald Ford, and Jimmy Carter and now the incumbent President is Ronald Reagan. I am no longer surprised when American political personalities ask me what one or another President thought about this or that international issue. You see, they have never met them.

My meetings with the great American Franklin Roosevelt have left me with a cherished memory. He was a wise statesman and had a wide range of interests. I remember when I handed him my credentials he said with his usual directness: 'Give me your speech, and here's mine; both will be in the newspapers tomorrow. We'll spend our time more profitably exploring the possibilities for a summer meeting between the three powers: the USA, the USSR, and Great Britain.'

The correspondence between Stalin and Roosevelt passed through the office of the Soviet Ambassador in Washington. These documents have now been published and become the property of the world.

As had been agreed, General Watson, the President's military aide, usually came to the Soviet Embassy in Washington, on 16th Street, whenever letters were received from Stalin to Roosevelt or from Roosevelt to Stalin. Everything was done in a rush. There were no matters of inconsequence in those days. I particularly remember my discussion with Roosevelt on some matters that were considered later at Yalta.

In 1945, soon after Yalta, the world learned of President Roosevelt's untimely death. In Yalta, when Roosevelt caught a cold and fell ill, the conference was postponed for one day, and Stalin, Molotov, and I called on the American President. He was resting in the former bed-chamber of the Tsaritsa in the Livadia Palace. On our way back, as the three of us descended the stairs, Stalin said: 'Is this man any worse than the rest of us, why has nature been harsh with him?' He obviously had in mind not the cold but the President's disabling malady—polio accompanied by the paralysis of both his legs. Frankly, Stalin liked Roosevelt.

Soon Truman came to power in the USA. As a statesman he was only a pale reflection, like the moon, of his predecessor. Grave tensions began to creep into Soviet–US relations.

In the post-war situation the main thing was to enforce the Potsdam Agreements. Although the agreements themselves were profound and far-reaching, the true face of the new American foreign policy was soon seen when the time came to translate them into reality. By working towards the formation of the Bipartite Zone, the Tripartite Zone, and then a separate West German state, Washington, London, and Paris demonstrated that they had jettisoned the idea of creating a single, genuinely democratic, demilitarized Germany. Subsequent Soviet proposals on this issue were invariably turned down.

I had many meetings also with British statesmen, including Winston Churchill, Clement Attlee, Ernest Bevin, Harold Macmillan, Anthony Eden, Hugh Gaitskell, Selwyn Lloyd, Philip J. Noel-Baker, R. A. Butler, Dugald Stewart, David Owen, Lord Carrington, Francis Pym, and Geoffrey Howe. Of course later, in 1952, I handed my credentials to Queen Elizabeth II. I had also met her father, King George VI.

I met the King for the first time in St. James's Palace at a dinner for heads of delegations at the First UN General Assembly. Getting up from the table on which were laid massive and, evidently, unique gold plate, all the guests went to a fairly spacious drawing room. On the way I found myself walking beside the King. He suggested a private word in, to my amazement, the centre of the drawing room. The guests stood mostly along the walls.

The King spoke warmly, saying that the relations that had taken shape between the Soviet Union and Great Britain during the anti-Nazi struggle should under no circumstances be weakened. Naturally, I was wholeheartedly in agreement and said so. Our conversation attracted attention but clearly caused no surprise, for the two countries had been allies in the war. I shall not conceal the fact that this conversation impressed me profoundly. Needless to say, upon returning to the Embassy I shared my impressions with the other Soviet delegates.

My second meeting with King George VI and Queen Elizabeth, the present Queen Mother, occurred at a reception for delegations to the UN session. They were very gracious to the Soviet representatives, including the representatives of the Ukraine and Byelorussia. Standing beside the King and Queen as they received the guests were the present Queen Elizabeth II and her sister Margaret. We had a short but extremely friendly conversation.

I would like to say frankly that even then Princess Elizabeth greatly impressed me with the considered nature of her views. I remember several of her remarks, which though brief were interesting and well thought out.

I had a similar impression of the Queen from my conversation with her at the presentation of my Letter of Credence in 1952. This conversation took place before the Coronation. Apart from the quality mentioned above, what struck me at the meeting with the Crown Princess was the fact that she talked in broader concepts on matters concerning the relations between the Soviet Union and Great Britain as well as world politics in general.

I remember vividly the extraordinarily long and disproportionately narrow reception hall at Buckingham Palace. We, the Soviet representatives, looked over the magnificent decoration in the hall and noted that if it were a few metres wider and higher it would perhaps give nothing away to St. George's Hall in Moscow's Kremlin. Its colour scheme is sombreish in the Anglo-Saxon style.

Naturally, I have vivid memories of my meetings with the late Winston Churchill. During the war I usually met the British Prime Minister at important Allied conferences, at which his Soviet negotiating partner was Joseph Stalin. In those days all political matters decided during negotiations came from the common table at which Stalin, Roosevelt, and Churchill sat. I contributed to the talks in my capacity as a member of the USSR delegation and as Soviet Ambassador in Washington.

When, in the discharge of my duties as Ambassador in Great Britain, I met the British Prime Minister after the war he invariably began our conversations with reminiscences of war-time summits, and also of the Potsdam summit held immediately after the end of the war. This summit began while Churchill was still Prime Minister, but witnessed his replacement in that capacity by Clement Attlee, leader of the Labour Party. Correspondingly, Anthony Eden was replaced as Foreign Secretary by Ernest Bevin.

I remember Churchill's confidence as he waited for the outcome of the elections. But life decreed otherwise. I repeat, Churchill later reminisced not about this dramatic episode of his life but about his meetings with the leaders of the other two war-time Allied powers. If I did not put in a word when he got off on the subject he would talk about it endlessly, and it was obvious that he derived pleasure from his reminiscences and that my presence spurred them on.

The same thing happened when I paid my last call on Churchill before leaving for Moscow to take up my duties as First Deputy Minister of Foreign Affairs.

After we had dealt with political matters, Churchill poured some whisky for me, while he himself drank Russian vodka. Then he asked me whether I liked London. I replied that I did, especially now, with the city decorated for the coronation of Queen Elizabeth II. I said that Piccadilly, which was, to all appearances, on the route of the Queen's coronation procession, looked particularly attractive. Churchill smiled with the twinkle in his eye that he reserved for such occasions and said: 'Indeed, Piccadilly and the city itself look beautiful for the forthcoming event. We British feel that it is better to go to a considerable expense once in the lifetime of our monarchs than every four years as the Americans do when they elect their presidents.' Frankly, this bit of typically Churchillian wit impressed me, and I said so, adding that I had personally observed American-style inaugurations during my stay in the USA. The talk ended on a friendly note and Churchill escorted me to the door of 10 Downing Street, where photographers were waiting to photograph my last meeting with him.

The people I have mentioned were of different political calibre, but I would say that what they had in common was the gradual realization that the 'crusade' against the Soviet Union had come to grief and that the cold war was prejudicing the interests of the British themselves. The vast majority of ranking Western statesmen came round to this sober conclusion in the 1960s and the 1970s. However, many irresponsible individuals still cling to cold war positions and now and then emit a shrill hawkish screech. But the future has never belonged and never will belong to them. The people want neither a cold nor a cool war. This is a political axiom and it cannot be refuted by those who like to 'play soldiers' in order to bury *détente*. Soviet people are firmly convinced of this.

The principles of Soviet foreign policy, formulated during the very first days of the Soviet state's existence when Lenin proclaimed the victory of the Great October Socialist Revolution, comprise the basis of this book.

The central idea in this collection of articles, speeches, and statements made in the USSR and abroad is that nations should live in peace and that the differences between them should not be settled by crossing swords and bloodshed. This is further confirmation of the self-evident truth that what Lenin, architect of the Decree on Peace, said at the dawn of Soviet power has become the immutable foundation of the day-to-day work of the Soviet Government.

The statements, articles, and speeches published in this book deal with a wide spectrum of problems—from questions of war and peace and the prevention of another world-wide conflagration to workaday matters concerning economic, political, and cultural relations between nations. Whatever the rostrum used by a representative of the USSR, in this case the Minister of Foreign Affairs, the world hears the Soviet Union passionately calling for peace, *détente*, and neighbourly relations. Moreover, it hears condemnation of those national leaders whose policies and actions deliberately or involuntarily undermine the foundations of peace and come into conflict with the principles and pledges that were worked out and proclaimed during and directly after the Second World War with the aim of upholding peace and preventing further aggression.

Of course, the opinion of some readers of this book may differ in some details from the standpoint of the author—in the final analysis I state the principles underlying the policy of the Union of Soviet Socialist Republics. But I profoundly believe that given an unbiased, honest approach to international affairs no person will fail to agree that there is no reasonable alternative to the course towards peaceful coexistence of countries with different social systems, to the course towards the extension of *détente*, to the course towards ever more diversified and extensive relations between nations.

Naturally, among the problems analysed by the author, considerable attention is given to the problem of disarmament, of ending the arms race, of the ways and means of delivering nations from the burden of armaments, and, as a first step, of actually lightening that burden. Is there any intelligent person in the world who would deny that this is one of the paramount problems of international life, one that must be resolved? The Soviet Union will continue to make every effort to resolve it. This was urged by Lenin, and it is urged today by Leonid Brezhnev, who enjoys enormous prestige in the world and expresses the will of the entire Soviet people.

The author of these lines would be gratified if the reader reflects over this and other international problems. Today, more than ever before, nobody can afford to ignore them.

The will and thoughts of the Soviet people, and their dedicated work to carry out the internal tasks confronting them, are invariably aimed at contributing to the maintenance of lasting peace. The Soviet Union is doing everything in its power to make peace really durable. It is, as it has always been, willing to co-operate with any nation prepared to follow in the same path. The Communist Party of the Soviet Union, its Central Committee and Politburo headed by General Secretary Yuri V. Andropov are firmly determined to keep to that path.

In conclusion, I should like to return once more to what I began with. It has so happened, and I am happy and proud of it, that in effect my entire independent life has been devoted to implementing the Leninist principles of the foreign policy of the world's first socialist state. In this field I have been working in one post or another for nearly forty-five years.

It would be proper to ask me, and indeed I ask myself, the question: am I satisfied with what I have accomplished?

In my position I could answer emphatically in the affirmative only if the sun of peace were shining unclouded over our planet, and memories of wars, of all types of armaments, of oppression of nations by nations were, to quote Pushkin, 'buried in the remote past'.

Regrettably, this is still not the case. Lasting peace in the world cannot be achieved by the efforts of only one side, however titanic these efforts may be.

Nevertheless, to the above question I can in the main reply in the affirmative because what has been achieved today inspires optimism for the future. The world has indeed become better than it was some decades ago.

One cannot help deriving profound satisfaction from the fact of having made one's modest contribution to accelerating this movement towards peace, towards justice.

People say that to be a pessimist is simple and safe. I have been and remain an optimist. My optimism is based on my faith in human intelligence, which throughout the centuries has illumined the road to a happier, more just and radiant life for all people.

During the special UN session on disarmament in 1978 I had a meeting in Washington with President Carter and other American foreign policy makers. After the meeting, correspondents, as is the custom in the USA, surrounded me on the lawn in front of the White House. The questions were mostly about a second strategic arms limitation agreement. I told them that the vast majority of the issues involved, particularly the substantive problems, had been settled, and that the range of outstanding problems was gradually narrowing. I added, of course, that there were questions on which no final agreement had been reached, that to speed up settlement of these questions we needed further meetings and, above all, positive motivation not only on our part but also on the part of the American side in the negotiations. In our view the efforts of the American side to reach agreement were feeble and did not give the proper rebuff to the opponents of agreement.

When I saw the faint and quite understandable disappointment on the faces of some of the journalists, I said: this agreement must evidently be built as houses are built—brick by brick.

This idea, which I expressed at the time, is still with me today when I think of the world as a whole, and as I end the Introduction to this book for the English-speaking reader.

To build, brick by brick, the edifice of a lasting peace for my people and all other peoples of the earth, and only world peace can be truly lasting—this has been the aim of my whole life, and one to which I intend devoting the years to come.

Practical Ways of Ending the Arms Race

Speech at a Special Session of the UN General Assembly Devoted to Disarmament, 26 May 1978

Mr. President,

Esteemed delegates,

No problem in international politics today is more important and urgent than one that has brought together in this hall representatives of 149 states of the world. To end the arms race and achieve real disarmament is the challenge of the entire course of world developments. The problem of disarmament is the focus of attention of the United Nations, and rightly so. Indeed, compliance with the main provision of the United Nations Charter—"to save succeeding generations from the scourge of war"—means, above all, especially in the present circumstances, to seek to curb the arms race. The very convening of this special session of the United Nations General Assembly attests to this.

Consistently following its fundamental line on disarmament issues, the Soviet Union has come to the current session with a firm intention to contribute to its success. The session will live up to the expectations of all peace-loving peoples and states, if it helps to bring closer an end to the arms race and disarmament. It is our firm conviction that the core of the whole problem lies in moving from good intentions and noncommittal recommendations, vague in practical terms, even if useful, to concrete— and I stress "concrete"—steps along this main avenue of world politics to lasting peace.

As far back as half a century ago, the founder of the Soviet state, V. I. Lenin, referring to the verbose pacifist phraseology of certain countries, which were much less prepared to take effective action to ensure peace, said that it would be better on this and similar issues to hear as few

17

general statements, solemn promises and high-flown phrases as possible, and to see as many as possible decisions and measures that would be truly simple and clear and would really lead to peace, not to mention the complete elimination of the danger of war.

War preparations in the world have grown to too dangerous proportions for the alarm not to be sounded. The arsenals of states already contain a destructive potential large enough to threaten, if activated, the very existence of man on earth. Is that not enough? Yet that potential continues to grow.

During the celebration of the sixtieth anniversary of the Great October Socialist Revolution, Leonid Brezhnev, described the essence of the current world situation as follows:

"International relations are now at a cross-roads, as it were, which could lead either to a growth of trust and cooperation or to a growth of mutual fears, suspicion and stockpiles of arms; a cross-roads leading ultimately either to lasting peace or, at best, to balancing on the brink of war. *Détente* offers the opportunity of choosing the road of peace. To miss that opportunity would be a crime. The most important and pressing task now is to halt the arms race which has engulfed the world."

We must realize the stark truth: if we miss this chance now, then, in certain highly important areas we could reach a point beyond which any possibility of concluding appropriate agreements would be altogether non-existent—and for obvious reasons, since certain types of weapons which are being developed simply do not lend themselves to joint control over their quantity or qualitative characteristics.

Unfortunately, scientific and technological progress which, though it is meant to serve exclusively the good of mankind, is being used in no small measure to create ever newer means of destruction. The pace of their development outstrips by far the progress of international talks on arms limitation. No sooner has an understanding, however limited, been reached on one type of weapon than two or three new types, often even more sophisticated and dangerous, emerge.

And what about the huge material and intellectual resources of mankind spent so unproductively on the manufacture of means of annihilation? Over 1 billion dollars a day is spent on armaments—I stress this—a figure which cannot even be imagined by a normal person. How much faster the peoples would advance along the road of socio-economic development if they were not saddled with the enormous burden of huge military expenditure.

We have witnessed a dramatic aggravation of such problems of global dimension as those of providing people with food, medical assistance and housing and supplying industry with raw materials and energy. The environment of this planet may be threatened, and in a very real way. To postpone the solution of such problems would only exacerbate the situation. Yet the funds needed for this are still being devoured by the Moloch of armaments.

From any viewpoint mankind is facing an immediate choice between halting and subsequently reversing the arms race, ending the madness imposed on the world and thus ensuring lasting peace and the possibility of solving the problems of economic development, and allowing the machine of material preparations for war to continue to gain speed, deprive the peoples—or, to be more precise, rob them—of their national wealth and push the world towards catastrophe.

The peoples' choice is perfectly clear. If we look at the United Nations voting record, which is a sort of mirror image of world politics, even if not always accurate, we see that decisions in favour of peace, *détente* and disarmament are carried by an overwhelming majority of states.

Why then are more and more twists being added to a spiralling arms race? There can be but one answer. The crux of the matter lies in the policy being pursued by certain states, which disregard both the will of the peoples and the decisions of the United Nations, even when they join in taking these decisions.

Coinciding with the work of the special session of the General Assembly of the United Nations on disarmament in New York, another kind of session will be held not far from here, that of the North Atlantic Treaty Organization (NATO) Council. Represented at that session will be a number of States on whose behalf statements are being made here in favour of disarmament. What are the items on the agenda of the NATO session? There is no secret about it; they deal with a further build-up of military preparations as projected into the 1980s. One is prompted to ask what is basic to the policy planning of those states: the continuation of the arms race or the possibility of disarmament?

Thus, we see how some governments display inconsistency in yielding to the pressure of those quarters which have thrown in their lot with military production, amassing fabulous profits from arms manufacture. In order to befuddle people, to whip up the arms race they deliberately create myths or, at worst, keep harping on old stories like that of a "Soviet military threat".

Every unbiased person knows that whenever the Soviet people have had to go to war it was to repel the aggressors, for wars have been imposed on the Soviet Union. The Soviet Union has never unleashed war, and it will never do so.

It has been claimed from this rostrum in a somewhat suggestive manner than the Soviet missiles termed SS-20 in the West are not aimed in one particular direction but can be turned to aim at any part of the world. In a word, that argument is introduced to confuse the issue of invoking the same trumped up "Soviet threat". Is it not time American nuclear and missile weapons can be turned in various directions? Yet first and foremost they can be turned in the easily predictable direction. Also, we may ask, why are they deployed in Europe at all?

Many of those present must have noticed that representatives of some countries generally find it difficult even to pronounce the word "disarmament"; they would rather speak of control. Control over what? Control over armaments; they say it openly, in so many words. But the volume of armaments in the world can be increased to five times the present level even if they are under control. But is that the road to peace? I must remind representatives that this special session has been convened to promote disarmament, and not to whip up the arms race. Therefore, the causes of the continuing arms race are well known to us, and not only to us.

We realize full well how many complications and obstacles there are on the road to disarmament. Nevertheless, our Party, our state, the socialist community are all decisively opposed to any feelings of despair. Peoples, states and responsible governments are capable of changing this situation if they go about it in the right way instead of pursuing a policy designed to deceive the peoples.

No small body of experience has already been accumulated in containing the growth of armaments in a number of areas. Bilateral and multilateral agreements, over 20 in number, have made it possible to close certain channels for the proliferation of weapons of mass destruction and to narrow other channels. Is not the Treaty on the Non-

Proliferation of Nuclear Weapons indicative of that? Therefore, it is possible to continue advancing beyond the ground gained.

Despite all its ups and downs, the current international political climate, of which *détente* has been a dominant feature for several years now is favourable to serious arms limitation efforts. There has been no such precedent in the history of the interrelationships between the two world social systems. Some degree of international trust has been created, though still, of course, insufficient. A powerful impetus to all these processes was given by the recent talks of Leonid Brezhnev with the leaders of the Federal Republic of Germany.

It is essential to make full use of the favourable conditions obtaining at present. Political *détente* should merge with military *détente*, otherwise the positive gains in international relations achieved through the years of hard effort by many peoples and states may well vanish. To admit that there is no reasonable alternative to the policy of *détente*, which is actually the case, means admitting that there is no reasonable alternative to disarmament.

There is yet another factor which favours disarmament. The reality of the present situation is such that approximate equality or parity exists in the military field, sufficient to ensure defence, and that is recognized by both sides. However, the existing balance of military power is somewhere at the level of the Montblanc. As things are going, it may soon reach still greater heights. To halt the build-up of armaments and then to reduce their level without upsetting the established correlation of forces, that is, without prejudicing the security of anyone, is an opportunity which must absolutely not be missed.

On behalf of the Soviet Union, the delegation of the USSR is able to say quite clearly that if other states are prepared to disarm the Soviet Union will not be found amiss. Military superiority is not our goal. There is not a single objective which our country intends to attain by military means. We perceive the security of our state and international peace in general through the prism of curbing the arms race, and of agreements on disarmament, agreements concluded in good faith, accommodating equally the interests of all contracting parties.

We do not claim to have exhaustive answers ready for all the questions arising with respect to disarmament, which is a vast problem, not easy to solve. However, we have our own clear ideas in that respect.

The call for disarmament has been inscribed on the banner of our socialist state since the very moment it was hoisted over the world.

Concrete initiatives in this field have been tried and tested in the course of the long struggle for disarmament waged by the Soviet Union and fraternal socialist states. The limitation of armaments, disarmament measures, are an integral part of the programme of struggle for peace and international cooperation and for the freedom and independence of peoples put forward by the Communist Party of the Soviet Union at its twenty-fourth and twenty-fifth Congresses.

From the high rostrum of the General Assembly of the United Nations in this special session on disarmament our country urges all participants and all the states of the world to agree on a number of immediate steps capable of halting the arms race, and to do so without delay.

What then, is to be done in the first place? We believe that the time has come to raise the question of the complete cessation of a further quantitative and qualitative build-up of arms and armed forces of states with large military potentials.

More specifically, and taking into account the fact that military arsenals consist of various components of armaments, the Soviet Union proposes that the following measures be implemented: cessation of the production of all types of nuclear weapons; cessation of the production and prohibition of all other types of weapons of mass destruction; cessation of the development of new types of conventional armaments of great destructive capability; the renunciation of the expansion of armies and the building-up of conventional armaments of the permanent members of the Security Council and of the countries which have military agreements with them.

Thus, appropriate measures which would radically alter the current most alarming situation and put an end to the frenzy of armaments would cover all the components of existing arms and armed forces. Such measures, if implemented, would not upset the present-day correlation of forces of states. No one stands to lose, while the gains for the cause of peace would be enormous.

Is it a simple thing to agree on such measures? Of course not. The Soviet Union is prepared to discuss all these measures in their totality, and, of course, it is prepared not only to discuss them but also to implement them within a specified limited period of time. To make a start we are even prepared to take up any of these measures. Since the main danger stems from the accelerating nuclear-weapons race specifically, priority could be given to the cessation of the production of nuclear weapons.

From the moment the atomic bomb was developed the Soviet Union proposed that it be banned. At that time our proposal was not accepted. Today it is much more difficult to solve the formidable problem of nuclear arms. Yet, it can be solved. A fatalistic approach to this undoubtedly most complex problem is alien to us.

Seeking to put the matter on a practical plane, the Soviet Union proposes that talks on the cessation of the production of all types of nuclear weapons and the gradual reduction of their stockpiles, up to their complete destruction, should get under way. How do we visualize such talks? Of course, all the nuclear powers must take part in them. Such a complex problem cannot be solved on a selective basis. Evasion by any power would place a heavy burden on its policy. That does not mean that the number of participants would be limited to just five. It would be useful if a certain number of non-nuclear states also joined in the talks.

Precisely how many and who will participate could be agreed on, for instance, within the framework of an appropriate preparatory committee. The same procedure could be followed in working out the agenda for the talks and in determining the specific questions to be discussed and acted upon. No one should nurture any illusions, since the problem is exceedingly complex in purely technical terms as well. But what is much more important is the political aspect. Unless we approach the matter in a practical manner it will not budge an inch.

It goes without saying that the elaboration and implementation of measures to end the production of nuclear weapons and gradually destroy their stockpiles should go hand in hand with and be inseparable from the strengthening of international legal guarantees for the security of states. It is not fortuitous that the General Assembly of the United Nations adopted some time ago the well-known decision on the non-use of force in international relations, along with the permanent prohibition of the use of nuclear weapons. The conclusion, in accordance with United Nations decisions, of a relevant world treaty on the non-use of force in international relations would be a major step forward in that direction.

We suggest that the current special session of the General Assembly should adopt a decision of principle to start negotiations on nuclear disarmament and on the question of the non-use of force. What is more, it should establish a procedure for their preparation and set a date for their beginning. That would reveal in deeds rather than in words, those who firmly intend to do their utmost to relieve mankind from the threat of nuclear was and those who would rather do the opposite.

Another major question which we are emphasizing in the context of slowing down the nuclear arms race is the prevention of the spread of nuclear weapons. The relevant treaty has played and continues to play a very useful role in this respect. However, further efforts are required.

This, like many other international issues, requires unilateral, bilateral and multilateral actions by states. For its part the Soviet Union is undertaking such an action. I believe it would not be an exaggeration to say that it is a significant action.

From the rostrum of the United Nations special session our country declares that the Soviet Union will never use nuclear weapons against those states which renounce the production and acquisition of such weapons and do not have them on their territories.

We are aware of the responsibility which would thus fall on us as a result of such a commitment. But we are convinced that such a step to meet the wishes of non-nuclear states to have stronger security guarantees is in the interests of peace in the broadest sense of the word. We expect that the goodwill evinced by our country in this manner will lead to more active participation by a large number of states in strengthening the non-proliferation régime.

The Soviet Union is prepared to enter into an appropriate bilateral agreement with any non-nuclear state. We call upon the other nuclear powers to follow our example.

Nuclear weapons, should they find their way into the hands of states in conflict with their neighbours, could trigger off an all-out nuclear conflagration. We never fail to draw attention to this danger to world peace. Here, a single mistake would be one too many. Incidentally, this is one of the main reasons why plans to develop nuclear weapons in the Republic of South Africa and in Israel cause such great concern.

Everything must be done to prevent these plans from being carried out.

We must support in every possible way the desire of states to see certain geographical areas free of nuclear weapons. That is precisely the attitude of the Soviet Union.

A few days ago, during the visit to Moscow of President Lopez Portillo of Mexico, our country signed Additional Protocol II of the Treaty for the Prohibition of Nuclear Weapons in Latin America—the Treaty of Tlatelolco.

Honestly speaking, we had some doubts on that score because of some well-known shortcomings and weak points in that Treaty. Nevertheless, we decided to assume the obligation to respect the denuclearized status of the Latin American continent. We proceed from the premise that such an obligation will remain valid only if the other nuclear powers respect the status of that zone and if its participants ensure a truly nuclear-free regime for it.

The Soviet Union will continue through practical action to contribute to the creation of nuclear-free zones in various parts of the world. In other words, here too our aim is the same: to reduce the threat of a nuclear conflict. It is of course important that they be truly nuclear-free zones.

Sometimes we hear it said: "You know, we too favour non-proliferation of nuclear weapons, but could that not harm international cooperation in the field of peaceful uses of atomic energy?" The answer is no; it would not harm it. It is possible, without infringing upon the interests of non-nuclear countries in this field, to preclude at the same time the possibility of someone—let us say in the deserts or jungles of Africa or Latin America—from trying to find some roundabout way of manufacturing nuclear weapons.

The Soviet Union has for many years now been helping a number of countries to have their natural uranium enriched at Soviet facilities. We have always been engaged in other forms of co-operation in this field. And this does not lead to a greater nuclear threat.

There is yet another way of preventing nuclear weapons from proliferating all over the globe—that of limiting the number of territories on which they are stationed. The Soviet Union submits for discussion by the participants in this special session the question of not stationing nuclear weapons on the territories of states where there are no such weapons at present. In fact, there is no technical difficulty that could stand in the way of its solution. All that is required is the political will on the part of nuclear and non-nuclear states. Indeed, some non-nuclear countries have already declared that they will not condone the emplacement of nuclear charges on their territories. This practice could well become universal.

For their part the nuclear powers would undertake not to station nuclear weapons—warheads, bombs, shells, mines—in those countries where there are no such weapons at present. As a result, we would thus be able to erect yet another obstacle in the way of the proliferation of nuclear weapons and to prevent a possible destabilization of the strategic situation.

As far as the Soviet Union is concerned, it is ready to assume an obligation to this end, and we call upon the other nuclear powers to do the same.

If they agree not to station nuclear weapons in areas where there are none at present, we believe that it would then not be difficult to couch such an agreement in treaty language.

Quite recently at the very highest level, the General Secretary of the Central Committee of the Communist Party and President of the Praesidium of the Supreme Soviet of the Union of Soviet Socialist Republics, Leonid Brezhnev, declared: "We are against the use of nuclear weapons; only extraordinary circumstances—aggression against our country or its allies by another nuclear power—could compel us to resort to this extreme means of self-defence."

If this attitude met with the support of all the other nuclear powers, the situation in the world would become much calmer.

It is useful to recall in this connection that the socialist countries of Europe addressed a proposal to all participants in the All-European Conference—including the United States and Canada—to sign a treaty on the non-first-use of nuclear weapons against each other. That proposal still stands and awaits implementation.

The specific feature of the arms race today is that it is becoming increasingly qualitative in character. Hence, it is particularly imperative to prevent the development of new types and new systems of weapons of mass destruction. This is another problem that could well have been tackled a number of years ago.

Unfortunately, the pace of talks on that subject has been slow. We favour redoubled efforts in order to reach agreement at last. Prototypes of new lethal and merciless weapons developed in laboratories and design offices must not be allowed to reach the mass production lines.

Some people express surprise at a powerful wave of protests on the European continent and throughout the world against plans to produce these weapons in the United States and subsequently to deploy them in Western Europe. However, the peoples and the world public have been quick to realize that this is a particularly inhuman means of mass destruction intended specially to annihilate all living things.

The Soviet Union favours a complete ban on neutron weapons by no means because it is unable to meet this challenge effectively. The record of atomic and thermonuclear weapons research and development is good evidence to this effect. We are against lending a new dimension to the arms race as a matter of principle.

We propose agreement on a mutual renunciation of neutron weapons manufacture before it is too late. Last March, jointly with other socialist countries, the Soviet Union submitted a draft convention on this issue to the Committee on Disarmament at Geneva. We expect a clear and unambiguous reply to that proposal.

The Soviet Union will not begin neutron weapons production unless the United States or any other state for that matter goes ahead with it. This is a clear commitment on the part of the USSR. Neutron weapons must be banned once and for all. We give clear warning to the peoples in the countries where support is sometimes voiced for neutron weapons: beware of deception, be vigilant, let reason prevail over folly.

This special session could give a fresh impetus to the disarmament talks now under way in various international forums, or on a bilateral basis. In some instances much work has already been accomplished, and this strengthens the conviction that the arms race can be curbed.

Let us first turn to the Soviet–American talks on limiting strategic offensive arms. Those talks arouse particular interest all over the world and the reasons for that are, we believe, understandable. Too much is at stake.

During all the years that these talks have been going on, the Soviet Union has consistently been seeking a mutually acceptable understanding. And we cannot be held responsible for the fact that the talks have dragged on for so long. But I do not wish to dwell on that here.

Now, many of the difficulties in the talks have been overcome. As we see it, possibilities exist for resolving the remaining issues as well. Indeed they exist objectively. We proceed from the premise that mutual efforts can make it possible to arrive at an agreement which would equally accommodate the interests of the security of both sides and serve the broad interests of a stronger peace.

Immediately after signing the agreement which is now being prepared, the Soviet Union would be ready to enter into negotiations which should lead, with all the necessary factors being taken into account, to a substantial reduction—I repeat reduction—of the levels of strategic arms and to a further limitation of their qualitative improvement.

It seems that there are grounds for expecting a successful completion of the talks on the complete and general prohibition of nuclear weapon tests. This is an area of curbing the arms race on which the efforts of many states have been concentrated for several years now. The role of our country in this is well known. What is required now is to bring the matter to a conclusion—to ban tests in all environments, that is to say, to ban underground tests as well.

Clearing the path towards constructive agreement, the Soviet Union has travelled its part of the way to meet its partners in the negotiations—the United States and Great Britain—and has done so on the issues that presented the greatest difficulties. We have agreed to verification on a voluntary basis, to a moratorium on peaceful nuclear explosions and to the entry into force of the Treaty—even if initially not all the five nuclear powers become parties to it, but only the USSR, the United States and Great Britain.

But it is not only important to ensure an early signing of the Treaty. It is no less important that the example set by the three powers with respect to the complete and general prohibition of nuclear weapon tests be convincing enough to be followed by others. An end must be put to nuclear weapon tests in all environments and by all those who conduct them.

It is necessary in the near future to complete the negotiations on the prohibition of chemical weapons. What is needed is a decisive spurt—as they say—and that is what we are calling for. The problem of control which has arisen can be resolved on the basis of national means of verification supplemented by well-considered international procedures.

A further type of mass destruction weapon—radiological weapons—must be banned. Those are weapons known to affect living organisms by non-explosive radio-active emanation. An agreement can be said to be in the offing; a relevant draft convention has already been partly agreed upon. Here again we stand for a speedy completion of that work.

The Soviet Union believes that it is an important and positive factor of the international situation today that talks in progress cover not only weapons of mass destruction but also armed forces and conventional armaments.

It is an established fact that 80 per cent of the world's military expenditures go for conventional armaments. What a great number of people in the postwar period alone have fallen victim to weapons called "conventional" but which now, as a result of their amazing accuracy and complete coverage of large areas, have a most devastating power. The talks carried on at Vienna dealing with the reduction of armed forces and armaments in Central Europe are highly important in that respect.

In that area the two most powerful military and political alliances confront one another. But here too an approximate military parity has been reached between them. Therefore, through agreed measures it is possible to reduce the level of that equilibrium without upsetting it in anybody's favour, without prejudicing anyone's security.

Such is our approach to those talks. Unlike the NATO countries, we have not expanded our armed forces in Central Europe for a long time, nor do we intend to increase them in the future by one single soldier, by one single tank. Our approach is also shown in our desire to do our utmost to find mutually acceptable solutions in Vienna; but far from everything depends on us.

We continue to hope that the talks will be concluded successfully, that the other side will abandon its desire to secure unilateral advantages for itself and to change the correlation of forces. Military *détente* on the European continent can and must make substantial headway.

The talks on the limitation and subsequent reduction of military activities in the Indian Ocean are now in progress between the USSR and the United States. But it is clear that the parties directly involved are not the only ones interested in their success. It can even be said that an agreement on the limitation of armaments in such a vast part of the world would have a noticeable effect on the international situation as a whole.

So far, the discussions concern "freezing" military activities in the Indian Ocean at the present levels. Of course, this is only a beginning. Later on we are prepared to seek ways of drastically reducing such activities, including the dismantling of foreign military bases. Thus, the idea of turning the Indian Ocean into a zone of peace, put forward by littoral states and supported by the majority of United Nations members, will take a more definitive shape.

As you can see, talks on various aspects of disarmament cover a broad spectrum of problems. I shall also mention here the Soviet–American consultations on the limitation of international trade and transfers of conventional armaments. This is, of course, an urgent problem, but a clear-cut political approach must underlie its solution. One cannot place on the same footing the aggressor and his victim ; one cannot allow any encroachment on the rights of peoples waging legitimate struggle for their liberation from colonial and racist oppression.

The strengthening of international treaties and agreements in force in the field of disarmament would be a significant lever for ending the arms race.

Why is it, I ask, that about one third of member states of the United Nations still have not acceded to the Treaty on the Non-Proliferation of Nuclear Weapons? Why is it that almost one third of United Nations member states are not parties to the Treaty Banning Nuclear Tests in the Atmosphere, in Outer Space and Under Water? Why is it that more than half of them are not parties to the Convention banning bacteriological weapons, or to the Treaty on the Prohibition of the Emplacement of Weapons of Mass Destruction on the Sea-bed and the Ocean Floor? Can one consider this situation as normal? It is a situation which calls, purely and simply, for accession to existing treaties and agreements rather than general statements on the desirability of disarmament. No excuse sounds convincing here.

We hope that the special session on disarmament will have its authoritative say and will strongly urge states to make their contribution to strengthening international treaties in force.

Before concluding, mention should be made of yet another practical step which could scale down the arms race and at the same time release additional funds for development needs. That step is the reduction of the military budgets of states.

This is not a new problem for the United Nations. Yet, despite all the resolutions adopted on that score, there has been no progress towards its solution.

The Soviet Union takes the initiative in order to get things moving. We propose that the states having large economic and military potential—and in the first place the countries that are permanent members of the Security Council—should agree to reduce their military budgets, not in terms of percentage points, but in absolute figures. Of course, the idea still stands that part of the amount thus freed would be diverted to meet the needs of developing countries. In other words, if that helps, we are prepared, along with others, to reduce our military budget on such a basis.

Such is the general outline of our approach to the problem of the arms race and disarmament. This is the essence of the document "On the Practical Ways to End the Arms Race: Proposals of the Soviet Union" which we are submitting for consideration by the special session of the General Assembly of the United Nations.

The Soviet Union believes that the steps proposed are essential if we wish to halt the arms race. They could actually lead to a breakthrough in achieving military *détente* and lead to a radical lessening of the threat of war. At the same time, all these steps are feasible in practice. They take into account the present balance of forces in the world. Their implementation will not result in unilateral advantages for anyone.

The special session of the General Assembly can realistically, without going to extremes, assess the state of affairs in the field of disarmament in the world. It must explicitly speak out on the objectives and priorities in this field, confirm, on the basis of the collective experience of states, the well-considered and fundamental approaches to the problem of disarmament. But what is required is that all participants display a genuine desire for peace, free from the risk of war and armed conflicts. The responsibility of all—practically of every country—for the present and the future of the peoples of the world is too great today for them not to cooperate in good faith in meeting a truly historic challenge, that of disarmament.

The more concrete the programme of action in the field of disarmament worked out at the session, the more clear-cut and definite its decisions, the greater will be its effectiveness. It is obvious that such decisions will be recommendations, but they will be recommendations in favour of peace and against the danger of war.

The Soviet Union, and we are not alone, favours the holding of a world disarmament conference, the forum which would be in a position to adopt at once effective decisions truly binding on all states. The success of the special session should help in convening such a conference. That means that we should give serious thought to a specific and early date for the holding of this world conference.

A few words concerning yet another item on the agenda of the special session : the international machinery for disarmament negotiations. We are convinced that here one should display a great degree of circumspection. It is easy to dismantle the well-adjusted machinery. But would that be beneficial for disarmament, or could it possibly play into the hands of those who actually oppose disarmament?

We see no need to give up the existing negotiating channels or to restructure them radically. Of course, the existing bodies should produce more results than has been the case so far; we are in favour of that. Indeed, any machinery, any subsidiary body or its work, can only be as good as the policies of the states represented on it. Changing the names or the signboards of such bodies would make little difference.

The Soviet Union will do everything in its power so that decisions of the General Assembly's special session and the document it adopts serve as real guidelines for states in their advance towards the radical solution of the problem of disarmament, up to general and complete disarmament, and to removing the very material basis of war. It goes without saying that, as always, we shall give thorough consideration to any constructive proposals in that direction which may be made here. Both within the United Nations and outside it we are prepared to cooperate constructively with all those who actually strive for disarmament. There exists in particular a natural and organic foundation and basis for cooperation between socialist countries and non-aligned states which contributes in no small measure to the strengthening of international security, freedom and the independence of peoples. The socialist countries, welded together by unity of purpose and ideals, both in the field of domestic policies and in their international activities, will continue to use all their influence and all their prestige to ensure peace.

One would wish that the loud appeals for peace and the denunciation of war, heard from this high rostrum, would reach the remotest corners of the world and shake it so mightily that the voices of the advocates of the arms race, uniformed or not, would be drowned by the powerful voices of the peoples themselves, who long to live in conditions of lasting peace and reliable security.

For the Security of Nations, for Peace on Earth

Speech at the 34th Session of the UN General Assembly, 25 September 1979

Mr. President,

Esteemed delegates,

The current session of the United Nations General Assembly is the last one to be held in the 1970s. This gives us certain grounds not only for considering the topical issues of today but also for summing up some of the political results of the decade which is about to close and for casting a glance at the past. For the problems of today, as indeed the future itself—what we could and could not do—are more clearly seen against the background of the lessons of the past.

It is worthwhile to recall the circumstances which brought about the United Nations. The war was still raging and the sword of just retribution had not yet fallen on those who instigated it, when the leaders of the major nations of the anti-fascist coalition took up the challenge, which today still retains its vital importance: the setting up of a reliable barrier against another world tragedy. That challenge was indeed enshrined in the United Nations Charter as the main goal of this Organization. The effectiveness of the United Nations in maintaining international peace has been and remains the main yardstick in judging all its activities.

Has the United Nations lived up to its mandate? There can be no simple answer to that question. Yet it should be recognized that it has done a lot of good for consolidating peace and promoting international co-operation. It is also evident that the United Nations could have done more than it has.

We are all aware that the manner in which the Member States of the United Nations act in international affairs cannot be reduced to one common denominator. Here the amplitude between different policy trends is great: some have not yet abandoned their claims to dominate the rest and even to hegemony in the world arena; others, naturally, cannot and will not reconcile themselves to this. Some countries make every effort to put an end to the arms race and demonstrate a serious and responsible approach to this task; others, on the contrary, hurl ever more funds into that race and inflate their military budgets. In short, the United Nations, as the broadest international organization shows up in the boldest relief the characteristic features of the world with all its contradictions and collisions and, at the same time, the growing hopes of the peoples for a peaceful future.

The Soviet Union has never abandoned the belief in the possibility of building a solid edifice of peace. At the beginning of the current decade there was a new lease on life, so to speak, through a series of treaties which have brought international relations in Europe in line with the realities of its post-war development. The first Soviet–American agreements on the limitation of strategic arms and the basic principles of relations between the USSR and the United States of America were also concluded at that time.

Special mention should also be made of the historic conference of the top leaders of 35 nations at Helsinki which sealed in a document the evolution of Europe towards stronger security and co-operation. In that period, long and serious negotiations resulted in the Soviet–American SALT II Treaty, whose entry into force, one can say, the whole world is looking forward to.

Indeed, all of us can say that the 1970s will hold an important place in history. These years have seen the positive trend in international affairs which was named "*détente*" becoming a broad process. *Détente*—and the Soviet Union stood at its cradle—expresses the aspirations of our entire nation and, we are sure, those of all peoples of the world.

The attitude towards *détente* is the best indicator of any country's political intentions. In recent years many a good word has been said about *détente*. But even very good words in favour of *détente* are not enough; they must be buttressed by deeds, by the policies of States.

There are still people in the world today who shrink when they hear the word "*détente*"; their faces wrinkle like that of a hungry cat tasting a cucumber in a kitchen garden.

Take, for instance, the questions of renouncing the spread of enmity and hatred among nations and the prohibition of war propaganda. This is, so to speak, a minimum for any State adhering to the policy of *détente* and desirous of promoting a healthy political climate in the world.

As far back as 1947 the General Assembly adopted a resolution against the propaganda for another war. Over 30 years have elapsed since then, but who would assert today that such propaganda has been stopped? In many States it has not even been outlawed. The Soviet Union did that long ago. The provision stating that war propaganda is banned in the USSR is a formal part of our Constitution, the fundamental law of our State.

On more than one occasion we have emphasized the urgency of this matter. Indeed, before the guns of the aggressors who unleashed the Second World War began to thunder, war propaganda had been in full swing for many years. Incessant calls had been made for the map of Europe and of the world to be carved up to suit the aggressors' designs. The Soviet Union mentions this fact because the forces that seek to condition people to think in terms of war and the arms build-up are still active.

It is becoming a tradition in some countries to play out scenarios of military conflicts. "Look," they say, "that is how things are going to unfold." And estimates are made of the casualties and the number of cities to be swept away. Tens or even hundreds of millions of lives are written off in those callous calculations.

The ancient Greeks, and not they alone, left us wise myths whose beauty lies in glorifying what is human in man. It is not to the credit of our contemporaries that other myths are invented today which are designed to stupefy man with pessimism and to make him despair of the triumph of reason. They depict war as totally unavoidable. There is no doubt as to the purposes for which these other myths are invented and the policies which they are designed to serve.

What a huge number of spurious films, books, articles and speeches of politicians and quasi-politicians are produced to make people believe the fictitious stories about the source of a threat to peace. One example is the campaign launched with regard to Cuba, in the course of which all sorts of falsehoods are being piled up concerning the policies of Cuba and the Soviet Union. But the truth is that this propaganda is totally without foundation in reality, and is indeed based on falsehoods. The Soviet Union and Cuba have already stated as much.

Our advice on this score is simple: the artificiality of this entire question must be honestly admitted and the matter closed. The Soviet Union and other countries of the socialist community have never threatened anybody, nor are they doing so now. A society which is confident of its creative forces and abilities needs no war. It needs peace. These words have been inscribed on the banner of our foreign policy ever since the days of Lenin.

The policy of peace and friendship among peoples, the policy of peaceful coexistence of States with different social systems, has invariably been expressed in the decisions of the congresses of the Communist Party of the Soviet Union. This policy course will be followed unswervingly in the future as well.

Naturally, the USSR and its Warsaw Treaty allies cannot fail to take into account the fact that some States are continuing their military preparations and stepping them up. In these circumstances the USSR and its allies are compelled to look after their security. At the same time our approach in this matter can be described as follows: "The defence potential of the Soviet Union," as Leonid Brezhnev has pointed out, "must be at a level that would deter anyone from attempting to disrupt our peaceful life. A course aimed not at achieving superiority in weapons, but at reducing armaments and easing military confrontation—such is our policy."

He who trusts this policy will never be deceived. The USSR and socialist countries can always be relied upon in the struggle for peace, disarmament and *détente* and for the freedom and independence of peoples. Those countries have common ideals and are guided by common goals. Shoulder to shoulder, their peoples are working hard in the grandiose effort of construction.

Indeed the whole world knows how many proposals, and what kind of proposals, have been submitted by the socialist States to other countries, first of all in the United Nations, with the aim of deepening the process of easing tensions in the world, of broadening peaceful co-operation among States, and of strengthening international security.

The countries making up the socialist community co-ordinate their policies for the sake of universal peace, the security of their peoples and the peoples of other countries. This was again confirmed with new vigour by the fruitful results of the latest series of meetings held by Leonid Brezhnev with top Party and State leaders of socialist countries which took place in the Crimea last summer. These meetings were widely reported throughout the world.

I feel that our opinion will not differ from that of most participants in this session if I say that a comparison of the United Nations Charter provisions with what is going on in the sphere of military activities in some countries reveals a glaring contradiction. Although those States affixed their signatures to the United Nations Charter and its peaceful purposes and principles, they are nevertheless doing everything to see that stockpiled mountains of weapons grow.

In the meantime, the world has long since crossed the line beyond which the arms race has become sheer madness. This is strong language, but this is the way it is—the arms race has become madness. He urged all Member States of the United Nations to counter this madness with common sense and the will to strengthen mutual trust. For its part, the USSR, together with other countries, will continue to work consistently to stop the arms race, to start dismantling the war machine part by part and to reduce the military arsenals of States down to general and complete disarmament.

Here at the United Nations and at various forums where the disarmament problem is under discussion, there is certainly no dearth of proposals that are well considered and based on the principle of equality and equal security. There are proposals relating both to weapons of mass destruction and to conventional weapons. We are still seized with the question of the reduction of military budgets. But, honestly speaking, who will tell us that that question is not of direct interest to the peoples of the world and a matter of deep concern to them?

There has been no small number of major initiatives directed towards a general improvement of the political climate in the world, including the proposal for a world treaty on the non-use of force in international relations. In our view, not a single State that sincerely strives for peace and good relations with other countries could possibly object to such a treaty.

There are also initiatives concerning various regions of the world. I should like to point, in particular, to the idea of the States bordering on the Indian Ocean that this ocean be turned into a zone of peace, which is supported by the majority of the Member countries of the United Nations, and the Soviet Union is certainly in favour of implementing this idea. It is actively working for an early resumption of the Soviet–American talks on the limitation and subsequent reduction of military activities in the Indian Ocean, talks which were interrupted through no fault of ours. An appropriate agreement on that subject would undoubtedly give this idea a more tangible shape, and this would have a favourable impact on the entire international situation.

Yet, on the whole, one has to note with concern that all or almost all proposals for ending the arms race and for disarmament as a rule encounter opposition on the part of a number of States. They frequently get bogged down in the quagmire of debate. And it takes tremendous efforts to bring them up to the stage of decision-making, though such decisions do not yet ensure real disarmament even in limited areas.

A considerable period of time has already elapsed since the question was raised about reaching an agreement on ending the production of all types of nuclear weapons and the gradual reduction of their stockpiles until they have been completely liquidated. In our days there is no more burning problem than that of removing the threat of nuclear war. Yes, there is no more burning problem confronting mankind today. Every reasonable person understands this. And it cannot be effectively solved without stopping the assembly line producing an incessant flow of weapons of monstrous destructive power—nuclear warheads, bombs and shells. And this is happening now, at this time when we are discussing vital problems confronting mankind.

As we have repeatedly stated, the Soviet Union is prepared to discuss this fundamental problem together with other countries, and it is proposing that specific negotiations be initiated. All the nuclear Powers without exception are in duty bound to take part in them.

It is sometimes said that ending the production of nuclear weapons and their liquidation are too difficult a task. Yes, it is indeed not easy; one can say that it is a complex task. But can this be a reason for not starting the search for ways and means to resolve the problem? We are sure that reaching an appropriate agreement is not beyond the realm of possibility if States, and first of all the nuclear States, adopt a responsible approach.

The complex of questions relating to nuclear weapons includes the ensuring of guarantees of the security of non-nuclear States and the non-stationing of nuclear weapons on the territories of States where there are no such weapons at present.

The General Assembly has already adopted resolutions of principle on these matters. It is now necessary to embody them in binding international agreements.

In our view, further efforts should be made to strengthen the regime of non-proliferation of nuclear weapons. Those who have already spoken on this topic at this session of the General Assembly were quite right. We have to strengthen the regime of non-proliferation of nuclear weapons. And the responsibility for this rests on all States. We hope that the forthcoming Review Conference of the Parties to the Treaty on the Non-Proliferation of Nuclear Weapons will be crowned with positive results. This Conference will be held soon.

Negotiations on a number of essential aspects of disarmament are already in progress, and on some they have been going on for a long time. I should like to single out a couple of questions whose solution could, in our view, be found in the not too distant future.

Progress has been achieved in the negotiations between the Soviet Union, the United States and the United Kingdom on the complete and general prohibition of nuclear-weapon tests. We would expect that no complicating elements will be introduced in the negotiations by our partners. We entertain high hopes on that score; but, unfortunately, these complications are being introduced to this day.

In the course of Soviet–American consultations, basic elements of an agreement banning radiological weapons have been worked out. If work on the agreement is not impeded artificially, it can be speedily prepared for signature. This means that, following the ban on bacteriological weapons, one more type of weapon of mass destruction will be prohibited.

The file of constructive proposals on various aspects of the disarmament problem is impressive and proper use should be made of it. This offers broad opportunities for action by the United Nations which, at its special session devoted to disarmament, adopted a programme which on the whole is a good one. The United Nations resolution should not merely remain on paper. For the time being, however, it is but a paper, though a well-written one.

It may be that many of us are somewhat shocked at this, but, unfortunately it is true. So far, this decision is nothing but a scrap of paper, although, I repeat, it is well written.

The signing of the Soviet–American Treaty of the Limitation of Strategic Offensive Weapons is convincing proof that, given goodwill and readiness to take into account each other's legitimate interests, it is possible to achieve agreements on the most difficult questions. The Treaty builds a bridge to the further limitation and reduction of strategic weapons. It also contains great potential for exerting a positive influence on other negotiations—and this is not without importance—on the limitations of the arms race and on disarmament.

It can be stated without exaggeration that a major step has been taken for the Union of Soviet Socialist Republics and the United States of America and the entire world. It is quite understandable, therefore, that, one after another, the representatives of States speaking from this rostrum, with very few exceptions—and we hope that it is only a mistake when there are exceptions—speak out in favour of that Treaty.

The strengthening of universal peace is inseparable from ensuring security in Europe. The situation in the European continent is not merely a part of the general picture of the world situation: today, as in the past, it has a profound impact on the course of international developments.

Since the historic moment when it raised the banner of a new social system, our country has been pursuing a consistent course towards creating conditions of reliable peace in Europe. Everything we have accomplished in the name of that goal is an open book, and we are proud of its every page.

Of course, we are far from underestimating the contributions made by other States. We give their due to the countries that took part in the Pan-European Conference, which was crowned by the adoption of the Final Act. That document provides guidelines for further efforts to deepen the process of *détente* in Europe.

Today the basis for the peaceful co-operation of States on the European continent is more solid than it was yesterday. Favourable changes have taken place in relations between socialist and capitalist countries in Europe.

Soviet–French co-operation is on the rise. There is a considerable degree of mutual understanding and agreement on major issues of European and world politics, and accordingly there is a possibility for the further development of fruitful co-operation.

The development of our relations with the Federal Republic of Germany has been following a positive trend. Both sides appreciate the mutual advantages of what has been achieved, recognizing that a good deal could yet be accomplished in the future. I should like to express the hope that there will be no move on the part of the Federal Republic of Germany that would reduce such possibilities for the future or that would run counter to the peaceful line in Europe and to the easing of international tensions.

We are interested in the consistent development of Soviet–British relations. We are hopeful that there is a desire for this in Britain, too.

We have good relations with Italy. The assets accumulated in these relations must be multiplied.

I should like to note the genuine and traditional good-neighbourly relations between the Union of Soviet Socialist Republics and Finland. We appreciate all the good achievements that have been made in our relations with other Scandinavian countries.

A positive shift is taking place in our relations with Spain.

The development of our ties with the rest of Western Europe is also a source of satisfaction.

On the whole, both in the field of bilateral relations with States having a different social system and in other fields, the Soviet Union is following the course charted by the Helsinki Conference.

The roots that political *détente* has taken on European soil cannot, however, be viable unless practical measures are taken in the field of military *détente*. In this regard, great prospects have been opened up by the proposals contained in the Declaration of the Political Consultative Committee of the Warsaw Treaty Organization adopted last November, and in the May communiqué of the Foreign Ministers' Committee of that Organization.

First of all, I wish to refer to the initiative concerning the conclusion between the participant States in the European Conference of a treaty on the non-first use of either nuclear or conventional weapons against each other. Its intent is self-evident.

Unfortunately, our Western partners have not yet shown themselves ready to engage in talks on this problem. Nevertheless, we expect that a sober approach and a sense of responsibility will prompt them to react positively to our proposal.

The socialist countries are still waiting for a response to yet another important initiative of theirs—concerning the convening, at a political level and with the participation of all European countries as well as the United States and Canada, of a conference on strengthening confidence among States, easing military confrontation and the subsequent lessening of the concentration of armed forces and armaments in Europe and their reduction. Each of those countries could make its own contribution to the work of that conference.

In the opinion of the Soviet Union, substantial work is needed on a bilateral as well as a multilateral basis to ensure the success of both the conference on military *détente* on the European continent and the Madrid meeting to be held next year of representatives of the participant States in the European Conference. Far from competing with each other, those two forums are complementary. As for the Madrid meeting, it should focus on truly urgent issues of *détente* in Europe. No narrow selfish interests should be allowed to prevent this.

Now a few words about the Vienna talks, the subject of which, it will be recalled, is the reduction of armed forces and armaments in Central Europe. This is not a problem of significance to Europe alone. Our country invariably adopts constructive positions at those talks and puts forward initiatives which also take into account the legitimate interests of the Western partners. Only strict observance of the principle of undiminished security of either party would bring the Vienna talks to the road leading to agreement, and the sooner that happens the better.

The review of problems relating to Europe would be incomplete if no reference were made to attempts undertaken from time to time by some countries to test the durability of the quadripartite agreement on West Berlin. This is contrary to the long-term interests which provided the basis for that agreement and which must serve as guidance for all States, particularly the parties to it.

The root cause of the complexities and contradictions of the present day international situation lies to no small extent in the fact that the existing sources of tensions and conflicts between States do not disappear and that now and then new ones keep springing up.

There is more than one such source in Asia. It was only six months ago that aggression was committed against the Socialist Republic of Vietnam. Practically the whole world branded the aggressors as such. But have appropriate conclusions been drawn from that event by all those who should have drawn them? This issue cannot be drowned in the artificially whipped up propaganda campaign concerning Indo-Chinese refugees, a campaign whose sharp edge is directed against Vietnam. No, that edge should be turned in another direction, towards a completely different quarter, and that direction and that quarter are well known.

It is also no secret who imposed and nurtured the blood-thirsty murderous regime of Pol Pot. Today that regime in Kampuchea has been done away with and there will be no return to the past. The legitimate representatives of the Kampuchean people must be given the opportunity to take the seat belonging to Kampuchea in the United Nations. Sooner or later that is what is going to happen, and we express the hope that all delegations in this hall fully realize it.

The policy of some States is shortsighted—there is no other name for it—States that are intensifying their interference in the international affairs of Afghanistan. That country, which has chosen the road of progressive democratic transformations, comes out in favour of good relations with its neighbours and pursues an independent foreign policy, a policy of non-alignment. The Soviet Union, which has long-standing ties of friendship and good neighbourliness with Afghanistan, considers that this inadmissible interference must be stopped. The Afghans alone are entitled to settle their internal affairs. Only they will settle them, the same as the people of any other sovereign State.

With respect to such Middle East States as Turkey and Iran, not only have we common borders but we also maintain relations of traditional co-operation with them. We take a positive attitude to the steps which those and other Asian countries take to protect and strengthen their sovereignty, and we are willing to develop relations with them.

We in the Soviet Union are satisfied with the friendly nature of relations between the USSR and India, that great Asian country with its consistently peaceful policy. The Soviet–Indian relationship is a major factor for stability and peace on the Asian continent.

We wish to maintain, on the basis of reciprocity, normal good relations with all States, whether in South or South East Asia or in the

Far East. This applies to Japan, Indonesia, the Philippines, Malaysia, Thailand, Pakistan, Bangladesh, Sri Lanka and other countries of those regions.

Like all peace-loving peoples, the Soviet people are gravely concerned over the state of affairs in the Middle East—one of the "hottest" spots on earth, where now there emanates a serious threat to peace.

The Middle East problem if divested of what is immaterial, boils down to the following: either the consequences of the aggression against the Arab States and peoples are eliminated or the invaders will be rewarded by being allowed to appropriate lands that belong to others. A just settlement and the establishment of lasting peace in the Middle East require that Israel should end its occupation of all—I repeat, of all—the Arab lands it seized in 1967; that the legitimate rights of the Arab people of Palestine, including the right to establish their own State, be safeguarded; and that the right of all States in the Middle East, including Israel, to independent existence under conditions of peace be effectively guaranteed. Is this not a just position? The separate deal between Egypt and Israel resolves nothing, despite the reams that have been written about that deal. It is nothing but a means designed to lull the vigilance of peoples. It is a way of piling up on a still greater scale explosive material capable of producing a new conflagration in the Middle East. Moreover, added to the tense political atmosphere in this and the adjacent areas, is the heavy smell of oil. We all understand that.

It is high time that all States represented in the United Nations realized how vast is the tragedy of the Arab people of Palestine. What is the worth of declarations in defence of humanism and human rights—whether for refugees or not—if before the eyes of the entire world the inalienable rights of an entire people driven from its land and deprived of a livelihood are grossly trampled upon?

The Soviet policy with respect to the Middle East problem is one of principle. We wish to point out that it is not dependent upon timely, topical elements. It is difficult—indeed, practically impossible—to carry out a serious policy by basing oneself on passing topical elements. We are in favour of a comprehensive and just settlement, of the establishment of durable peace in the Middle East, a region not far from our borders. The Soviet Union sides firmly with Arab peoples who resolutely reject deals at the expense of their legitimate interests.

By adopting in 1960 the Declaration on the Granting of Independence to Colonial Countries and Peoples—one of the most significant acts of the United Nations—the world community acknowledged the indisputable fact that the hour of colonialism had struck. Since then an overwhelming majority of peoples have cast off the yoke of colonialism. But humanity's conscience continues to revolt against the fact that the shackles of colonialism and racism have not yet been completely broken. And it is above all of southern Africa that we should be talking here.

For many years now the peoples of Zimbabwe and Namibia have been waging a selfless struggle for their freedom and independence. The Soviet Union is entirely on the side of their noble cause. We have raised and shall continue to raise our voice in their support, and we shall cooperate with those States, especially African States, which adhere to the positions of justice, of upholding the inalienable rights of those peoples.

All kinds of combinations, no matter how superficially clever, which are aimed at preserving the domination of racists and colonialists with the help of hastily formed puppet regimes should be resolutely rejected.

Is it possible to achieve a political settlement in southern Africa? Yes, it is possible and there are ways leading to it. But so far the racists and their stooges have replied with bullets to proposals that a choice be made in favour of a just and peaceful solution. And this, of course, applies to their friends abroad.

The session of the General Assembly of the United Nations will be right if it clearly states its resolute support for the liberation struggle of the peoples of southern Africa and condemns attempts to drown this struggle in blood as a crime against humanity. It is a direct duty of the United Nations to make those who ignore the decisions of the United Nations on southern Africa respect them.

The Soviet people are well aware of the contribution of the peoples of Latin America to the struggle for peace and national liberation. This contribution will be all the greater the more the stand of Latin American States in defending their independence is resolute and the less their policies are influenced from the outside. In this connection, we note with satisfaction the growing prestige of Latin America in international relations.

In its approach to all continents, to all countries of the world, the

Soviet Union does not apply different yardsticks when it comes to the sovereignty of States, the freedom of peoples and genuine human rights. One cannot hold aloft the United Nations Charter in one situation and hide it under the table in another. The provisions and principles of the United Nations Charter must be applied equally to any State and any people.

The Soviet Union has repeatedly stressed, notably in the United Nations, the significance of the movement of non-alignment and its peaceful orientation. We are confident that non-aligned States will continue to make use of their entire political weight in the interests of peace, disarmament and *détente*. This confidence of ours is supported by the successful results of the summit conference of the non-aligned States which recently ended in Havana. It was an important forum and a major international event.

What is needed in the first place to resolve any important international problem of a political, economic or other nature is an atmosphere of peace. And whether peace will be more durable or less stable depends to an important extent on the state of relations between the Soviet Union and the United States. That conclusion is objective and indisputable.

The leadership of the Soviet Union makes no secret of its desire to have normal and, what is more, friendly relations with the United States. We have said this many times—for instance, during our Party congresses. It was mentioned by Leonid Brezhnev at the recent Twenty-fifth Congress of the Communist Party of the Soviet Union. This only requires the observance of principles which have become well-established in international relations; and they are recorded, in particular, in the well-known Soviet–American documents—that is, the principles of peaceful coexistence between States and of non-interference in the affairs of others. We shall not allow anybody to meddle in our internal affairs. Concern for Soviet–American relations is a matter for both sides. It is only on this basis that the relations between the USSR and the United States can develop successfully.

Our position was stated with exhaustive clarity and precision by Leonid Brezhnev in Vienna, in particular, in the course of his meeting with United States President Jimmy Carter. The meeting has shown that, given the wish on both sides, the USSR and the United States are able to find mutually acceptable solutions and to co-operate in the interests of international *détente* and peace.

Leonid Brezhnev has stated:

> "There is no country or people in the world, in fact, with which the Soviet Union would not like to have good relations; there is no topical international problem to the solution of which the Soviet Union would not be willing to contribute; there is no source of danger of war in the removal of which by peaceful means the Soviet Union would not be interested."

In the succession of post-war developments, along with positive events there were also dangerous ones which gravely threatened the foundations of peace. A closer look at these developments would easily reveal that the evolution of the international situation largely depends upon the States which have the most powerful levers to influence it.

When those levers are activated to attain objectives contrary to, or even openly defying, the United Nations Charter, conflict situations and international crises arise. The instigators of such events usually seek to whitewash themselves and, in that, they do not hesitate to pin all kinds of labels on others. That is a procedure that is, unfortunately, sometimes followed.

One such tactic consists in juggling with the term "hegemonism", which in recent years has been increasingly used in international political practice. Although of recent origin, the term "hegemonism" denotes a phenomenon that is far from new. On the contrary, it has been known, so to speak, from time immemorial. It means striving for world domination, for domination over other countries and peoples.

The Soviet attitude towards hegemonism and domination is clear. Since its very first days, the Soviet State has resolutely objected to anyone's being a hegemonist with others submitting to his will, and to any States' holding a position of domination over others.

Twenty million human lives were sacrificed by our people to defeat Hitler's designs for world domination and to bury hegemonism in its fascist attire. This figure alone is indicative of our score with hegemonism.

Hegemonism is a direct antipode to the equality of States and peoples, an antipode to the ideal which the October Revolution proclaimed for the whole world and which the United Nations, as prescribed by its Charter, should promote in every possible way in international relations. Its manifestation in our day constitutes a serious obstacle to the process of *détente* to which there is not and cannot be any reasonable alternative.

The time has come for all United Nations Member States to take an unambiguous position with regard to hegemonism—to condemn it and to block any claims to hegemony in world affairs. Its inadmissibility should be raised to the level of a principle that must be rigorously observed, of an international law that must be respected.

Guided by all this, the Soviet Union is proposing the inclusion in the agenda of the current session of an important item entitled "On the inadmissibility of a policy of hegemonism in international relations" and is submitting an appropriate draft resolution to be considered at the session. Its purport is that no States or groups of States should claim, under any circumstances or for any motives whatsoever, hegemony in regard to other States or groups of States.

We are convinced that all those who approach the conduct of international affairs on the basis of equality and in the interests of *détente* and peace cannot oppose the adoption of such a draft resolution. It is to be hoped that the General Assembly will consider the draft with a high sense of responsibility.

Following the General Assembly, the United Nations Security Council, with the five nuclear Powers as its permanent members, could also express itself against hegemonism. It would be a good idea subsequently to couch the renunciation by States of a policy of hegemonism in all its manifestations in terms of a broad international agreement and to conclude such an agreement or treaty.

In conducting its policy our country scrupulously complies with the principles of the United Nations Charter and invariably pursues its purposes. We never lose sight of the fundamental basis of the activities of the world Organization, that is, concentration of its efforts on ensuring that the peoples can live in conditions of peace. The Soviet Union has consistently come out in favour of strengthening the United Nations, of no one's being allowed to erode it.

The peoples will assess the results of the current session, like those of previous sessions, of the General Assembly primarily in terms of what it will have achieved to make people feel more secure. Hence, great responsibility rests with all United Nations Member States and with their representatives assembled in this hall.

Everything positive that we can achieve today will help us in the 1980s to consolidate and to develop the successes of the 1970s. That in turn will largely determine the thoughts and feelings, the memories of the past and the faith in the future that mankind will take with it into the next millennium.

We wish, and we shall do all in our power to ensure, that the work of the thirty-fourth session of the General Assembly may culminate in the adoption of resolutions that will be commended by the peoples of the world.

To Secure Peace for Nations, A Task for All States

Speech at the 35th Session of the UN General Assembly, 23 September 1980

Mr. President,

Esteemed delegates,

Speaking today from this rostrum, I should like to emphasize at the very outset the great importance which this session of the General Assembly would have if its work were successful.

In view of the specific character of the situation in the world arena today, it is essential for the work of the session to be conducted in a constructive atmosphere. Its participants will have to display to an even greater extent than before a sense of realism, a considered approach to key international issues and a genuine interest in finding solutions to them. Thereby the Member States of the United Nations would demonstrate their commitment to the principles and purposes of this world Organization and awareness of their responsibility for the destinies of peace. Indeed, this is now a vitally important task for them individually and collectively. We focus attention on this because the state of affairs in the world has lately become more complicated as a result of a sharp turn in the policies of the United States of America and some other members of the North Atlantic Treaty Organization (NATO).

Let us look at the facts—they are more eloquent than words.

Back in May 1978, the NATO countries decided automatically to increase their annual military expenditures almost to the end of this century. Last December, they took a decision to produce and deploy in Western Europe new American medium-range nuclear missile systems designed to change the military and strategic situation to the unilateral

51

advantage of the NATO bloc. Simultaneously, Washington also announced its own multi-billion dollar buildup programme.

The course chosen by the United States of America, which cannot be called anything but militaristic, is expressed in the so-called "new nuclear strategy". Under the cover of arguments that have nothing to do with reality concerning the possibility of some "limited" or "partial" use of nuclear weapons, the architects of this strategy seek to instill in the minds of people the idea of the admissibility and acceptability of a nuclear conflict. This foolhardy concept exacerbates the risk of a nuclear catastrophe, which cannot but cause concern throughout the world.

And is it not contrary to the expectations of the peoples of the world that Washington should have indefinitely postponed ratification of the Soviet–American treaty on the limitation of strategic offensive arms (SALT II)? It has demonstrated that it sets a low value on the assurances and promises it gave earlier.

Several theses have recently been adopted by American foreign policy which, by all appearances, are regarded as its credo. Here is one of them. A given region of the world is chosen at will—especially if it is rich in energy resources or important from the point of view of transport and communications, or simply if the Pentagon has taken a fancy to it—and that favoured area is declared with naked bluntness to be a United States "sphere of vital interest".

And if, to boot, it is a sphere of American interests, not just anyone's, and on top of that—God only knows why—of "vital" interests, efforts are made simply to deprive the peoples who live in that area of the right to be masters in their own home and masters of their own wealth. It is even hard to understand that at the end of the twentieth century generally recognized rules of international law hallowed by time should be so blatantly and so rapaciously flouted.

Another proposition is that any internal changes in any State—merely because they are not to Washington's liking—are considered to be a good enough pretext for United States interference in the affairs of that State, including the dispatch there of armed forces and commandos. It is precisely these functions that have been assigned to the rapid deployment force. And it is surely those countries which cannot defend themselves that become the first victims.

And what about the treatment of Cuba? This is a striking example.

Contrary to the legitimate demands of its Government and people, a part of Cuba's territory, Guantanamo, where a United States military base is located, is held by force. But in Washington they reason in the following way : we want this base—so that is that. It is of no importance to them that the sovereign rights of Cuba and its people are thus flagrantly ignored, once American interests stand to gain.

And what a host of statements are made to justify such a policy. Those deal at length with human rights, the rights of States. It is simply amazing how such a policy can be combined with genuine respect for the rights of States, the rights of peoples, and human rights. If such statements are to be believed and they are, incidentally, repeated with the importunity of commercial advertising—then all manuals and all books on international law, and indeed the United Nations Charter itself, which strictly protect the sovereignty of States, should all be discarded. But no verbal acrobatics, no diplomatic contrivances can conceal the real essence of such a policy.

The methods of pressure and blackmail in foreign policy are making themselves felt in various parts of the globe. Blatant violence is employed against Iran. Everybody knows this. United States actions in the Persian Gulf area threaten the sovereignty not only of that country but of other countries of the region as well.

A build-up of the United States military presence is under way in East Africa, where, most recently, new American military bases have been coming into being. This is taking place in particular in Somalia, a country whose leadership continues to make groundless territorial claims in respect of its neighbours. The Soviet Union fully supports those States which raise their voices in protest against the establishment of such bases. Surely, those who offer their homes for American military bases assist in the accumulation of inflammable material in that area, with all the ensuing dangers.

The anti-Arab Camp David deal has as its direct consequence unabated tension in the Middle East, where the situation is fraught with perilous and unforeseen developments. That should not be overlooked. That deal, which runs counter to the interests, and slights the just demands of Arab States and the inalienable rights of the Arab people of Palestine, whose only legitimate representative is the Palestine Liberation Organization, is intended to satisfy Israel's annexationist claims and to establish an American military presence in the Middle East.

In short, since the time of the separatist collusion among the United States, Israel and Egypt, the situation in that region has proved to be further from genuine peace than ever before. It is for that reason that Camp David is rejected by Arab States and denounced by all those who are interested in a just and comprehensive settlement in the Middle East, not in a settlement dictated by imperialist interests. That has been graphically demonstrated by the recent decisions of the emergency special session of the United Nations General Assembly on the Palestinian question, and by recent decisions of the United Nations Security Council.

In another region, the Far East, Washington is striving to strengthen its political and military position and is heating up militarist trends that are far from being on the wane in certain quarters in Japan. Peking is acting in unison. Yet one would think that the Japanese leadership would display the ability to see things as they are and succeed in resisting the outside influences prodding that country onto the road of hostility towards the Soviet Union, a road that has already led Japan to a catastrophe.

The United States, whose troops, contrary to the decision of the thirtieth session of the United Nations General Assembly, still remain on South Korean territory, shares with the puppet Seoul regime the responsibility for the fact that the Korean problem is still unresolved. It obstructs the normalization of the situation on the Korean Peninsula and the reunification of Korea on a peaceful and democratic basis without any outside interference, as is proposed by the Government of the Korean People's Democratic Republic.

The United States adds to the destabilization of the situation in Indo-China and in the whole of South-East Asia. Here, too, the United States acts in league with the Peking hegemonists who, having committed aggression against the Socialist Republic of Vietnam, continue their demonstrations of military force on the Sino-Vietnamese border and stage provocations against the People's Democratic Republic of Laos and the People's Republic of Kampuchea, whose voice, we are sure, will sooner or later be heard from this rostrum. Other countries of that region are also under constant pressure from Peking and Washington.

In recent years, the United States and some other Western countries have resorted ever more frequently to playing the "China card"—they love it—in order to use to their own advantage the great-Power ambitions of Peking, which is itself keeping pace with the most zealous proponents of the position-of-strength policy and is stubbornly and cynically advocating the idea of the inevitability of another world war—with never a thought of giving up this idea. I stress this idea of the inevitable nature of a new world war.

While these countries are intent on having China follow ever more closely in the wake of their policy, Peking, for its part, in seeking a rapprochement with them, attempts to put them on the track of the cold war and confrontation with the Soviet Union, although our country, I would note here, stands for the normalization of relations with the People's Republic of China, as has been repeatedly stated at the most authoritative level.

Even if we leave aside the question of who is playing whose cards more, it must be emphasized that this game is dangerous to the cause of peace.

The facts I have enumerated suffice to lead us to the conclusion that influential circles in some countries would like to squander away the substantial assets of the policy of *détente* that were accumulated, especially in the 1970s, as a result of prolonged and strenuous efforts by many States.

Not long ago, in Vienna, where the SALT II Treaty was signed, there was a frank conversation between Leonid Brezhnev and President Carter of the United States. The latter also recognized the need to maintain the existing approximate parity of military strength between East and West, the Soviet Union and the United States. This was recognized also by the leaders of other NATO countries. At present, contrary to their previous statements, the leaders of the NATO bloc are seeking to change the strategic balance of forces in the world in that bloc's favour. That is the root cause of the aggravation of the present international situation.

Attempts to give a different interpretation of world developments and to cast aspersions on the foreign policy of the USSR by once again resorting to the myth of a Soviet military threat constitute a gross deception.

Only the gullible could heed the groundless assertions to the effect that the aggravation of the world situation has been caused by the temporary introduction of a limited Soviet military contingent into Afghanistan. As has already been explained repeatedly, our move was made to assist the Afghan people in protecting their country's sovereignty and repelling armed incursions into its territory from the outside, as well as to prevent the emergence of a direct threat to the security of the USSR on its southern border. That assistance was rendered in response to repeated appeals by the Government of Afghanistan, and it is in full accord with the Soviet–Afghan Treaty of 1978 and the United Nations Charter. I believe that there still exist in the United States persons who signed the United Nations Charter, which contains a provision relevant to this.

Now that the situation in Afghanistan is gradually returning to normal, some of our military units have been brought home by agreement with the Afghan Government. Not infrequently, and notably at the United Nations, one may hear persons speak in favour of a complete withdrawal of the Soviet military contingent. To that we reply that the USSR will withdraw its contingent by agreement with the Government of Afghanistan as soon as the reasons that made the introduction of a contingent necessary have been removed, but not before.

It will be recalled that the Afghan Government has put forward a programme for a political settlement of the situation around Afghanistan. It is quite possible to achieve such a settlement on that basis and the Soviet Union is firmly in favour of that. But any attempts that run counter to the sovereign rights of Afghanistan are futile. The truth about the nature and essence of events in Afghanistan and around that non-aligned State is steadily gaining ground.

The allegation being bandied about in certain Western countries that the Soviet Union is building up its military might on a scale that exceeds its defence requirements is also patently false. There are some experts who make such claims. Our country believes that the strategic parity of forces obtaining in the world is sufficient to protect its own security and that of its allies and friends. Our country aspires to nothing more.

Let us take Central Europe, the area with the highest concentration of military forces confronting each other. There, the Soviet Union, unlike the NATO countries, has not for a long time now increased its forces by a single soldier, a single tank, a single aircraft. On the contrary, it has been reducing them.

As for the medium-range nuclear systems deployed in the European part of the USSR—we do not deploy them on the territories of other States at all—in terms of the number of launchers and the yield of their nuclear warheads, such systems have recently even been somewhat reduced. The leaders who, with a specific purpose in mind, are trying to mislead people are also fully aware of that. However, being at odds with the truth, they systematically feed public opinion with fraudulent propaganda whenever they talk about the foreign policy or the armed forces of the Soviet State. The products of such propaganda are often to be seen floating around this hall.

Against that background, it is obvious that those who speak of some unprecedented build-up of our country's defence potential are in fact trying to turn attention away from their own plans to deploy hundreds of new United States nuclear systems on the territories of several West European countries.

In order to prevent another round of the arms race, the Soviet Union has proposed negotiations to be held on the basis of equality and with observance of the principle of equal security. In order to remove the obstacles to negotiations arising from the NATO decision, we propose that discussions be initiated without delay on the question of medium-range nuclear weapons in Europe and the question of United States forward-based systems, concurrently and in organic interrelation. It is understood that eventual agreements would be implemented after the entry into force of the SALT II Treaty.

The USSR has not so far received a substantive reply to its initiative. The Soviet proposal is talked and written about; various assessments of it are made and it is sometimes alleged that it is unclear or even mysterious. But those who are supposed to respond to it have as yet said nothing intelligible. And the reason for all this is that the Soviet Union's proposal is designed to find a genuine solution to the problem of strengthening European security and to erect a barrier to prevent Europe from becoming an even more dangerous staging area for military confrontation, with enormous quantities of nuclear weapons in readiness day and night.

It would seem that the delays in making a constructive reply to the substance of our proposal are intended to muffle the positive international response which it has evoked. We express the hope that common sense and a responsible approach to improving the situation in Europe will yet prevail. We would like to believe that. The Soviet Union is ready to start talks with its partners on the aforementioned just basis at any time.

Of course, if there is any lack of clarity as to the substance of our proposal, we would not be adverse to removing it through consultations and exchanges of views. But it is essential that the participants in such exchanges of views should join us at the negotiating table in good faith and not just to kill time.

At the same time it must be clearly understood that the Soviet Union and the Warsaw Treaty countries will not allow the military-strategic balance they have achieved between them and the member States of the North Atlantic Treaty Organization (NATO) to be upset. Any calculations aimed at disrupting this balance should be discarded.

The USSR and other countries of the socialist community have never sought, and are not seeking, any military superiority. They have not had, and will not have, any strategic doctrine other than a defensive one. As Leonid Brezhnev stated once again, with all clarity, in his recent speech in the city of Alma-Ata,

"Our country's foreign policy is a clear and honest policy of peace which is not directed against anyone else. We do not encroach on anybody's land; we do not interfere in anybody's internal affairs. But we shall always manage to defend our rights and legitimate interests."

Peaceableness is an inherent feature of the foreign policy of socialism, which is a social system having no classes interested in war. A world without wars, said Lenin, is the very ideal of socialism.

The source from which the policy of the socialist countries draws confidence in its strength is the identity of their objectives in constructing a new society, in defending the cause of peace. To this end the perfecting of relations of full equality, fraternal unity, comradely mutual assistance and fruitful co-operation in all spheres of life is constantly in the forefront of their attention, and this was once again borne out by the results of the meetings held in the Crimea last summer between Leonid Brezhnev and the leaders of fraternal parties and States.

The Soviet Union and the socialist community have been and will continue to be in the vanguard of the struggle for international security. However, we do not claim a monopoly in this field. We shall stand in the same line with all States which consistently pursue a policy of peace and of averting the threat of another world war; a policy of *détente*.

The concrete deeds of the socialist countries are shown in a whole series of initiatives, in particular those they have advanced since the previous session of the United Nations General Assembly. These are: the proposal put forward by the meeting of the Political Consultative Committee of the Warsaw Treaty Member States for holding a top-level conference of the leaders of States of all regions of the world to discuss problems related to the elimination of hotbeds of international tension and to the prevention of war; the measures for curbing the arms race, for disarmament and for strengthening peace in Europe and throughout the world contained in the declaration which was adopted at that same meeting; the initiative of the USSR with regard to holding negotiations on medium-range nuclear weapons in Europe in close interrelation with United States forward-based systems; the recent withdrawal by the Soviet Union of 20,000 troops, 1000 tanks and other materiel from the German Democratic Republic, a process which has been completed; the proposal submitted by the socialist countries at the Vienna talks providing, among other steps recommended, for the reduction of United States military personnel by 13,000 and of Soviet military personnel by 20,000, in addition to the Soviet military contingent which has been unilaterally withdrawn from the territory of the German Democratic Republic; and the withdrawal of some Soviet military units from Afghanistan.

A comparison of the list of the initiatives we have advanced during the past year alone with NATO's record immediately reveals the contrast between the two main lines in world politics. The facts are self-evident in showing which policy line is consonant with the aspirations of the peoples and which is in conflict with them.

It certainly seems to be far from easy to create a distorted picture of our foreign policy in the minds of the peoples. Misinformation and, primarily of course, slander directed against it, backfire on those who resort to them.

Given the present state of international relations—when the policy of

détente is being put to a severe test, when the danger of war is growing—
it is essential to multiply efforts in order to arrest this course of
developments. Even if the initial steps were not to be the most radical
ones possible they would still be steps which could infuse an invigorating
spirit into the international political climate.

Proceeding from this, the Soviet Union proposes the inclusion in the
agenda of this session of the United Nations General Assembly of an
important and urgent item entitled "Certain urgent measures for
reducing the war danger", and we are submitting for the Assembly's
consideration a relevant draft resolution.

What is proposed here is the adoption in the immediate future of the
following measures.

First, an important step would be for the States members of military
alliances to renounce the expansion of existing military–political
groupings through the admission of new members, and for countries
which are not members of such groupings to renounce joining them. All
States, without exception, should avoid any action conducive to the
establishment of new military alliances or to assigning military functions
to regional organizations which have no such functions at present.

At the same time, the statements repeatedly made by the USSR and
the other socialist countries concerning their readiness to disband the
Warsaw Treaty Organization if, simultaneously, the North Atlantic
Treaty Organization (NATO) bloc were dissolved and, as a first step, to
eliminate the military organizations of the two groupings, starting with a
mutual reduction of their military activities, remain fully valid.

Second, it is essential that all States, and first of all the permanent
members of the Security Council and countries which have military
agreements with them, undertake not to increase as from a certain
date—say January 1 of the coming year—their armed forces and
conventional armaments, as a first step towards their subsequent
reduction.

Third, proceeding from the premiss that an early conclusion of an
appropriate convention, with the participation of all nuclear and non-
nuclear States, would best serve to strengthen security guarantees for
non-nuclear States, the USSR is also prepared to consider other possible
solutions to this problem, provided the other nuclear Powers adopt a
similar approach. We call upon all nuclear countries to make identical

and solemn declarations concerning the non-use of nuclear weapons against non-nuclear States which have no nuclear weapons on their territories. Such declarations, if they serve the aforementioned objective, could be reinforced by an authoritative decision of the Security Council.

At the same time, the Soviet Union reaffirms that it will never use nuclear weapons against those countries which renounce the production and acquisition of such weapons and do not have them on their territories.

Fourth, we are convinced that, if our partners in the negotiations, the United States and the United Kingdom, show corresponding readiness, it is quite realistic to expect a successful conclusion within a short time-limit of the elaboration of an international treaty on the complete and general prohibition of nuclear weapons tests. We consider this to be possible. There are no insuperable obstacles.

To this end, the USSR proposes that all nuclear Powers declare themselves ready to renounce within a period of one year, beginning on a date to be agreed by them, all nuclear explosions. The point is to have a one-year moratorium while negotiations would continue with a view to achieving a more radical solution.

A prompt implementation of all these measures would blunt the edge of some of the issues in international relations. It could be instrumental in easing the burden of military expenditures of States, strengthening the regime of the non-proliferation of nuclear weapons, and creating favourable conditions for progress in the field of the arms race limitation.

We hope that the United Nations General Assembly will give these proposals careful and due consideration, and that it will support them.

In today's international conditions, the Soviet Union considers it an imperative duty of the United Nations Member States to intensify their efforts in all major directions of the struggle for peace. As hitherto, the Soviet Union will maintain and deepen the dialogue and co-operate with all States that display political will towards this end.

By the way, with regard to "dialogue", this is a term often used nowadays. One way of reasoning goes like this: if there is something I do not like in the policy of a State, I will not speak with it. But to our mind such capriciousness, such vagaries, have been widely condemned, and rightly so. There should be no place for them in politics.

At the current session, we consider it necessary to recall the United Nations decisions which have yet to be implemented, proposals put forward by the USSR and other countries, as well as to set forth our views on enhancing the efficiency of efforts in specific sectors of this historic struggle. To this end, the USSR is submitting to this session a memorandum entitled "For peace and disarmament, for international security guarantees". This memorandum will soon be in delegations' hands—indeed, many of them may already have it.

There is hardly any need to prove that the greatest threat to peace on our planet is posed by the unabated nuclear arms race. There is, however, a need to say again and again that it is inadmissible to put up with a situation where people live under the burden of a constant fear of a nuclear disaster.

While recognizing the complexities of the problem of nuclear disarmament, once should not toe the line of those who shirk even its discussion. It is for people to resolve this burning problem. People have created the nuclear weapon, and it is they who can and must outlaw and destroy it. There is no denying that man's mind is stronger than his fists.

Nonetheless, the fact remains that the negotiations proposed by the Soviet Union for ending the production of all types of nuclear weapons and gradually reducing their stockpiles until they have been completely destroyed have never started, owing to the negative position of certain Governments. We stand for the talks getting under way and for the Governments concerned to adopt a serious attitude towards them, so that the relevant decision of the special session of the United Nations General Assembly devoted to disarmament may be fulfilled.

The conclusion by States of an agreement on the renunciation of the use of force in international relations would be of great importance for the cause of peace and *détente*. In statements made from this rostrum the Soviet Union has repeatedly stressed the importance of such an agreement and of the resolution adopted by the United Nations General Assembly in 1972 entitled "Non-use of force in international relations and permanent prohibition of the use of nuclear weapons". In the current situation, the duty of the United Nations to pronounce itself in favour of the prompt completion of efforts in this field is becoming ever more imperative.

To lessen the threat of nuclear war it is of decisive importance to check the further growth of the strategic potentials of States and subsequently to reduce strategic nuclear-weapon systems quantitatively and to limit them qualitatively.

And could anyone deny how significant would be the entry into force of the Soviet–American Treaty on the limitation of strategic offensive weapons (SALT II)? The USSR is ready to ratify the SALT II Treaty and afterwards strictly to comply with all its provisions. It is also the intention of the Soviet Union to participate in the negotiations on the further limitation and reduction of strategic arms, with strict observance of the principle of equality and equal security.

But it would not be out of place to say in this connection that, although the Treaty has not yet entered into force, the American side is already laying a mine under it in the shape of a plan whose implementation would open up the possibility of excluding from appropriate verification a large number of strategic nuclear-missile systems. I think that this is well known to all representatives in this hall.

Now that the nuclear missile arsenals of States are being constantly inflated, the question of elaborating and adopting more reliable measures to prevent the possibility of the accidental or unauthorized use of nuclear weapons is becoming ever more acute, and repeated false nuclear alarms in the United States armed forces give ground for serious thought in this regard.

Indeed, the fact that the alarm was false becomes known later— afterwards. And this surely leads to certain conclusions.

Such things should not take place if the leadership of a State deals with all questions pertaining to nuclear weapons with a sense of responsibility.

It has always been the stand of the Soviet Union that the strengthening of the regime of the non-proliferation of nuclear weapons should be a subject of unfailing concern. The failure to see that transfers of nuclear equipment, materials and technology intended for peaceful purposes could serve as a channel for spreading nuclear arms is fraught with the most negative consequences.

An important step would be taken if an international agreement were reached on the non-stationing of nuclear weapons on the territories of countries where there are no such weapons at the present time, regardless of whether or not these countries are allies of a given nuclear

State. However, owing to the opposition of certain Powers, progress in negotiations on this question is slow to say the least.

The lethal power of such means of mass destruction as chemical weapons does not at all pale in comparison to the monstrous destructive force of nuclear armaments. The negotiations on their prohibition have been dragging on for many years, with the distance to the finishing line— the signing of a relevant international convention—remaining almost as long as ever. It will be impossible to cover the remaining distance without energetic efforts on the part of all participants in the negotiations. We, for our part, have been persistently working towards that end.

The Soviet Union, as before, is fully in favour of observance of the Convention on the prohibition of bacteriological weapons. It has always been, and remains, faithful to the spirit and letter of the Convention, which constitutes a measure of real disarmament.

Sometimes representatives of military quarters float allegations that the Soviet Union does not always respect the obligations it assumes under international agreements. But such allegations are a ploy that is as old as the universe. The reasoning of their authors is obviously as follows: if peoples are to be deceived, let the deception be huge to make an impression. But in the contest between truth and deception, truth has always been victorious sooner or later. The Soviet Union has not violated one single international agreement and it does not intend to do so.

Those who resort to such allegations attempt to weave them into a thick shroud to cover their own unseemly deeds. Look at what is taking place in the country whose representatives indulge in such statements: plans are openly being discussed there for building new plants to produce chemical weapons. I said plans are being discussed there, but it would be more accurate to say that they are being discussed here, and this is being done at a time when representatives of that very country are sitting at the negotiating table where the question of banning chemical weapons is being discussed.

And how often has the Soviet Union made representations regarding non-compliance with agreements by those who aim such allegations at the Soviet Union? Those for whom these words of ours are meant know that very well.

That is how things are with attempts to cast a shadow on the attitude of the Soviet Union towards its international obligations.

The world is not safeguarded from the possible emergence in the not-too-distant future of new types and systems of weapons of mass destruction. This is particularly dangerous now, since forces have appeared that are counting on achieving military superiority. The USSR favours the adoption of additional measures to ensure the conclusion of an international agreement banning the development of new types and systems of weapons of mass destruction, as well as the conclusion, as necessary, of special agreements on individual types of such weapons.

Vigilance and perseverance are required in the struggle against the neutron weapon—that barbarous means of annihilation. The position of our country, which declared in the past that it would not begin production of neutron weapons unless the United States did so, remains valid and it also applies to the possible emergence of such weapons in any other State.

Objectively there is a basis for the early completion of work on a treaty banning one type of weapon of mass destruction—radiological weapons.

Due to the opposition of certain Powers, the question of what are called conventional armaments has actually been left outside the sphere of concrete negotiations. The solution of that question should be speedily moved to a practical plane. Representatives of certain countries wish to talk endlessly and willingly on that subject, while doing nothing, however, to facilitate agreement.

The danger of war could also be reduced in no small measure by the limitation and cessation of the arms race in particular geographical areas as well. That applies first of all to Europe. Developments in Europe have always had a most significant impact on the state of world affairs.

The Soviet Union, like other countries of the socialist community, is seeking to ensure a steady continuation of the process initiated by the European Conference and compliance with all the provisions and principles of the Final Act adopted by that forum.

As we are staunch advocates of the Leninist principle of peaceful co-existence, we have always striven to ensure that no avenue in our relations with States belonging to a different social system, including the

United States, should remain unexplored. We expect those States to do likewise. Indeed, an overwhelming majority of them do build their relations with us in that fashion.

The course for maintaining and strengthening security in Europe and for reducing the level of military confrontation on the continent was convincingly demonstrated last May at the meeting of the Political Consultative Committee of the Warsaw Treaty Member States. It was also manifested during the recent talks held by Leonid Brezhnev with French President Valéry Giscard d'Estaing and with the Chancellor of the Federal Republic of Germany, Helmut Schmidt.

In the series of proposals made by the countries of the socialist community with regard to Europe, a prominent place belongs to the initiative for the conclusion by all participant States in the European Conference of a treaty on the non-first-use of either nuclear or conventional arms—I repeat, nuclear or conventional arms. Does anybody who stands for peace object to this proposal?

The socialist countries have taken steps, some of them quite recently, which provide a solid basis for reaching agreement at the Vienna talks on the mutual reduction of armed forces and armaments in Central Europe. Success in that work is being obstructed by those who do not wish to give up attempts to gain unilateral advantage to the detriment of the security interests of the Warsaw Treaty States.

The holding of a conference on military *détente* and disarmament in Europe is a matter of paramount importance. We express the hope that all States concerned will contribute to the realization of this idea. This is a good idea.

A significant role in achieving general agreement on the convocation and the subject matter of the conference is to be played by the Madrid meeting of representatives of participant States in the European Conference. We wish the meeting to be businesslike and to be crowned with positive results on all sections of the Helsinki Final Act. We urge other countries to display the same constructive approach to the Madrid meeting.

The problem of lessening tensions in the Indian Ocean is increasingly important. The Soviet Union has invariably supported the initiative of the littoral States to turn the Indian Ocean into a zone of peace. For the purpose of implementing that initiative we shall continue to co-operate with all States concerned, *inter alia*, at the international conference on the Indian Ocean scheduled for 1981. The same objective would be served by the resumption of the Soviet–American talks, suspended by the United States, on the limitation and subsequent reduction of military activities in that ocean. We are ready at any time to sit at the same table with the United States and to continue negotiations on that matter. It is now up to the United States.

The Warsaw Treaty countries favour discussion within the framework of the United Nations of the question of limiting and reducing the level of military presence and military activities, be it in the Atlantic, the Indian or the Pacific Ocean, in the Mediterranean or in the Persian Gulf. Agreements in that field would serve the interests of peace and stabilization of the international situation. The Soviet Union is prepared at any time to come to the negotiating table to discuss this issue with the States concerned.

More than once has the United Nations tried its hand at achieving agreed decisions on the reduction of the military budgets of States. However, each time it encountered resolute opposition and all means of misinformation are employed here to frustrate any progress towards agreement in this extremely important field.

As a result, the military appropriations of States have been growing from year to year. And what a variety of methods have been devised by certain governments to extract from the taxpayer ever greater sums to be fed into the grinder of military production. And this is taking place at a time when hundreds of millions of people in the world are suffering from starvation, have no access to proper medical services and education or have no roof over their heads. Resources which could be used for the benefit of people are being consumed by the arms race. Regrettably, the United Nations has not so far pronounced its weighty opinion on that score. It has great possibilities for speaking out.

Now as before, the USSR is prepared to proceed to negotiations on specific reductions, in absolute figures or in terms of percentage points, of military budgets of States permanent members of the Security Council as well as of other States with large economic and military potential. We are also prepared to reach agreement on the amounts which each State reducing its military budget would allocate for increased economic aid to developing countries.

The Soviet Union believes that thorough preparations should be carried out for the special session of the United Nations General Assembly devoted to disarmament which is to take place in 1982. That session should be followed by a world conference on disarmament to ensure that a profound consideration of disarmament issues may result not merely in recommendations, but in decisions to be implemented by States fully, without any exception.

There must be implementation of the United Nations Declaration on the Granting of Independence to Colonial Countries and Peoples, adopted 20 years ago on the initiative of the USSR.

We welcome the emergence this year of new independent States.

In southern Africa there is the Republic of Zimbabwe, which was born in the flames of the long struggle of its valiant people. We are convinced that the day will come when the people of Namibia, too, will win their freedom and independence.

Everything must be done to bring nearer the moment when here in this hall of the General Assembly final victory will be solemnly celebrated over the monster which has taken the lives of or crippled many millions of human beings, which for centuries has mercilessly exploited many a people and whose name is colonialism.

The Soviet Union has always shown respect for the legitimate aspirations of States which have freed themselves from the yoke of colonialism. We have good relations with most of them. We note with satisfaction the increasing role of these States in international politics and appreciate the peaceful anti-imperialist orientation of the Movement of the Non-Aligned Countries.

Our country has consistently supported the developing States in their desire to attain economic independence, their inalienable right to dispose of their natural resources and their legitimate demand for the restructuring of international economic relations on the basis of equality, without any discrimination.

Problems affecting all mankind are becoming ever more conspicuous in the broad spectrum of the concerns of our time. I shall make special mention of one of them; preservation of the earth's nature. The Soviet Union wishes to see man show greater care and concern for nature, and to see natural resources used in the interests of all nations on a scientific basis.

However, everybody knows what immense material and intellectual resources are being deflected from the solution of this problem by the arms race, how ruinous and perhaps irreversible is the damage inflicted on the entire human environment by military activities of States, such as tests of various types of weapons and above all of nuclear weapons, the stockpiling of poisonous chemical agents, and so on to say nothing of the disastrous consequences which a nuclear war would have not only for people but also for nature in general.

It is the bounden duty of the United Nations to draw the attention of the States of the world to their historic responsibility for preserving the nature of the earth, which is indispensable for the life of present and future generations and to make its contribution to the development of international co-operation in this field. We have submitted an appropriate draft resolution for consideration by the General Assembly at the current session.

Our views and specific proposals on important measures which should be adopted in the evolving situation stem from the peaceful nature of the foreign policy of the Soviet Union. We are convinced that the necessary possibilities for staving off the threat of war and putting international peace on a more solid foundation exist. There are forces able to do that. For it is the will of the peoples and the policies of States, not fate, that determine the trend of world developments.

No responsible politician in the world can remain indifferent to the course pursued by those countries in whose policies the cult of war is becoming the dominant factor. Indeed, even here and now in the host country of the United Nations Headquarters there is massive propaganda in favour of nuclear war before the very eyes, it can be said, of the public. But it is not only a question of propaganda; plans for such a war are being worked out and discussed, and this is all being done at government level.

In the atmosphere of militarist frenzy which has of late become so widespread in the United States, there is ever less room left for sound and sober assessments of the world situation and well-considered conclusions on the conduct of policy.

The United Nations would be right to issue a firm warning to those who seek a dangerous exacerbation of tension and war hysteria. It would be a good thing to say to those responsible: "Gentlemen, do not push the rock down the hill, for there is a risk that you will not be able to stop it later on."

Saving mankind from the scourge of war is the goal towards which the States should direct their efforts instead of preparing for war. If the General Assembly took that stand it would add a bright page to the book of modern history.

Despite all the differences in social systems, levels of economic development, national characteristics and historical destinies of the States represented in the United Nations, all peoples want to live with confidence in their future. No country, no Government, if it expresses the aspirations and will of its people, can remain aloof from the struggle for disarmament, for the relaxation of tensions and for peace. This is the basis on which the Soviet Union acts.

"We shall continue to spare no effort," stressed Leonid Brezhnev, "to preserve *détente*, everything positive that was achieved in the 1970s, to ensure a turn towards disarmament, to uphold the right of peoples to free and independent development, to preserve and consolidate peace."

Our country and its representatives are prepared to participate in a most constructive manner in the work of this session and to contribute actively to its success.

To Guarantee Peace for the Common Good of Mankind

Speech at the 36th Session of the UN General Assembly, 22 September 1981

Mr. President,
Esteemed delegates,
Speaking from this rostrum today, I should like first of all to recall that the United Nations enjoys solid credibility among the peoples of the world as a forum whose principal objective is to serve as an effective instrument for the maintenance of peace.

It is well known that the birth of the United Nations was the result of the peoples' determination to preclude another world tragedy. Its establishment reflected the awareness, deeply rooted in people's minds following the great victory over fascism, of the need for them to unite closely in the name of peace and to prevail over the forces of militarism and aggression. That is why the very first lines of this Organization's Charter proclaimed the goal "to save succeeding generations from the scourge of war". These are clear and emphatic words. I should like to express the confidence that these words will never fade and will never lose their profound meaning. They are a solemn oath taken by the founding States when creating the United Nations. Today that is the duty of all the 155 countries represented in the United Nations.

True, there are some who now try to contend that there are things more important than peace. However, it is obvious that the peoples have never authorized those leaders to say this on their behalf.

Peace is a priceless asset of all people on earth; it is a decisive prerequisite to progress in any sphere of human endeavour. That was true in the past, and it is all the more true now. As Leonid Brezhnev has stressed,

> "the safeguarding of peace—no other task is more important now at the international level for our party for our people and for all the peoples of the world. By safeguarding peace we are working not only for the people who are living today, and not only for our children and grandchildren; we are working for the happiness of countless future generations".

Acting on that fundamental assumption, the 26th Congress of the Communist Party of the Soviet Union—the highest forum of the Soviet Communists—recently put forward a whole series of proposals on the key problems of international life, which have evoked a broad response in the world.

They provide for far-reaching steps designed to limit arms, eliminate hotbeds of tension and strengthen confidence among States. They cover both the political and the military fields, deal with nuclear-missile weapons and conventional armaments and bear upon the situation in Europe, in the Near, Middle and Far East and in other regions of the world. Underlying these proposals is one single desire: to improve the international climate, to ward off the threat of war.

In the international arena the Soviet Union stands shoulder to shoulder with other socialist States. Recently, during their meetings in the Crimea, the leaders of the parties and countries of the socialist community had an opportunity once again to harmonize those countries' assessments and actions in the light of the situation taking shape in the world. The same purpose is served by regular meetings of the Political Consultative Committee of the States members of the Warsaw Treaty and by the activities of the Council for Mutual Economic Assistance.

The foreign policy of the socialist countries has been and continues to be a policy of peace. It follows from the very nature of our social system, of whose advantages we are deeply convinced. It is determined by the fact that under this system there are no social strata which would make profits out of war and war preparations or derive benefits from militaristic policies. Nevertheless, we do not impose our social system on anybody. The peoples themselves determine, and should determine their destinies. That has always been and remains the cornerstone of the scientific world outlook that guides us in both our domestic and our foreign policies.

In building a society free from social and national exploitation and oppression, the socialist countries are following an unexplored path. This is not always easy; but the laws of social development and the strength of our ideals ensure for the socialist countries a steady advance in all spheres of life.

Futile are the attempts by certain circles in Western countries to interfere in the internal affairs of the socialist States. Such attempts are being made, in particular, with regard to the Polish People's Republic. No small effort is being made to shake loose the socialist foundations of the Polish State. It will be recalled, in this connection, that the leaders of the Member States of the Warsaw Treaty made the following statement:

"It was reiterated that socialist Poland, the Polish United Workers' Party and the Polish people can firmly count on the fraternal solidarity and support of the Warsaw Treaty countries. The representatives of the Polish United Workers' Party stressed that Poland has been, is and will remain a socialist State, a firm link in the common family of the countries of socialism."

The Republic of Cuba is coping with the tasks of socialist development and pursuing a policy of peace in difficult external conditions. The Soviet Union has invariably supported and will continue to support the Cuban people in their struggle to safeguard their sovereignty.

Hostile, criminal intrigues against Cuba on the part of the United States, which have of late been stepped up, must cease. Washington does not like socialist Cuba, but it may well be asked whether the social system of the United States is to everybody's liking. No one has the right to tell the Cuban people how they should manage their internal affairs.

In a bid to besmirch the socialist countries, their social system and their peaceful policies, all kinds of fabrications are being resorted to, and those who resort to them seem to be competing with one another as to who can come up with the most preposterous invention. Some even go so far as to predict an early sunset of socialism. I wonder how long it took them to find that word "sunset". These people seem to be endowed with a remarkable gift of inventiveness, but I must say that they do not seem to have a very good idea of the objective processes of historical development. Are they looking for the sunset in the right country? Is that where they should be looking? Are they not looking in the wrong direction?

How many were the prophets who predicted the downfall of socialism, but what of it? Their prophesies have invariably fallen by the wayside, while history has continued inexorably to follow its course.

The Soviet Union has never threatened and is not threatening anybody. Since the days of Lenin, peace and friendship among nations have been inscribed on the banner of the Soviet State, and we have invariably been true to this ideal. Today it is as dear to the people of our country as it was in Lenin's day.

In examining and solving international problems we rely on the ideals of the freedom and progress of nations, on the principles of respect for the independence of all States and all peoples, and aim to consolidate the foundations of life rather than prepare the funeral of mankind.

There exists, however, another trend in world politics, which has quite different goals. It is the course followed in the militarist circles of imperialist States. The sum and substance of that course is to seek domination over other countries and peoples, a domination that means imposing one's will upon them, their economic exploitation and the use of their territories for military strategic purposes. Washington is ever more frequently heard to speak about the American leadership of the world, though no one has entitled the United States to claim such leadership.

The architects of that course see as the main instrument for achieving their objectives the whipping up of international tensions and the use, as they put it themselves, of methods of force in politics. Even when they occasionally recognize in words the possibility of a diplomatic alternative they hasten to make it clear that diplomacy, unless it relies on force, does not suit them.

The most typical manifestations of that policy line are: a further whipping up of the arms race; an overt claim to military superiority over the Soviet Union; the setting up of a wide network of military bases and the stationing of American troops on foreign territories; the undermining of the basic principles of Soviet–American relations worked out earlier as a result of tremendous effort; pressure on other States, particularly in Europe, to curtail their political, trade and economic ties with the socialist countries; and slanderous propaganda against countries adhering to the positions of peace and rejecting claims to world leadership by no matter whom.

And what great pains are taken to drag the NATO allies into following that policy. When arguments are lacking—and there is a constant lack of them to support such a hopeless and dangerous course—crude pressure is brought to bear, so as to give no respite to those who are not always eager to accept militaristic schemes alien to their interests.

It is sometimes said that Washington's present policy does not rule out prospects for developing relations between the USSR and the United States. However, in the same breath it is immediately demanded that our country should change—neither more nor less—its conduct in international affairs to satisfy American interests. In other words, the Soviet Union must give up defending its legitimate interests, give up its foreign policy.

To put forward such demands is to show a lack of seriousness. The Soviet Union will continue to pursue its course of Leninist peaceful policy. Our country does not intend to deviate from it. We do not encroach on the legitimate interests of others, but nor shall we forgo legitimate interests of our own, including commitments to our allies.

It is to be hoped that Washington will yet be able to take a more sober view of the actual state of affairs, adopt a more realistic approach to international affairs and not overestimate its capabilities while under-estimating the capabilities of others.

In order to build policy on a realistic basis one should seek, not clashes and conflicts with other countries, even though those other countries have a different social system, but rather the settlement of controversial problems at the negotiating table.

For our part, we reaffirm once again—and the USSR delegation is authorized to say it from this rostrum—that the Soviet Union has not sought, nor is it seeking, confrontation with the United States of America. We should like to have normal businesslike relations with the United States.

P.N.   F

As is known, we are in favour of a dialogue in order to seek mutually acceptable solutions to controversial problems. But we are not begging for such a dialogue, we are proposing it.

At every session of the General Assembly many States emphasize quite rightly, that the peoples are greatly endangered by the policy of crude interference in the internal affairs of other countries, support for bloodthirsty dictatorial regimes hated by their own peoples and an all-out encouragement of oppressors and hatchet-men of every stripe, including the Pol Pot experts in genocide.

The methods and forms employed in pursuing such a policy are varied. Recently, the United States has all but launched a crusade against "international terrorism", levelling accusations against one country after another. These accusations, however, are misdirected. They are utterly false. Terrorism is looked for not where it should be sought and where it really is to be found.

The scheme here is simple—to tag the label of terrorism on the struggle of peoples against colonialism and its vestiges. In other words, it is the policy of oppression, cursed by peoples, which is pictured as a struggle against terrorism. At its basis lies unwillingness to take into account the rights of peoples to manage their domestic affairs as they see fit, and refusal to accept social changes occurring in the world.

And surely, the events in El Salvador are a fitting illustration of the policy of imperialist interference in the affairs of other peoples. A real massacre has been committed there before the eyes of the whole world. Patriots defending the independence of their country, thousands of peaceful civilians are being killed. It is well known who is in charge there. And all this goes on at the very moment when we are all sitting in session here in the United Nations General Assembly hall.

What is happening in El Salvador arouses the legitimate indignation of all honest people on earth. Regrettably, the United Nations has not yet lifted a finger to assist in putting an end to these crimes against a whole nation.

And how should one view the policy of shameless pressure exerted on Libya and, in particular, the recent armed provocation against that country? Or take the so-called "rapid deployment force". Apparently, its formation is regarded in Washington as a great invention. But there is nothing great in it. It is nothing but a policeman's club intended to ensure crude interference by the United States in the affairs of independent States and to stifle the freedom of peoples.

At this world forum one cannot ignore either the concept of "American vital interests cited in justification of such a policy. This concept is importunately repeated in almost every official statement by Washington on the subject of the international situation. It is interpreted in such a way as to enable the United States to declare any part of the world a sphere of its interests and to take any steps there, all the way up to the use of force.

Europe, Asia, the Middle East and Latin America, they are all there. It seems that the only area still missing is the South Pole, but it too may soon be added. Everything is there except the right of the United States to do all this. Neither the United States nor any other country has been granted the right to hold sway over the entire globe. This is nothing but arbitrariness.

As is known, a whole United States naval armada has been assembled in the Persian Gulf. This action is directed against Iran, against the Soviet Union and against a number of independent countries of Asia and Africa. The United States Navy must leave this area. It has nothing to do there, nothing to defend. That would be a sensible act.

Neither the size nor the power, nor the resources of this or that State give it the right to impose by force or threat of force its will on other countries and arbitrarily to declare any part of the world as a sphere of its vital interests.

If such a right were to be recognized for any country or group of countries, then, apparently, all instruments of international law should be destroyed. Indeed, little would be left then of the United Nations Charter itself.

The ruling circles of a number of North Atlantic Treaty Organization (NATO) countries now worship but one god—an unrestrained arms race. Everything that serves this end is acceptable to them.

This arms race is invariably accompanied by a torrent of speeches and permeated with militarist frenzy, including speeches by top-level statesmen. Those who advocate inflated arms programmes resort to any means imaginable. Deception is held in special esteem by them. They deceive one another, they deceive the people, they deceive their kin and strangers alike.

The most salient element of deception is the myth of a "Soviet threat". It is repeated endlessly, to the point of stupefaction, day and night. In this manner it is easier to confuse people and extort money for armaments.

In these conditions decisions are taken on a huge increase in military expenditures such as history has never before known.

The urge to expand their military presence wherever possible has not acquired the element of a real Bacchanalia, with half a million United States troops stationed in more than a dozen countries.

Today the policy of the United States is beset by such an obsession, especially in setting up military bases near the borders of the Soviet Union and the areas adjacent to it. Of course, the States against which these bases are aimed have to take all this into account so as safely to protect their security.

Who would believe that it is concern for peace that motivates the accelerated pace of the development of ever-new types of weapons, including MX intercontinental ballistic missiles, Trident submarine-launched missiles, the new strategic bomber, various types of cruise missiles and many other things.

What is the purpose of all this? The purpose is to try to upset the established strategic balance, obtain military supremacy and, on this basis, impose one's will upon others.

The Soviet Union condemns this policy as adventuristic. The whipping-up of the arms race is madness. This has been repeatedly recognized by many political and public figures in the world, scientists and men of culture. Mankind must be saved from it. The present balance of military power is fully in line with the interests of peace and international stability.

Our country has never sought, nor is it now seeking, military superiority. I repeat this again: our country has never sought, nor is it now seeking, military superiority. Leonid Brezhnev has said this to the entire world many times and, *inter alia*, directly to American Presidents on various occasions. But we shall not permit others to become superior to us. We shall of course adequately meet any challenge so as to maintain the balance of power.

However, the Soviet Union has not done, and is not doing, anything beyond what is absolutely necessary to ensure a peaceful life for its people and the security of its allies and friends. We believe that the ruling circles of the North Atlantic Treaty Organization (NATO) know all that. Yet, they do not want to admit that there is no Soviet threat whatsoever, nor do they want to give up practising deception.

Indeed, what would then be left of exhortations about the need for the notorious "additional armament" of the West? Nothing would remain. That is the reason why use is made of incomparable indicators and of falsified data on strategic arms, on medium-range nuclear systems in Europe, on armed forces strength of the two sides in Central Europe or on any other aspect of the correlation of forces.

If, by any chance, some NATO official happens to concede that the Soviet Union has really never overtaken the United States and that parity is still there, there immediately follows a tongue-lashing from above. And then the record of "Soviet military superiority" is played again in order to support another increase in military appropriations and to substantiate some freshly-baked militaristic doctrine.

In some capitals such doctrines pop out as if rolling off the assembly line. Things may well reach the stage where any bureaucrat, especially if he is in the spotlight, will, once installed in an executive office, immediately come up with a strategic doctrine of his own concoction. Thus, quite recently, the world was presented with a "discovery" according to which nuclear war in general should not be feared too much, that it is "admissible" and "acceptable". This is a shameless deception designed to mislead the peoples and paralyse their will to struggle against the nuclear threat.

If the arguments of the proponents of the militaristic policy course are left free of deliberate vagueness and extravaganza, and of claims to originality, there remains only one thing, namely, the urge to intensify the arms race, in breadth and in depth, without any restraint.

But have the authors of these militaristic doctrines asked 500 million Europeans, 470 million Africans, 360 million Latin Americans, 2.5 billion Asians and, finally, their own people whether they want to perish in the flames of war? Certainly not. They just do not care.

The instigators of the arms race would like to discard everything that hampers their plans. If to this end it is necessary to renege on the obligations already assumed, that is what they do. Thus, the United States refuses to ratify the SALT II Treaty.

Negotiations had been under way for many years before the Treaty was finally agreed upon and signed. Now they say that this Treaty is not to the advantage of the United States and that it is inequitable. Of course, this is not true.

The balance of interests of the sides was accurately established and preserved in the Treaty. This is known to anyone familiar with its contents. Therefore, that is not the point. The point is that it is this very principle of equality and equal security reflected in the Treaty which is not to someone's liking.

Counting on people's ignorance, they seek to sap the Treaty by alleging that it does not envisage strategic weapons reductions. But this is not true either. The Treaty explicitly envisages such reductions, and on a substantial scale.

It is also obvious that, once agreement has been reached on strategic arms limitation and the initial reduction of their levels, it is easier to solve the task of their more radical reduction so that the balance reflects a lower arms level.

All that convincingly proves that the significance of the Treaty already agreed to and signed is as great today as at the time of its signing.

How numerous were the cases when talks on the limitation of armaments were held both in the period between the two world wars and after World War II. Yet any unbiased person will undoubtedly admit that none of those talks produced results that could be compared even to a small extent to the SALT I agreement, which is in force, and especially to the SALT II treaty, which has not become operative.

Now a question arises: why smear both the treaty and the SALT process itself? Yet exceptionally reckless politicians are now saying that the entire problem is not urgent at all, at least not till the United States implements its most sweeping arms buildup plans.

Just think of the absurdity of such a stand. The nation which claims to be the most powerful in military terms says "Let me first increase by so many times my armaments and then perhaps I shall talk about their limitation."

What is the main factor in such a stand: aggressive designs in politics, great-Power expansionist ambitions, a striving to impose on the world monstrous plans for an ever greater stockpiling of weapons for the annihilation of people instead of manufacturing things of material goods, or a desire to have an inexhaustible source of excess profits for those who manufacture armaments? It is hard to say. Most likely it is a complex mixture of all these things.

The United States decision to start the production of the neutron weapon aroused great indignation in the world. That decision is a new step towards intensifying the arms race, towards aggravating the world situation.

The peoples clearly say that they strongly oppose the fiendish neutron weapon, rightly considering it to be a particularly inhuman type of mass-destruction weapon. The neutron weapon must be totally banned. A ban must be imposed on both its production and its use.

Washington has long been making attempts to hold back or even to wreck the negotiations initiated earlier on a number of important problems. Unfortunately, quite a lot has already been done to that end. That was the case, for example, with the talks on the Indian Ocean, on limiting conventional arms transfers, on the complete and general prohibition of nuclear-weapon tests, and on the prohibition of the production of chemical weapons and the destruction of their stockpiles.

It is also appropriate to mention here the current efforts to cast aside the results of many years of work by States within the framework of the United Nations Conference on the Law of the Sea.

Other developments in international life also have their impact on the world situation. Attention is attracted to the ever-increasing closeness between Washington and Peking.

Who would object to the desire of two countries to have normal relations between them? Nobody would, of course. It is the basis on which this is done that matters. In this particular case the basis is openly hostile to many States, above all to the Soviet Union, and hostile to the cause of *détente*.

It has been proclaimed to the world that the United States intends to sell weapons to China and to help it build up its military potential. And this is done at a time when Peking is pursuing a policy that runs counter to the interests of peace, a policy of hegemonism and aggression.

The establishment of military co-operation between the United States and China—with Japan, for reasons that no one knows, getting involved in it—will be duly taken into account by the Soviet Union and, we believe, by other States.

For its part, the Soviet Union has repeatedly expressed the conviction—it was recently reiterated by Leonid Brezhnev from the rostrum of the Congress of the Communist Party of the Soviet Union—that the Chinese people's interests would best be served by a policy of peace. The Soviet Union would like to build its relations with the People's Republic of China on a good-neighbour basis. We have repeatedly reaffirmed that our proposals for normalizing these relations remain valid.

These are the main reasons, as we see them, for the recent exacerbation of the international situation.

What is the conclusion that follows from all this? According to the ideologists of militarism, mankind is to expect a pitch-dark night, an endless spiralling arms race, further conflicts and clashes.

The USSR and, we are sure, many other countries hold different views as to the prospects for world developments. Pessimism and a feeling of doom are alien to our nature. We are convinced that to prevent war is not only necessary but also possible if this is actively fought for.

Hand in hand with all States, our country is prepared to wage the struggle for curbing the arms race, removing the threat of war, settling outstanding problems. In this respect we are not politically allergic to any partner, irrespective of differences in social systems or ideologies.

The immediate and most pressing task today is to struggle for easing world tensions, curbing the arms race, eliminating the threat of war.

The Soviet Union proposes that the General Assembly, acting on behalf of all Member States, adopt a declaration solemnly proclaiming that States and statesmen who would be the first to use nuclear weapons would commit the gravest crime against humanity.

There are and can be no grounds or motives, there are and can be no circumstances or situations which would give a State the right to be the first to use nuclear weapons. It would be a crime against all the peoples, against life itself on earth.

It is likewise necessary to warn that there will never be any justification or pardon for statesmen who would make the decision on the first use of nuclear weapons.

To proclaim this in a declaration so that these words be heard in every capital, in every part of the world, would be to remind statesmen who, by virtue of their official position, are involved in making decisions on the use of nuclear weapons, that each and every one of them is personally responsible for the destinies of mankind.

We propose that the declaration further state loudly and clearly that any doctrines allowing for the first use of nuclear weapons are incompatible with human moral standards and the lofty ideals of the United Nations.

It is also most important to draw the attention, especially of leaders of nuclear-weapon States, to the fact that their supreme duty is to act in such a way as to eliminate the risk of outbreak of a nuclear conflict.

The declaration should stress that the nuclear-arms race must be stopped and reversed by joint effort, through negotiations conducted in good faith and on the basis of equality.

What is meant here is that the energy of the atom should be used not against life but for the sake of life, not for the production of weapons but for scientific progress, for improvement of the living standards of people, that is, exclusively for peaceful purposes.

This is the essence of the political document that we are proposing for adoption. We hope that this proposal will meet with wide support.

The adoption of such a document may become a major landmark on the path towards complete elimination of the threat of a nuclear conflict. No single country should stand aside from the solution of this problem.

The Soviet Union is in favour of a dialogue on all aspects of the problem of ending the arms race, on all controversial international issues, in favour of a bilateral or a multilateral dialogue.

From time to time statements are made which seem to express willingness to negotiate. However, attached to this willingness are all sorts of conditions, linkages and unequal approaches of all sorts.

If someone really intends to negotiate in this vein, we must say outright: nothing will come of it. Negotiations can be successful only if they are conducted on the basis of compliance with the principle of equality and equal security.

The Soviet Union is prepared and has been prepared for a long time to resume negotiations with the United States on the limitation of strategic weapons. Given mutual desire, headway in the solution of this problem can be made, relying on what has already been achieved and preserving the results achieved.

The Soviet–American negotiations on the limitation of nuclear weapons in Europe will apparently be resumed unless winds start blowing again in Washington in a different direction. Of course, the question of limiting medium-range nuclear weapons and those of corresponding forward-based nuclear systems of the United States should be examined and settled concurrently and in organic inter-relation, with due account of all factors determining the strategic situation on the continent.

Our country has proposed that the moment negotiations begin a moratorium should be imposed on the deployment in Europe of new medium-range nuclear-missile systems of the North Atlantic Treaty Organization (NATO) and the USSR. This proposal is based on the existing approximate parity of their respective armaments. The establishment of a moratorium would certainly exert a favourable influence on the climate of the negotiations.

The Soviet Union is prepared to reach agreement on limiting and, what is more, on reducing medium-range nuclear systems in Europe. As Leonid Brezhnev stated in Berlin on 6 October 1979:

". . . we are prepared to reduce the number of medium-range nuclear weapons deployed in the west of the Soviet Union from their present level, but only, of course, in the event that no additional medium-range nuclear weapons are deployed in Western Europe."

At the same time we must make it quite clear that should the other side artificially drag out the negotiations and start to deploy new medium-range nuclear weapons in Western Europe, the Soviet Union will have to take measures to restore the balance.

For the purpose of strengthening peace in Europe, it is also important to break the deadlock at the Vienna negotiations on the reduction of armed forces and armaments in Central Europe. The socialist countries have done a good deal to ensure progress at the Vienna negotiations. Should the Western partners show a minimum of goodwill, a solution could be found.

Of great significance is the question of convening a conference military *détente* and disarmament in Europe. As is known, this question is under discussion in Madrid at the meeting of representatives of the States participants in the European Conference.

Wishing to contribute to success, the Soviet Union has gone far to accommodate the West and has declared its willingness to include the entire European part of its territory in the zone of confidence-building measures, provided, of course, the Western side makes a corresponding step in turn. What is required now is precisely such a step.

Military *détente* on the European continent is intended to strengthen and complement political *détente*. But this does not depend on us alone.

The Soviet Union is prepared to hold negotiations on all areas of limiting the arms race and of disarmament.

Under current conditions, it is becoming increasingly important to prevent military competition from extending to outer space. Each day brings new evidence that outer space can become an arena of the arms race.

The Soviet Union has submitted to this session of the General Assembly an item entitled "Conclusion of a treaty on the prohibition of the stationing of weapons of any kind in outerspace". The Governments of all States represented here have had an opportunity of familiarizing themselves with the Soviet draft of that treaty. The draft takes into account all major aspects of the problem. We would like the exchange of views on the basis of the USSR proposal and its outcome to be constructive.

With reference to the need to take measures for curbing the arms race and for disarmament, special note should also be made of the importance of efforts to resolve conflict situations in various parts of the world and to prevent the emergence of new hotbeds of tension. States are capable of coping with this problem provided they strive to ensure a more durable peace.

The struggle of Arab peoples to defend their legitimate rights, trampled underfoot as a result of Israel's aggression, elicits understanding and support on the part of an overwhelming majority of countries. If justice has not so far been restored and the situation in the Middle East remains dangerous, it is because those in Israel's ruling circles persist in their expansionist policies and do not stop their brutal terror against the people of Lebanon, while influential forces outside that area actually encourage this policy and seek to follow the pattern of the anti-Arab Camp David deal.

Peace and stability in the Middle East can be assured only through a comprehensive political settlement which would not infringe the rights of any country or people of that region. Such a settlement must envisage the withdrawal of Israeli troops from all Arab territories occupied in 1967 and the exercise of the national rights of the Arab people of Palestine, including the right to establish their own State.

The Soviet Union consistently comes out in support of the Arabs' rights and stands for the elimination of the consequences of Israeli aggression. There is growing understanding that the path to a Middle East settlement lies through the convening of an international conference with the participation of all the parties concerned, including the Palestine Liberation Organization (PLO).

A political settlement is needed for the situation created around the Democratic Republic of Afghanistan, against which an undeclared war is still being waged. The principal role in this is played by the United States, and Peking is not far behind.

Unfortunately, Pakistan, whose territory serves as the main bridgehead for armed incursions, in effect avoids negotiations with the Democratic Republic of Afghanistan. Yet, who else but Islamabad should be primarily interested in establishing lasting peace in the region?

There has been some talk recently about the proposal by certain Western countries to convene an international conference on Afghanistan. But what is striking is that, while the conference is to be on Afghanistan, the main party concerned, the Democratic Republic of Afghanistan, has been forgotten. This forgetfulness conceals the attempt to have the internal affairs of Afghanistan, a sovereign non-aligned State, examined in a forum composed of other States, without even the participation of the Afghan Government. Of course that approach is unacceptable.

There is a basis for a political settlement; it is simple and, given goodwill, can be translated into reality. The constructive programme to this effect was set forth in the statement by the Government of the Democratic Republic of Afghanistan on 24 August of this year.

The political settlement must ensure the termination and non-resumption of armed or other interference in the affairs of Afghanistan.

Such a settlement, including reliable international guarantees, would permit the establishment, by agreement between the Afghan and Soviet sides, of modalities and timing for the withdrawal of the limited contingent of Soviet troops from Afghanistan.

In South-East Asia, too, there is no other way but negotiations to reduce tensions in the area. We support the well-known proposals by Vietnam, Laos and Kampuchea, including the proposal on holding a regional conference with the participation of the countries of Indo-China and the Member States of the Association of South-East Asian Nations (ASEAN).

However, no one should assume that the manoeuvres under way around the non-existent Kampuchean question can result in anything but harm. It is inadmissible that, under the cover of some pseudo-conferences, executioners overthrown by the people of Kampuchea or former princelings should be imposed once again on that people. They have already made their choice.

Also doomed to failure are the attempts to cast a shadow upon the Socialist Republic of Vietnam, which extended a helping hand to the Kampuchean people in their struggle for freedom and independence.

Attention is drawn to the fraudulent allegation put forward in typical Washington wrappings that someone somewhere in South-East Asia used toxic chemical substances said to be of Soviet make. It is quite obvious that at work here are those who are themselves guilty of such crimes. Now they are trying to cover their traces.

The situation in the Far East, too, offers possibilities for positive political action. One such could be an agreement on the application of confidence-building measures in the region. The implementation of such measures on a collective or a bilateral basis would make a useful contribution to the cause of *détente* in that region. The Soviet proposal on this question has been communicated to all the States concerned. We expect that in this regard they will display the required sense of responsibility.

The Korean question—still unsettled and thus an old source of tension in the Far East—can and must be solved by peaceful means. In our opinion, a suitable basis for solving the problem is provided by the proposals made by the Democratic People's Republic of Korea.

Recently the Mongolian People's Republic has taken a timely initiative by proposing a convention on mutual non-aggression and renunciation of force in relations between the States of Asia and the Pacific. Our country supports that idea.

The Republic of India is making a major contribution to maintaining stability and peace in Asia and ensuring international security. We value highly its peaceful constructive policy. Soviet–India relations, which rest on the solid basis provided by the Treaty of Peace, Friendship and Co-operation, are in the interest of our two peoples and positively serve the interests of peace.

Political means can also be effective in settling other dangerous situations and controversial problems, including the conflict between Iraq and Iran, the Cyprus problem, the situation in Western Sahara and that in the Horn of Africa. The indispensable requirement in this regard is that nobody be allowed to pit one State against another and to capitalize on conflicts between them. There should be no room for imperialist intrigues in those areas.

As is well known, the South African racist regime and its accomplices are engaged in manoeuvres aimed at thwarting the decolonization of Namibia. It is a matter of honour and is the immediate duty of the United Nations to help the people of Namibia gain their freedom. The racists and all those on whom they rely must realize that the time of colonialism is past.

An end must be put to South Africa's aggressive gangster-like actions against the People's Republic of Angola and a number of other African countries. It is necessary to condemn those actions, to demand that South Africa cease its armed intervention and to adopt international sanctions against it.

It is precisely this approach that has recently been manifested by the overwhelming majority of members of the Security Council. However, the United States has prevented that United Nations body from taking an appropriate decision, thus openly defying the African peoples and world public opinion.

The United States support for South Africa constitutes direct assistance to the aggressor. Such a course must be resolutely condemned. The United Nations should do everything that is needed to put an end to the aggression and call the aggressor to order. The decision recently adopted by the General Assembly at its special session on Namibia is a step in the right direction.

The Non-Aligned Movement, which has recently marked its twentieth anniversary, has become an important factor in world politics. The Soviet Union expresses its solidarity with the anti-imperialist orientation of the Non-Aligned Movement and supports its activities in the interest of strengthening peace.

Much is now being said about the problem of relations between the industrialized and the developing States. Various bodies, narrow and broad, of the North–South type are being proposed.

It is obvious, however, that no body will produce positive results unless developed capitalist States radically change their approach to developing countries, cease discrimination in economic relations with them and renounce the economic plundering of those countries.

Our country will continue to give developing States the necessary support in their struggle for economic independence and for the restructuring of international relations on a genuinely equitable and democratic basis.

The activities of the United Nations cannot be assessed in terms of standard units of measurement. A formal one-dimensional assessment cannot be applied to them. There are, however, grounds for saying that the United Nations has done quite a lot to enable the peoples of the world to live with greater confidence in their future.

Working actively with other socialist countries in all areas of international politics, the USSR continues to make proposals aimed at strengthening peace.

No problem, no matter what its magnitude, can or should overshadow the principal purpose for which the United Nations was created, that is, to preserve peace. It is the individual and collective duty of all States and the duty of every statesman to do for this purpose everything within the capability of human beings, of their intelligence, of their energy and of their dedication to life and its most noble ideals.

It is clearer now than ever before how enormous are the challenges confronting the peoples—to meet the rapidly growing needs in the fields of energy, food, health and education, to explore the oceans and outer space, to preserve nature. These problems can be solved provided mankind saves itself from war.

Everything should be done to ensure that in the remaining two decades of the twentieth century people can live in conditions of peace and can cross the threshold of the third millenium of our era, not with fear for the future of our civilization, but with confidence in the boundless prospects for its development. All nations, large and small, that work towards this end will always find the Soviet Union at their side.

Father Andrei Matveevich and mother Olga Yevgenevna, 1916.

During a working period in the U.S.A. The beginning of the 1940s.

A. A. Gromyko in his study.

Speech on arrival at Geneva. The '60s.

Heads of delegations from countries who are permanent members of the Security Council with the UN General Secretary, Kurt Waldheim, New York, 27 September 1972.

Meeting with Indira Ghandi during the official visit of friendship to India, 12-14 February 1980.

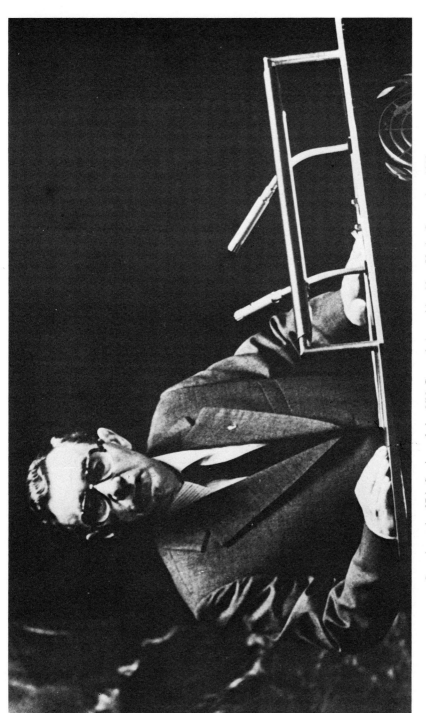

Speech at the 37th Session of the UN General Assembly. New York, September 1982.

With the UN General Secretary, Perez de Cuellar (Moscow, 1982).

To Safeguard Peace, To Prevent Nuclear War

Speech at the Second Special Session of the UN General Assembly Devoted to Disarmament, 15 June 1982

Mr. President,

Esteemed delegates,

The message of Leonid Brezhnev, General Secretary of the Central Committee of the Communist Party of the Soviet Union, President of the Presidium of the Supreme Soviet of the USSR, that has just been read out contains a condensed exposition of the Soviet Union's attitude towards the most pressing problem facing mankind today, that is, how to preserve peace.

Peaceful co-existence between States with different social systems and the settlement of all controversial issues among them by peaceful means constitute the underlying foundation of the foreign policy of the USSR. This is the essence of the Programme of Peace for the 1980s adopted by the 26th Congress of the Communist Party of the Soviet Union.

This has been convincingly borne out by all the peace initiatives of the Soviet Union and its allies, the socialist countries members of the Warsaw Treaty. This is eloquently evidenced by the statements of Leonid Brezhnev, permeated with a profound concern that the nuclear war threat be removed.

Our country is taking yet another step of exceptional importance: the Soviet Union has pledged not to be the first to use nuclear weapons. It is doing so unilaterally. If the other nuclear Powers follow suit, the likelihood of an outbreak of nuclear war will in fact be reduced to zero.

At the time the United Nations was being created, the winds of the world war could still be felt. In the United Nations Charter the founding

Member States expressed the people's aspirations by formulating a universal international obligation similar to a vow, an obligation to prevent another war.

The idea of uniting the efforts of the peoples for maintaining international security is the cornerstone of the very foundation of this world Organization. States with different social systems and ideologies fought shoulder to shoulder in the great battle against fascism that sought to impose upon the world the rule of vandals and butchers.

And today no one, particularly no politician at the helm of State policy, can remain indifferent to the clear-cut provisions of the Charter concerning the need to save succeeding generations from the scourge of war.

It is no wonder then that every year an overwhelming majority of States in the United Nations has been expressing concern lest mankind trip up and fall into the abyss, concern for preserving the most precious thing on earth, namely, peace or, in other words, life.

This session specially devoted to disarmament problems should, in a more distinct way than any of the previous sessions, express the will to rein in the demon of war.

Any responsible political leader, scientist or reasonable person, asked what a nuclear conflict could entail, would give but one reply: the consequences would be catastrophic for all peoples. Is that perhaps an exaggeration? No. Today, hardly any serious person would venture to argue against that.

Is there indeed anyone who would wish to be consumed by the flames of a nuclear war? Just knock at random on any door in any town or village and ask that question. It would be correct to say that there is no nation, big or small, that does not long for a stable peace.

If all that is so, then how can that peace be achieved? One should not expect miracles. One has to work for peace.

It is people who have created not only rifles and grenades but also highly accurate missiles and highly lethal nuclear weapons. That means that people themselves must and can scrap the tools of war, should they so wish. We are convinced that States are equal to that task, provided they pursue a policy of peace.

It is being said that the disarmament problem cannot be solved at one stroke. It is hard not to agree with that. But if that problem is to be solved step by step, one should indeed try to do so, rather than take cover behind rhetoric that frequently serves to conceal everything except a genuine desire to tackle the problem.

The Soviet Union continues to advocate a practical approach to the solution of the problems of containing the arms race, of disarmament and of removing the risk of another war through agreements between States. That is the essence of Leonid Brezhnev's message to the United Nations. The Soviet delegation has come to this session actively to promote that objective as well.

However, another course in world politics is also known to exist. That course is predicate on the continuation of the arms race and on its escalation. Concoctions of all sorts are produced on a grand scale to provide propagandistic cover for that course. One can hear statements to the effect that arms limitation is not enough, that deep and impressive cuts are needed. The words themselves are not that bad. A closer look reveals, however, that it is the Soviet Union—and it alone—that is to make those deep and impressive cuts.

It is also being asserted that, in order to proceed to the reduction and limitation of arms at some future stage, mountains upon mountains of weapons, primarily weapons of mass destruction, should be accumulated in the arsenals of the North Atlantic Treaty Organization (NATO)—and the more the better. Indeed, such weapons are being accumulated with something of an obsession. Washington and the NATO bloc as a whole have announced such militaristic programmes.

The intent behind all this is to upset the existing military balance between the Union of Soviet Socialist Republics and the United States of America, the Warsaw Treaty and NATO, to move into a position of strength, to act from that position and to inflict one's will to others, notably at the negotiating table.

Nowadays, some NATO politicians are talking about the position of strength perhaps even more often than during the cold war. Calls are made from the highest political pulpits of that bloc to the effect that the United States should be ahead of everyone else militarily, that it should and must be in the lead, and that is that. All those statements, interviews, resolutions and communiques designed to stun people invariably smack of unbridled ambition. In fact, such things are becoming a glut on the market.

At times such plans are discussed without any great sublety, quite bluntly. More often, however, they are camouflaged. It is asserted, for example, that the Soviet Union has gained an edge in armaments, although that is a fraud, since both facts and figures totally disprove that argument. The obvious intention is to mislead people.

Most recently, word has been spread that the Soviet Union has at its disposal "a most destabilizing factor". What it essentially boils down to is that only one type of weapon—land-based intercontinental ballistic missiles—is singled out in the entire range of strategic nuclear arms. These, they say, are the missiles that the Soviet Union should reduce in the first place.

What is behind all this? It is not all that cunning a trick. It is being proposed that reductions should apply to the type of strategic systems in which the USSR has a numerical advantage—if this factor is regarded in isolation, and only in isolation. At the same time, the issue of other strategic arms in which the United States has an advantage, and a big one, such as long-range cruise missiles, on which Washington is known to place particularly high reliance, and strategic aircraft, in which the United States also has a considerable edge, is being deliberately blurred. They are also hushing up the fact that the United States has several times more warheads on its submarine-launched ballistic missiles than the USSR. The United States forward-based systems and the nuclear capabilities of America's NATO allies are totally ignored.

The same approach is taken to medium-range nuclear weapons in Europe, and with the same purpose in mind—that is, to misrepresent the line-up of nuclear forces of the two sides there, too. Fabrications take the place of truth and are dressed up to look plausible.

What all this adds up to is a desire to wreck the existing parity in the field of nuclear arms, which is determined by the totality of the arms that the two sides possess, rather than by the quantities of some of the individual types. Why is this truth concealed from people? Why is it kept under lock and key? They do not want people to know it. In this way it is easier to secure decisions in favour of the arms race and easier to defend bloated military budgets.

Whenever Washington has something against the weight of certain Soviet missiles, for instance, it immediately starts saying that they destabilize the strategic situation. To set the record straight, it should be recognized that such missiles form part of the over-all equilibrium that has been carefully balanced and agreed by the Soviet Union and the United States over many years of negotiations. That is exactly what they now want to upset.

Once the veil is taken off Washington's strategic arms plan it will be revealed that it is designed to undercut the security of the other side and to retain a completely free hand in implementing its own military programmes. This lopsided and twisted approach is unrealistic and unacceptable.

Actually, it is the unprecedented arms race launched in the United States that constitutes the destabilizing factor. See how fast the wheels of the American military-industrial machine are turning. In effect, the arsenals of that country are being stocked with every possible type of armaments, including such barbaric ones as chemical and neutron weapons. Scientific and technological progress is geared to march in step with the arms race policy. It has been squeezed into a military uniform.

Each day brings new evidence that the United States foreign policy is becoming pervaded more and more with a spirit of militarism. This militaristic frenzy breeds all sorts of frenzied military doctrines. A first nuclear strike is being talked about as if it were something casual or routine, whereas what is involved here is a criminal concept of unleashing nuclear war. The idea that a nuclear war is winnable provided the theatre of that war is moved to some place further away from home—for example, to Europe—is being presented as something of a masterpiece of military strategy.

When one comes to the country where the United Nations Headquarters is located one really finds oneself in an altogether different world. In newspaper articles and television appearances officials of various ranks are driving home but one point: we must go on and on arming ourselves so that the United States becomes the world's foremost military power. In other words, the idea being impressed on people's minds is this: you want peace, go all out in preparing for war; dig in, hide yourselves wherever you can, but prepare.

The Soviet Union is in principle against a policy of military superiority. It does not seek military superiority for itself, nor does it grant anyone else the right to do so. Of course, our country is capable in any circumstances of taking care of its security and the security of its allies and friends. Leonid Brezhnev's statements to that effect are well known.

A genuine concern for peace requires the maintenance of the military-strategic balance. It has been ordained by history that such a balance between the two countries should evolve. This has been reflected in the relevant agreements between the USSR and the United States. So would it not be better to use it as a springboard from which to work towards agreement to lower its levels in accordance with the principle of equality and equal security?

Why is that not acceptable? The arguments against that are moulded after a very simple pattern: supremacy over the Soviet Union is needed to keep it in a state of fear. It is as simple as that—to keep it in a state of fear.

But then the Soviet Union would also have every reason to keep the other side in a state of fear. If we are going to talk in such terms, both the strength and the fear should be equally shared by the two sides. It should not be argued "We, the United States, keep the strength and you keep the fear that is the Soviet Union's share."

We are convinced however that this entire fear–strength logic is faulty. The security of either side and of the world as a whole should be built neither on fear nor on a quest for military superiority. The search for agreements, dialogue and mutual confidence should guide and motivate States in their relations with each other. The basis for this is the recognition and maintenance of the existing parity and all possible efforts aimed at achieving a lower and lower level of armaments.

How can Washington's policy of gaining military superiority be explained? It is hard to rid oneself of the impression that someone has been carried away by the imperial dream of dominating the world. How else can we explain the fact that vast areas in one part of the world or another are declared without any grounds whatsoever to be zones of United States vital interests? This is viewed as enough justification for dispatching the navy or an expeditionary force to the other end of the world, to foreign shores and borders closer to other peoples' wealth.

Amid vociferous declarations about the need to defend United States vital interests a naval armada was dispatched to the Persian Gulf. The plan to reimpose a vassal status on Iran by threat and force has fallen through yet the armada is still in that area.

That area is only a stone's throw from the Soviet Union as can be seen from a look at the map. What conclusion should be draw from this?

What is it that the United States has lost in the Indian Ocean? Why does it need a strategic military base on Diego Garcia? It is developing another springboard so as to threaten the Soviet Union and many other countries from there too.

Nor does it seem to be an accident that the United States has been stubbornly resisting the demands of the littoral states that the Indian Ocean be turned into a zone of peace and disregarding their interests.

Outside interference, which goes as far as the dispatch of armed interventionist gangs is continuing against Afghanistan. Even those who are doing all this have apparently come to realize that the Afghanistan of the past has ceased for ever to exist. There exists a new Afghanistan with a new democratic regime replacing the former reactionary one, there exists an independent non-aligned Afghan state. The proposals put forward by the government of the Democratic Republic of Afghanistan provide a good basis for political settlement of the situation around Afghanistan and the Soviet Union supports those proposals.

It was suggested that a world fiesta of sorts be staged to mark the withdrawal of the Israeli occupation force from the Sinai Peninsula. But what actually happened was that its place was promptly taken by American soldiers and by soldiers from other states, including some in which the old habit of cracking the colonial overseer's whip has not yet been totally abandoned.

Is the assertion of the United States military presence in the Middle East conducive to a just settlement in that area? No, it is not. It only encourages Israel to pursue its policy of flouting the legitimate interests in the Arab states and the national rights of the Palestinian people.

In full view of the entire world while we are sitting here, Israel has committed another act of aggression against the sovereign state of Lebanon. Breaching the cordon of United Nations contingents in southern Lebanon, Israeli troops moved on sowing death among the Lebanese and particularly among the Palestinians who had taken refuge in that country. Tel Aviv makes no secret of the fact that its aim is to slaughter the Palestinian people.

Can the United Nations look on impassively while this crime is being perpetrated and while its decisions are being trampled into the dirt? No.

The United Nations and the United Nations Security Council must assert themselves and adopt measures under the United Nations Charter to stop the Israeli aggression.

Israeli troops should be withdrawn forthwith from Lebanon and the ancestral lands of the Arabs previously seized by Israel should be returned to them. The Palestinian people should be given an opportunity to exercise their inalienable right to create a state of their own.

Special emphasis should be laid on the responsibility that the United States bears for the actions of the aggressor. Proof of this can be found in the position the United States took in the Security Council, as a result of which the Council was unable to take a decision calling on Israel to stop its aggression in Lebanon. It is clear to all that if Washington had lifted a finger to put an end to those actions Tel Aviv would not have dared to defy the United Nations.

The situation in South East Asia cannot be viewed as tranquil. The atmosphere is being poisoned by a hostile policy of interference in the affairs of the countries of Indo-China. The aim of that policy is to prevent the peoples of Vietnam, Laos and Kampuchea from building a new life in conditions of independence and freedom. But they are moving along a path of their own and will continue to do so. As to the People's Republic of Kampuchea, it should, and no doubt will, take its legitimate seat in the United Nations.

For many years now socialist Cuba has had to resist blockade and pressure. Military exercises are staged off its very shores, troops are landed defiantly on its territory, and the Guantanamo Base is still being unlawfully retained by the United States.

The people of Nicaragua are also being threatened now. Nicaragua is a small country, yet does not its people, like any other, have the right to be master of its destiny? It surely does.

The bloody massacres in El Salvador have aroused indignation all over the world. The Salvadoran murderers are being armed and advised by those who formally associated with the anti-popular dictator regime.

Developments in the South Atlantic are but another manifestation of the policy of the use of crude force in international affairs. It would be proper for the United Nations to call emphatically for an immediate cessation of all hostilities in the area and for a just, anti-colonial political settlement of that acute issue.

In Latin America, Asia and southern Africa peoples are legitimately protesting against imperialist arbitrary rule. They are waging a just struggle for independence and freedom, and against the remnants of hated colonialism. The Soviet people's sympathies are on their side.

And look at the efforts aimed at swaying those United States allies which realize the need to search for solutions conducive to easing tensions in the world and establishing international co-operation.

The developments of the last few days have once again confirmed that certain people have set themselves the goal of poisoning the atmosphere even more, of increasing confrontation, of creating additional incentives for escalating the arms race and pitting more and more states again each other.

All this is being done while we are gathered here under the same roof trying to find common ground on the issues of preventing war, ending the arms race and strengthening peace.

The problems of war and peace should not be treated lightly by anyone. Yet, the reasoning of some politicians apparently continues to go like this: since the United States and NATO have the USSR and other socialist countries as partners in the talks on those problems, it remains to be seen whether or not to work for agreement with them, in so far as they belong to a different social system and have a different ideology. It is no wonder that sober-minded people all over the world shrug their shoulders, so to speak, when facing the question of how politicians responsible for the conduct of state policy can accept such reasoning. It would be in order to say: could not certain people in Western capitals be more serious in their pronouncements on issues of war and peace? The same applies also to prophecies on the subject of socialism and its future which at times verge on political necromancy.

The situation in the world causes legitimate concern among peoples. It has found its expression in parliamentary debates, discussions at international forums and in the upsurge of a mass antiwar movement for which the Soviet people has profound esteem. The fundamental question is how to counter the policy of war preparations.

There is an answer to that question, and it is a convincing one. The policy of war preparations must be countered with a policy of peace and peaceful co-operation. The instigators of the arms race are out to erode people's will in the struggle for peace, and to sow doubt in their minds as to the outcome of that struggle. We reject that. Faith in the strength and ability of peoples to safeguard peace is inherent in the Soviet Union's foreign policy. The Soviet people is firmly determined to uphold peace.

Since its birth the Soviet state has drawn inspiration from Lenin's words: "What we cherish most is the preservation of peace . . ." Those are truly undying words! Today those words continue to express the most cherished thoughts of the Soviet people, which is engaged in creative effort, they underlie the policy of the USSR, including its foreign policy, our moral ideals, and our spiritual creative endeavour in all its variety.

It has long been recognized that time is the most impartial judge of the policies of states on issues of war and peace. The Soviet people has drawn the sword only against aggressors, to defend the freedom and independence of its country. The feat of our people, who made a decisive contribution to the great victory over the fascist aggressor, will shine through the centuries.

The instigators of the arms race have worked hard to find an argument in favour of that race and in justification of the astronomical figures of military budgets. They have obviously decided that the best thing to do would be to scare people with the threat that purportedly emanates from the Soviet Union, in the hope that they will relax their efforts.

But the deception Washington so frequently resorts to in international affairs is an unreliable foundation for a long-term policy. Fewer and fewer people are being taken in by that deception, even though the propaganda machine continues to churn out one fabrication after another about the Soviet Union's armaments and armed forces and about its foreign policy. Confronted with reality, those fabrications fail the test. The Soviet Union is not threatening any state on any continent. The step announced in Leonid Brezhnev's message today is further convincing proof of that.

The USSR has no claims to a monopoly on proposals conducive to lessening the threat of war. We are receptive to such proposals, even when they are made by politicians whose political views and world outlook greatly differ from our own.

The message emphasizes that the idea of a mutual freeze on nuclear arsenals as a first step towards their reduction and eventual complete elimination is close to the Soviet point of view.

The Soviet appeal that agreement be reached without delay on a complete prohibition of chemical weapons has also been prompted by the grave realities of today.

We strongly reject the absurd tales implicating the USSR in the use of those weapons. This fraud bears too obvious a trade mark to allow those who are peddling it to capitalize on it. Obviously they are attempting to conceal their own notorious sins in that respect.

The Soviet Union is submitting to the special session for its consideration a draft document entitled "Basic provisions of a convention on the prohibition of the development, production and stockpiling of chemical weapons and on their destruction".

The draft takes into account other states' wishes, including those that deal with verification. It is our view that a breakthrough in reaching an international agreement could be made on the basis of the Soviet draft.

The Soviet Union is in favour of moving towards solving disarmament problems on a broad front, through negotiations. Negotiations that are currently under way should be revived and those that have been suspended should be resumed and new negotiations should be started in those areas where the situation calls for it.

The current Soviet–United States talks in Geneva on the limitation of nuclear arms in Europe are being closely watched everywhere. They deal with one of the key problems of European security and, indeed, of international security as a whole.

What is the goal of the Soviet Union? It is to deliver Europe totally from both medium-range and tactical nuclear weapons. If that solution is not acceptable to our Western partners, we are prepared to agree on a total renunciation of all types of medium-range nuclear weapons targeted on Europe. We are also prepared to reduce gradually but substantially, by the hundreds, the medium-range nuclear weapons of both sides, the USSR and the North Atlantic Treaty Organization.

The Soviet Union is backing with practical deeds its desire for the Geneva talks to be successful. Our country has unilaterally ceased further deployment of medium-range missiles in the European part of the USSR. Moreover, the Soviet Union is already reducing those missiles by a considerable number. We have stated in no uncertain terms that no medium-range missiles will be additionally deployed in areas where Western European countries would be within their range.

Now, what about the other side? As we have already said, its attitude is that it is only the Soviet Union that should reduce its medium-range nuclear arms.

The interests of the European peoples require neither confrontation nor an undermining of *détente*. The right path towards consolidating security and developing co-operation in Europe has been charted in the Helsinki Final Act.

To be true to the spirit of Helsinki means to abide scrupulously by the principles and understandings of the Final Act and to refrain from interfering in each other's internal affairs.

To be true to the spirit of Helsinki means to complete the Madrid meeting successfully, and to crown its work with a decision to convene a conference on confidence-building measures and disarmament in Europe. As before, the Soviet Union will do its best to contribute to the positive outcome of the Madrid meeting.

There is not a single state unaware of the importance of talks between the Soviet Union and the United States on strategic arms limitation and reduction.

The Soviet Union has invariably advocated the resumption of these talks. Now, following the consent of the United States, the opening date for the talks has been agreed upon. This is undoubtedly a positive fact.

However, the SALT II Treaty, already finalized and signed, is known to have been shelved by the American side. Needless to say, that dealt a heavy blow to international confidence and international security.

Two other important treaties between the USSR and the United States limiting activities in the nuclear field—the 1974 Treaty on the Limitation of Underground Nuclear Weapon Tests and the 1976 Treaty on Underground Nuclear Explosions for Peaceful Purposes—are yet to be ratified.

It is worth recalling all this at a time when the United States delegation is returning to the table of strategic arms negotiations.

What is most important is that the talks should strike the right note from the very outset. From this standpoint, the position with which the United States side is coming to the talks, as described in Washington's official statements, cannot but give cause for wariness.

In connection with those statements, it would be proper to point out that our partners in the talks both on the problem of strategic arms and on the problem of medium-range nuclear weapons in Europe just cannot assimilate the obvious truth that the Soviet Union and the United States are equally interested in the solution of those problems and in talks on them. It would be a gross mistake to think that the Soviet Union was holding out its hand begging for talks. No. Each side should extend its hand to the other if they both want to discuss their differences and to find mutually acceptable solutions to their problems.

In his recent speech Leonid Brezhnev clearly indicated what is needed for the Soviet–United States talks to result in an agreement. First, the talks should actually pursue the objective of limiting and reducing strategic arms rather than serve as a cover for the continuation of the arms race and to upset the existing parity. Secondly, the two sides should conduct them with due regard for each other's legitimate security interests and strictly in accordance with the principle of equality and equal security. Lastly everything positive achieved earlier should be preserved, including the SALT II treaty. It is also essential to block securely all channels for the continuation of the strategic arms race in any form. This means that the development of new types of strategic weapons should be either banned or limited to the extent possible in accordance with agreed parameters. We are prepared to agree now that the strategic arms of the USSR and the United States be quantitatively frozen the moment the talks begin, and that their modernization be limited to the maximum extent possible.

Neither the United States nor the Soviet Union should take any step that could upset the stability of the strategic situation. Aside from its intrinsic importance, the proposed freeze could also be conducive to progress towards a radical limitation and reduction of strategic arms. The Soviet Union has consistently advocated a substantial reduction of those arms.

It is hoped that the other side will give serious consideration to these Soviet proposals. There are, however, some alarming signals. The very moment that the Soviet Union proposes a freeze on strategic arms Washington defiantly announces that the implementation of the programme for the production and deployment of new MX strategic missiles is to be stepped up.

It cannot be denied that today Washington has mastered the art of destroying bridges that could lead to agreement. Building those bridges is far more difficult and important. It will be recalled that Leonid Brezhnev made a concrete proposal to meet United States President Ronald Reagan. The Soviet Union proceeds from the premiss that a summit meeting should take place and that, of course, it should be well prepared. It is obvious that such a meeting would inevitably centre on the problems of reducing armaments and of disarmament, that is, problems which are also in the focus of this special session of the General Assembly.

The Soviet Union believes that it would be useful to elaborate and adopt a nuclear disarmament programme to be implemented stage by stage. One of its initial stages could be the cessation of the production of fissionable materials for manufacturing various types of nuclear weapons. Many other states are also making statements along similar lines. The Soviet Union is prepared to consider this question in the over-all context of limiting and ending the nuclear arms race.

The consolidation in every possible way of the regime of the nonproliferation of nuclear weapons has been and remains a priority task in terms of curbing the nuclear arms race. A situation cannot be allowed to arise in which on the one hand measures would be taken to lessen the threat of nuclear war, while on the other hand nuclear weapons would spread all over the planet. Our approach to this problem takes into account the views of many other states and above all of non-nuclear ones. The Soviet Union is agreeable to placing under the control of the International Atomic Energy Agency part of its peaceful nuclear installations, atomic power plants and research reactors.

Non-nuclear countries parties to the Non-Proliferation Treaty, have been raising the question of guarantees of their security on the part of the nuclear Powers. Their interest is only natural. This question could be solved by concluding an international convention. The USSR is also prepared to conclude bilateral agreements on guarantees with states which do not possess nuclear weapons and do not have them on their territory.

The problem of the complete and general prohibition of nuclear weapon tests also calls for a solution. It can be tackled either radically or step by step. The Soviet Union believes that the trilateral talks with the United States and Britain which were suspended by them at the final stage should be resumed without delay.

An increasing number of states have been declaring that they do not want to have nuclear weapons on their territory. There have been suggestions for the creation of zones free of such weapons. For our part we shall contribute to the search for generally acceptable solutions concerning the establishment of nuclear-free zones in various regions of the world.

An agreement should be reached to ban the stationing of weapons of any kind in outer space. The draft international treaty on that subject submitted by the Soviet Union has been widely acclaimed by United Nations member states. Why not begin concrete discussion of it in the Geneva Committee without delay?

The time is ripe for reaching agreement to limit the naval activities of states, especially those possessing powerful navies. A whole range of important issues could be considered in this respect.

The United Nations should speak out against extending the spiral of the arms race into the vast expanses of outer space and the depth of the oceans of the world. The significance of those environments as regards a peaceful future for mankind is growing steadily.

Modern armies are equipped with enormous quantities of weapons which have come to be called conventional. Yet in terms of their purpose and characteristics they are not much inferior to weapons of mass destruction. Therefore this area of the arms race and consequently of the policy of states also requires the most serious attention.

The Soviet Union stands for substantial reductions of the current levels of armed forces and conventional armaments. A situation where many millions of people are withdrawn from the productive sphere and placed under arms cannot be considered normal. To start with, agreement could be reached, for instance, not increasing armed forces and conventional armaments, to be followed by negotiations on their reduction both on a global scale and in specific regions.

With regard to Central Europe, such talks are under way in Vienna. The Soviet Union, together with other socialist countries, reiterates its appeal to its Western partners finally to get down to work on preparing an agreement on the reduction of armed forces and armaments in

Central Europe. It is high time to discard the policy of upsetting the balance between the sides in this area as well.

Foreign trade in, and transfers of, conventional weapons are currently running into tens of billions of dollars. Given a sensible approach, this channel for spurring the arms race could also be at least narrowed.

The Soviet–United States talks on this subject were in progress only some time ago, but they were suspended by the United States, which has developed a sort of conditioned reflex with regard to negotiations on a number of cardinal issues. After two or three years of talks, the United States breaks them off. The Soviet Union is ready to resume talks on this subject as well.

It is beyond the power of any economist to prove that such acute social and economic problems facing states as unemployment, inflation and growing taxation, could be solved through militarization. The burden of military expenditures is becoming increasingly felt also in the developing countries, on some of which poverty and hunger are known to pay frequent and cruel calls.

Disarmament is a sure path leading not only to a safe but also to a more prosperous life for the peoples. Progress in the field of disarmament would make it possible to release huge resources through freezing, let alone reducing, military budgets. Part of the saving of resources currently devoured by arms production could be used to assist developing states.

The Soviet Union is submitting to this session for its consideration a memorandum entitled "Averting the growing nuclear threat and curbing the arms race". It recapitulates our country's positions of principle as well as its major specific proposals. We express the hope that they will be studied most carefully and supported by the United Nations member states.

The special session of the United Nations General Assembly devoted to disarmament should not become an ordinary event in international relations. This will not happen, given the will of the states represented in this hall. This session will leave a visible imprint on world politics if it gives a significant impetus to solving the most pressing problems of curbing the arms race and disarmament.

The United Nations has adopted quite a few well-intentioned resolutions yet, no matter how good a resolution may be, it will remain on paper unless followed by deeds. This entirely depends on states and on whether or not they recognize the fact that any chance offered by history in the name of the triumph of life must be seized. That is what the Soviet Union is calling for.

To Defend Peace on Earth

Speech at the 37th Session of the UN General Assembly, 10 October 1982

Mr. President,

Esteemed delegates,

A session of the United Nations General Assembly is a unique opportunity to review the international reality in all its diversity and to sense more profoundly what is of greatest concern to people on different continents. And, one becomes convinced once again that of the multitude of problems in today's world the main problem, the one that stands out, is that of averting the threat of nuclear war.

Virtually everyone agrees that world developments have been evolving in an alarming way. People are asking themselves whether the insane arms race can be halted and the slipping towards the abyss prevented. What should be done to counter the policies of those who are playing out various scenarios of nuclear war as if it were some kind of a game of chance rather than a matter that affects the destinies of mankind?

Those are legitimate questions. The Soviet Union is firmly convinced that peace, which is of the greatest universal value, can and must be preserved; and it must be a just peace, worthy of those heights which civilization on earth has attained. We draw this conviction from history itself, which contains many a tragic page but also examples of brilliantly devised solutions to the most acute international problems.

Let us recall how the United Nations Charter, which is a universally recognized code of rules that must govern relations between States, came into being. The establishment of this Organization and its Charter crystallized, as it were, the experience of the struggle against and the great victory over fascism. At that time the hope was held out to the world that it would be possible to avert another global tragedy. For almost 40 years now, that hope has been a reality.

Now let us look at the changes in international relations brought about in the 1970s, when the peoples of the world were given an opportunity to breathe the air of *détente*. Surely the differences in social systems and ideologies or in the world outlook were no less then than they are today. But even taking these differences fully into account, States and the leaders who guided their policies did find ways leading to constructive relations between nations. This constant in the experience of peaceful coexistence has taken root in the minds of peoples and in the fabric of inter-State relations, and it is not easy to discard. The urge to give orders to other countries, to dominate the world, must not be allowed to overshadow the experience of the past or muffle the voice of reason.

The Soviet people reject the gloomy view that mankind has no other path to follow than building up piles of armaments and preparing for war. It would be a mistake to underestimate the rising menace of war. But it is an even greater mistake to fail to see that possibilities do exist for putting up an insurmountable barrier against war. The Soviet Union and the Soviet people are placing all their political and moral potential and all the prestige of their policy on to the scales of peace.

This is surely demonstrated by the obligation unilaterally assumed by the Soviet Union not to be the first to use nuclear weapons, an obligation solemnly stated in the message of Leonid Brezhnev to the second special session of the United Nations General Assembly devoted to disarmament. That was an act of historic importance and it was seen as such throughout the world. Is it not time for our Western partners, the countries of the North Atlantic Treaty Organization (NATO), to assess in earnest the opportunities opened up by the Soviet Union's initiative? We expect them to weigh it carefully once again. In seeking to minimize the importance of the Soviet Union's peace initiatives, many Western leaders speak of the need for trust in relations between States. But how would that purpose best be served? It would be best served by renouncing preparations for war, the policy of the arms race and of whipping up world tensions. Why do they not assume the obligation, as the Soviet Union has done, not to be the first to use nuclear weapons?

Sometimes one can hear it said that it is not merely a question of nuclear weapons alone, for there are conventional weapons as well. Yes, there are. But there is a convincing reply to that too : we insist that all

States assume an obligation to renounce any use or threat of force in their relations.

As far back as 1976 the Soviet Union proposed that a world treaty be concluded on the non-use of force in international relations and it submitted a draft treaty to the United Nations for its consideration. The draft treaty expressly provides that States would refrain from the use of force involving any types of weapons—and I emphasize, any types of weapons. It would be a good idea to inscribe this on the doors of every agency in Washington that is concerned with United States foreign policy.

We note with satisfaction that the initiative concerning the non-use of force was endorsed by the overwhelming majority of Member States of the United Nations. Indeed, an *ad hoc* committee was even established to draft such a treaty. Why, then has no such treaty been worked out? Because Member States of NATO are thwarting it. Can the situation be remedied now? Yes, it can. The Soviet Union is prepared even today to come to the negotiating table in order to formalize strict obligations not to use force in settling disputes and differences which exist between States. No one would venture to deny that quite a few such disputes and differences have accumulated. But there are no problems among them that would not lend themselves to peaceful solutions. There are none in any part of the world or in any area of world politics—if, of course, one is motivated by the objectives of peace.

It has to be noted, however, that the United States of America has chosen a different policy for itself. The essence of this policy is the desire to impose its will upon other States and peoples. That desire underlies all plans for the production of weapons. It underlies United States foreign policy. The Soviet Union has repeatedly drawn attention to the fact that such a policy poses a serious threat to peace.

The objective of gaining an edge in armaments has been openly proclaimed in the United States. The idea that it has to be number one militarily has become something of an obsession. Huge sums are being allocated for building up the United States war machine and the pyramid of weapons is getting higher and higher. In the meantime there is continuously at work an assembly line fabricating all kinds of falsehoods about the Soviet Union's armed forces and its foreign policy. People are being deliberately misled.

Why is all this being done? Simply because in an atmosphere of lies, hysteria and chauvinistic intoxication it is easier to get astronomical military budgets approved; it is easier to divert the country's resources to war preparations and away from peaceful purposes such as eliminating unemployment and fighting inflation, away from using them for the benefit of people, which is what the Soviet Union is calling for.

There is no dearth of versions of nuclear war being planned by the apostles of the arms race: a *blitzkrieg*, a protracted war, a limited war, an all-out war. Every conceivable and inconceivable definition is being put into circulation. With the cold-blooded composure of grave diggers, they are speculating on the number of casualties the sides would sustain in a nuclear catastrophe. They deliberately hush up the fact that if a nuclear war were to break out under present conditions, there would be no winners, and few people today would disagree with that.

The Soviet Union has, on a number of occasions, including the sessions of the United Nations General Assembly, pointed to the dangerous nature of Washington's course aimed at upsetting the military equilibrium which has evolved between the USSR and the United States of America, and on the whole, between the Warsaw Treaty Organization and the North Atlantic Treaty Organization. Everywhere, on land and on sea, the United States is seeking to impose or strengthen its military presence and to set up new bases. Look at the bloody orgy that is taking place in the Middle East where a frantic search is under way for new clients to be harnessed to the Pentagon's militaristic strategy.

It should, of course, be clear that the Soviet Union does not recognize anyone's right to military superiority. And it will see to it that that does not happen.

One of the principles recognized by the United Nations is non-interference by States in the internal affairs of other States. It has been reiterated many times in United Nations decisions.

However, the world is witnessing today a flagrant flouting of this principle.

Who, we might well ask, has given Washington the right to tell sovereign States what they should and what they should not do in their own house? Who has given it the right to try to punish those who cherish their sovereignty and would not yield to pressure, to apply all kinds of sanctions, to impose economic blockades, and even to brandish arms?

From what some say, it would appear that United States interests are being endangered almost everywhere in the world. This is an absurd thesis. Yet it is being used to justify crude interference in the affairs of others, used on a sweeping geographic scale, as regards both nearby countries and those situated many thousands of kilometres away from the United States.

The Soviet Union has never permitted, nor will it ever allow, anybody to interfere in its internal affairs. This is the stand of the States of the socialist community, as well as of other countries which respect their independence and their legitimate rights.

I should like to express the hope that no calls for outside interference in the affairs of other sovereign States will be made from this rostrum either. Otherwise, this high rostrum will cease to be what it is intended to be. And may the United Nations emblem, which is before the eyes of all those present in this hall, serve as a warning to those who fail to distinguish between what is theirs and what belongs to others.

No review of the international scene can overlook the situation taking shape in some regions of the world. In the first place, attention is rivetted on the Middle East, for this session of the General Assembly is taking place at a time when ashes have not yet settled in the streets of the ruthlessly destroyed ancient city of Beirut and when the blood of tens of thousands of victims of aggression has not yet been completely absorbed by the soil.

All honest people all over the world feel outrage and disgust over the orgy of bloodshed staged by the aggressors in the Palestinian camps in west Beirut where defenceless Palestinians, mostly women, children and old people, were massacred.

Could Israel commit aggression and perpetrate genocide against the Palestinians but for its so-called "strategic consensus" with the United States?

As far as one can judge, in Israel they are now rubbing their hands gleefully. But this is what is called a Pyrrhic victory. The aggression was bound to turn, and has in fact turned, into a serious political and moral defeat for Israel. The rift between Israel and its neighbours has widened. New seeds of hatred and animosity have been sown, and they can bear the grapes of wrath.

Those who determine Israel's policies seem to give little thought to the future of their country. And that is too bad, indeed. They are clearly hampered by chauvinistic intoxication.

The root cause of the Lebanese tragedy lies in Camp David. It should be clear now to every unbiased person that separate anti-Arab deals only put off the establishment of a just peace in the Middle East.

The aggressor and its accomplices say that Camp David means peace. Such an assertion makes a mockery of the profound, humane and noble idea of peace. What kind of peace it makes is evident from the fact that more blood has been shed since Camp David than during the Israeli aggression in 1967.

Washington's recent statements, which it is serving up as a Middle East settlement plan, confirm that they are still thinking there in terms of *diktat* and enmity with regard to the Arabs, rather than in terms of peace.

The overwhelming majority of States hold it as a political axiom that there can be no durable peace in the Middle East unless the question of an independent Palestinian State is resolved. The Washington plan, however, states explicitly that the United States is against the creation of such a State.

It is widely accepted and recorded in United Nations decisions that the problem of fulfilling the national aspirations of the Palestinians cannot be solved without the participation of the Palestine Liberation Organization (PLO), whereas the American plan makes no mention at all of the PLO as a party to the settlement. In fact, Washington also fully evades such a fundamental matter as Israel's withdrawal from all the Arab territories seized by it.

All decisions taken by the United Nations proceed from the premiss that genuine security in the Middle East can only be such as would be common to all States and peoples in that region. The so-called Washington initiative focuses everything on the security of Israel alone, and its interests are made paramount, with the United States itself, naturally, maintaining its arrogant and unjustified claims to a leading role in Middle East affairs.

We regard positively the views on a Middle East settlement expressed at the recent Arab summit. On the whole these views are on the same lines as those of the Soviet Union regarding a Middle East settlement.

As Leonid Brezhnev has recently stressed once again, a just and durable peace in the Middle East can and must be based on the following principles.

First, the principle of the inadmissibility of seizure of foreign lands through aggression must be strictly observed. That means that all the territories occupied by Israel since 1967—the Golan Heights, the West Bank of the Jordan river and the Gaza Strip, the Lebanese lands—must be returned to the Arabs. The borders between Israel and its Arab neighbours should be declared inviolable.

Secondly, the inalienable right of the Arab people of Palestine to self-determination and to the establishment of its own independent State on the Palestinian lands which will be freed from the Israeli occupation—on the West Bank of the Jordan river and in the Gaza Strip—must be ensured in practice. Palestinian refugees must be given the possibility envisaged in United Nations decisions to return to their homes or be given appropriate compensation for the property they left behind.

I ask the following in this connection: has anybody annulled the decision adopted by the United Nations in 1947, which envisages the establishment in the former mandated territory of Palestine of two sovereign States—an Arab State and a Jewish State? Nobody has annulled it. Then what are the grounds for talking about the legitimate existence of the Jewish State alone, while impeding in every way the establishment of the other, Arab, State for over three and a half decades? There have been no such grounds, nor are there any now.

Thirdly, the eastern part of Jerusalem, which was occupied by Israel in 1967, where one of the main Moslem shrines is located, must be returned to the Arabs and become an inseparable part of the Palestinian State. Freedom of access by believers to the holy places of the three religions must be ensured throughout Jerusalem.

Fourthly, the right of all States in the region to a safe and independent existence and development must be ensured, naturally on the condition of full reciprocity, for the security of some cannot be ensured by flouting the security of others.

Fifthly, the state of war between the Arab States and Israel must be terminated and peace between them must be established. That means that all parties to the conflict, including Israel and the Palestinian State, must assume an obligation reciprocally to respect the sovereignty, independence and territorial integrity of each other and to settle the disputes that may arise by peaceful means through negotiations.

Sixthly, international guarantees of the settlement must be worked out and adopted. The role of the guarantor could be assumed by, say, the permanent members of the United Nations Security Council or by the Security Council as a whole.

The path to a durable peace in the Middle East lies through collective efforts by all the parties concerned, including the Palestine Liberation Organization, and the best way towards this end is to convene an appropriate international conference.

For almost two years now bloody hostilities have been going on between Iran and Iraq. This is a senseless war from the point of view of the vital interests of the peoples of the two countries. This conflict is also fraught with grave consequences. The fire should be put out before it spreads further.

The most reasonable thing to do would probably be for Iran and Iraq to put aside arms, to slip covers over the muzzles of their guns and to settle their differences at the negotiating table.

The Soviet Union has invariably come out in favour of putting an end to the war between the two States, with which our country has maintained traditional ties, and it is doing all in its power to bring that about. We expect that other major Powers will abandon attempts to take advantage of the conflict.

Dangerous scheming is still going on around the Democratic Republic of Afghanistan. The foes of the Afghan people, including those who flaunt their commitment to democracy, are trying to hinder the building of a new and truly democratic life in that country. While in words a political solution to the problems which have arisen around Afghanistan is being advocated, in deeds the achievement of such a solution is being impeded in every possible way.

Opportunities for such a solution do exist. They are embodied in the constructive proposals of the Government of the Democratic Republic of Afghanistan, which the Soviet Union fully supports. Only one thing is required, and that is to stop the armed intervention from outside against Afghanistan and not interfere in the internal affairs of that sovereign non-aligned State.

In the Soviet Union we view as a step in the right direction the start of negotiations in Geneva between representatives of the Democratic Republic of Afghanistan and Pakistan through a personal representative of the United Nations Secretary General.

We fully understand the legitimate concern of the coastal States of the Indian Ocean over the expansion there of the United States military presence. One can literally watch it grow, posing a threat also to the security of the USSR from the south. We cannot but draw our own conclusions from this.

The Soviet Union endorses the idea put forward by the non-aligned countries to turn the Indian Ocean into a zone of peace. If it were not for the attempts by certain Powers, above all the United States of America, to frustrate implementation of the United Nations resolution on this matter, an international conference which could be of tangible benefit to the whole of that vast region would have been convened long ago.

Even now, without waiting for the conference to be convened, we call upon all the States whose ships use the waters of the Indian Ocean to refrain from any steps that could complicate the situation in that region. This means not sending there large naval formations, not conducting military exercises and not expanding or modernizing military bases of those non-coastal States which possess such bases in the Indian Ocean.

One example of the way in which States with different social systems can fruitfully co-operate to mutual advantage and in the interests of universal peace can be seen in Soviet–Indian relations. This co-operation is a concrete and impressive contribution to the cause of security on the South Asian subcontinent and in the international arena as a whole. A new and powerful impulse has been given to it by the results of the recent talks in Moscow between Leonid Brezhnev and the Prime Minister of India, Indira Gandhi.

In another part of the Asian continent, South-East Asia, the Soviet Union supports the efforts aimed at turning that region into a zone of peace. A series of initiatives put forward jointly by Vietnam, Laos and Kampuchea opens up prospects for both deepening the dialogue between them and the ASEAN countries and in general normalizing the situation in the area. These initiatives have been reaffirmed by such a display of goodwill as the partial withdrawal of Vietnamese troops from Kampuchea.

The peoples of Vietnam, Laos and Kampuchea have chosen their own road of social development. In their march along that road they are repelling those forces which are seeking to prevent them from building a new life. The USSR resolutely sides with those States. It is rendering and will continue to render them necessary assistance and support.

The Soviet Union is prepared to seek, together with all the Far Eastern States, ways of enhancing the security of that region. Not so long ago we proposed that the time-tested experience gained in carrying out certain measures to build mutual confidence in Europe be considered from the point of view of its application to the Far East. The Soviet Union is ready to discuss this matter in a practical vein with the participation of the People's Republic of China and Japan.

For decades now the situation on the Korean peninsula has not been normalized, which increases tensions in the Far East. The Korean problem can and must be settled by peaceful means without any outside interference, as is proposed by the Government of the Democratic People's Republic of Korea.

Socialist countries are taking the initiative in strengthening security on a scale embracing the entire Asian continent. This is the intent of the proposal made by the Mongolian People's Republic for the conclusion of a convention on mutual non-aggression and non-use of force in relations between the Asian and Pacific States. The Soviet Union supports this useful initiative.

When a centre of tension appears in some part of the globe there can be no doubt that it is caused by the actions of those who have no regard for the legitimate interests of others. Not infrequently they are inspired by attempts to retain by force positions inherited from the colonial past.

One case in point is the South Atlantic. It is to be hoped that the peoples have drawn appropriate conclusions from the recent events in that region. The Soviet Union has on a number of occasions publicly stated its position that a just settlement of the problem that has arisen there can be achieved through negotiations within the United Nations framework and on the basis of United Nations decisions. That continues to be our position today.

Another case in point is southern Africa, where the South African racist regime, with the connivance of Western Powers, is actually waging an undeclared war against Angola and some other States of the region. Pretoria has been blatantly defying United Nations decisions on the granting of independence to Namibia. There is no doubt, however, that the Namibian people will attain freedom and independence.

Still another case in point is the region of Central America and the Caribbean, where a campaign of pressure and threats is going on unabated against Cuba and Nicaragua, whose only fault is that they want to live according to their own standards. Attempts are being made to portray them as the troublemakers in that region. Those are attempts made in bad faith. Together with other peoples and States of the Caribbean, Cuba and Nicaragua are in favour of turning it into a zone of peace, independence and development, and the Soviet Union has full sympathy for this goal.

Is there anyone who does not know whose advisers and instructors, both uniformed and otherwise, are now in El Salvador, and who rule the roost there, trying to prop up the corrupt and unpopular regime? The USSR has opposed and will continue to oppose such actions.

The sympathy and support of the Soviet people are entirely on the side of all the peoples fighting for their freedom and for national and social progress.

If there was any lack of evidence that the peoples and States consider the continuing arms race to be one of the most critical issues of our time, the second special session of the United Nations General Assembly devoted to disarmament has provided such evidence in abundance.

Ardent appeals to avert nuclear war and halt the arms race were voiced from its rostrum. The session failed to reach agreement on concrete steps in this field, and it is well known who is responsible for that. Still, the determination of the overwhelming majority of States to ensure peace and achieve disarmament was expressed in no uncertain terms.

The Soviet Union submitted to that session a detailed programme of measures to curb the arms race, ranging from nuclear and chemical weapons to limiting conventional weapons and naval activities of States.

As has been repeatedly emphasized by Leonid Brezhnev, there is no type of weapon which our country would not be prepared to limit or ban on the basis of reciprocity. And if the accumulation of arms is not only continuing but accelerating, if this tragic competition is proceeding at a pace that leaves behind accords on arms limitation, and if the agreements already reached in this field are called into question, all this is the direct result of the United States policy aimed at building up its military muscle. It makes no secret of this policy line; indeed, it is bragging about it.

To take a problem such as the limitation and reduction of strategic arms, that is, the most destructive weapons, the problem which is of utmost importance under present-day conditions, there had been many delays on the part of our partners before the Soviet–American talks started. Undoubtedly, the fact that they are being held is in itself of positive significance. But that alone is not enough. What is required is the desire on both sides to seek agreement.

Without going into the details of the talks, it should, however, be emphasized that so far the other side has failed to show the desire to come to agreement. Surely one cannot take for such a desire the attempt to single out from the totality of weapons possessed by the USSR and the United States only those types of weapons—in this particular case land-based missiles—which constitute the backbone of the Soviet Union's strategic potential, and to make them alone the subject of reduction, leaving out all the rest, that is, submarine-launched missiles, strategic bombers and cruise missiles, where the United States preponderance is obvious?

Certainly this lopsided approach promises no hope for the success of the negotiations. The principle of the equality and equal security of the sides must remain their unshakable foundation. Accuracy, science, balance of parameters, together with a careful evaluation of all elements of the problem—all these must be taken into account. There must be no room for deception, guile or juggling with facts, either in large or in small doses.

It should be recalled that the Soviet Union has put forward an important proposals, namely, to agree to freeze the strategic armaments of the USSR and the United States quantitatively as soon as the talks begin, and at the same time to restrict their modernization to the utmost. We have proposed that for the duration of the talks the sides should take no actions that might upset the stability of the strategic situation.

That is our concrete response to the sentiments mounting in many countries of the world in favour of a freeze on the existing levels of nuclear arms, to be followed by their drastic reduction, which is advocated by the Soviet Union.

Unfortunately, those who are conducting negotiations with us on this problem shudder at the mere words "a freeze on arms". What has actually been frozen on their side, and quite deeply at that, is the realization that the talks must be frank, in good faith and free from any lopsidedness.

What is the state of affairs at the Soviet–American talks on the limitation of nuclear arms in Europe?

Sometimes encouraging statements are heard from the United States side in this respect. But this is an assumed optimism. The so-called zero option—or, to be more precise, pseudo-zero option—proposed by the United States does not offer a solution to the problem. It provides for the elimination only of Soviet land-based missiles, including those which the Soviet Union has possessed for over 20 years now. As to the medium-range nuclear forces of the North Atlantic Treaty Organization (NATO), they are not to be subject to reduction by a single unit and can even be built up.

We have no doubt that Washington realizes that the Soviet side would not agree to a one-sided solution that would run counter to the security interests of the USSR and its allies. Therefore, what is doubtful is whether Washington is really seeking an agreement.

The Soviet Union's desire to come to agreement with the United States is buttressed by practical steps. As is well known, it has unilaterally discontinued further deployment of medium-range missiles in the European part of the USSR. And, what is more, it is carrying out the reduction of a part of that force. Finally, we are not stationing any additional medium-range missiles beyond the Urals, from where Western Europe would be within their reach.

The Soviet Union has faithfully kept its word in this matter too.

Throughout the post-War period, since the emergence of the first atom bombs, the Soviet Union has been persistently seeking approaches to putting an end to the nuclear arms race. At that time it was much easier to ban the atomic weapon than it is nowadays, when there exists a huge arsenal of nuclear armaments.

But even today this problem can be resolved. Mankind has no other reasonable option but to reduce the nuclear threat gradually though consistently, step by step, and ultimately eliminate it.

In this context, it is extremely important to erect a barrier against the development of ever new types and systems of nuclear weapons—a process which tends to destabilize the strategic situation for it entails the emergence of weapons which because of their characteristics, would hardly lend themselves to verification. If this is so, the working out of relevant international agreements on their limitation and reduction is becoming more difficult.

That is the reason why it is becoming increasingly urgent to stop nuclear weapons tests and to erect a tangible physical barrier to the development of ever new kinds of nuclear weapons and thus slow down the arms race.

The States of the world, with very few exceptions demand a ban on all nuclear-weapon test explosions in all environments and for all times. Their will was reflected in a series of decisions adopted at the United Nations. Moreover, when signing the Treaty on the Non-Proliferation of Nuclear Weapons, all the parties to it, including the United States undertook to do away with nuclear-weapon tests for good.

In our view, it is the direct responsibility of the United Nations to demand that all countries, and the nuclear Powers in the first place, do their utmost to achieve that goal.

As a nuclear Power, the Soviet Union declares that for its part, it is ready to do that. We propose the inclusion in the agenda of this session of an important and urgent item entitled "Immediate cessation and prohibition of nuclear-weapon tests".

What is proposed specifically? It is proposed to speed up the working out and signing of a treaty on the complete and general prohibition of nuclear-weapon tests and to put the talks on that subject in the Committee on Disarmament on a practical footing.

The Soviet Union is submitting to this Assembly for its consideration "Basic provisions of a treaty on the complete and general prohibition of nuclear-weapon tests", a document which takes into account the measure of agreement reached during the discussion of that problem in recent years. It also takes into account the views and suggestions advanced by many States, *inter alia* on questions of verification.

In order to create more favourable conditions for the elaboration of the treaty, we propose that all nuclear-weapon States declare a moratorium on all nuclear explosions, including peaceful ones, as of a date to be agreed upon among them. Such a moratorium would be effective pending the conclusion of the treaty.

In the context of the problem of the complete and general prohibition of nuclear-weapon tests, I wish to single out two more aspects of importance.

First, the Soviet Union is prepared at any time to ratify—on a reciprocal basis—the treaties concluded with the United States on the limitation of underground nuclear-weapon tests and on nuclear explosions for peaceful purposes.

Secondly, we are in favour of the resumption of the trilateral talks between the USSR, the United States and Britain.

Those talks were under way. Then they were broken off, and it is public knowledge who was responsible for that.

In the context of the struggle to lessen the nuclear threat, there is still another important problem to which the Soviet Union would like to draw the Assembly's attention.

The number of non-military nuclear facilities, above all power installations, is increasing in various countries. This is an inevitable process, which is bound to grow in scope in the future.

However, intentional destruction, even with the help of conventional weapons, of atomic power plants, research reactors and other similar installations might cause the release and dissemination of a huge amount of radioactive substances, which would have fatal consequences for the population. In other words, it would be tantamount in its effect to a nuclear explosion.

As calculated by experts, the consequences of the destruction of a large atomic power plant are comparable to the radioactive contamination occurring after the explosion of a one-megaton nuclear bomb. Therefore, the need for ensuring a safe development of nuclear energy is closely linked with the task of preventing the unleashing of nuclear war.

Being desirous of lessening the nuclear threat in this area too the Soviet Union proposes the inclusion in the agenda of this session of an urgent item entitled "Multiplying efforts to eliminate the threat of nuclear war and to ensure a safe development of nuclear energy".

The Soviet Union proposes that the General Assembly declare the destruction of peaceful nuclear facilities with conventional weapons equivalent to an attack involving the use of nuclear weapons—that is to say, it should equate such destruction with those actions which the United Nations has already qualified as the gravest crime against humanity.

The question of a speedy elimination of chemical weapons presents itself in all its magnitude. This weapon is one of the means of mass annihilation. The unrestrained build-up of chemical weapons in the West, far from enhancing anybody's security, is only aggravating the risk of military conflicts with the use of these lethal weapons.

The Soviet Union has consistently been advocating the exclusion of chemical weapons from the arsenals of States. The relevant proposals submitted by it have been referred to the Committee on Disarmament. We hope that its members will proceed, with all due sense of responsibility, to the elaboration of an international convention on the prohibition and elimination of these barbaric weapons.

There is an increasing danger that the arms race will acquire a qualitatively new dimension unless the necessary measures are urgently taken. Washington is now planning a military thrust into outer space.

We are convinced that the arms race must not be permitted to spread into the boundless expanses of outer space. The United Nations can and must play its part in this respect.

For a number of years now the Soviet Union has been seeking the conclusion of an international treaty prohibiting the stationing of weapons of any kind in outer space. The expanses of outer space should be an area only for the peaceful co-operation of States.

A separate question and a major one is the reduction of conventional armaments and of the numerical strength of armed forces. The Soviet Union wishes to see this problem, too, firmly integrated into the fabric of international negotiations and agreements.

In relation to Central Europe, these problems are under discussion at the Vienna talks. For nine years now, these talks have been, figuratively speaking, marking time, and the time to find agreements that would ameliorate the situation in an area with the highest concentration of the opposing armies is long overdue. The Soviet Union and its Warsaw Treaty allies are doing their utmost to achieve that.

It is a favourite allegation in the West that the Warsaw Treaty countries are superior to NATO in terms of conventional armaments in Europe. Yet at the Vienna talks the socialist countries are proposing to establish for both sides equal levels of armed forces stationed in Central Europe.

Unfortunately, the conduct of our Western partners in the negotiations is not conducive to reaching such an agreement. Although some rouge, figuratively speaking, has recently been applied to their position, the essence has remained unchanged.

So what is left of the so-called concern of the Western countries regarding the alleged superiority of the Warsaw Treaty over NATO?

And what is worse, steps are being taken outside the framework of the talks, which can only be described as provocative. What is there to say, for instance, about the recent agreements between the Federal Republic of Germany and the United States concerning the bringing from overseas of additional contingents of American troops under far-fetched pretexts? In other words, instead of reducing forces in that region, conditions are being prepared for increasing them by several more divisions. That is, of course, a mockery of common sense. The same applies to the planned redeployment of United States military units to the immediate vicinity of the borders of the German Democratic Republic.

In Europe, as well as on other continents, the Soviet Union is countering the policy of confrontation with the policy of good-neighbourliness and co-operation. We understand and appreciate the desire of the Europeans to follow the path opened up by the Conference on Security and Co-operation in Europe.

There exists a possibility of further progress towards making Europe a continent of peace and stability. The attainment of this goal would be largely facilitated by the implementation of the idea of convening a conference on confidence-building measures and disarmament in Europe.

That is one of the principal issues at the Madrid meeting of the States participants in the European Conference. If all its participants adopt a constructive approach at its resumed session in November, general agreement could be reached both with regard to the convening of the conference and to ensuring the success of the Madrid meeting.

Seeking to alleviate tensions throughout the world, we have recently proposed that the decision-making bodies of NATO and the Warsaw Treaty Organization make declarations on the non-extension of the sphere of action of the two military and political groupings to Asia, Africa and Latin America. That would constitute a major step towards *détente*. All the members of the Warsaw Treaty support this proposal. We hope that the NATO countries will study this proposal and respond to it in a positive manner.

In recent years serious obstacles have emerged in restructuring international economic relations on a democratic and equal basis. The root cause lies in the policies of certain Western Powers aimed at keeping the developing countries in an unequal position, at facilitating the attempts of the monopoly capital to exercise its sway over those countries.

A recent vivid example of that is the attitude of some Western Powers to the enormous work accomplished by States in preparing an international convention on the law of the sea. Many years of effort have produced a document whose provisions do not prejudice anybody's interests. And what has become of it? The United States is hampering the adoption of that convention. We would like to express the hope that it will stop being in opposition to a vast majority of States and will adhere to the convention.

The USSR is in favour of democratization of both political and economic relations between States. As to our participation in rendering assistance to the newly-freed States in overcoming their economic backwardness, in this respect too the Soviet Union is doing at least as much if not more than any of the developed capitalist countries.

It is common knowledge that the foreign policy course of any State is an extension of its domestic policy. Our country sets itself economic and social tasks of vast magnitude. We need peace to accomplish them.

The Soviet Union is extending its hand to every State which, for its part, is willing to maintain and develop good relations with us.

That applies to Europe. We are prepared for a further expansion of co-operation with West European countries on a peaceful and mutually beneficial basis.

That applies to Asia, where the Soviet Union has longstanding and stable ties with many States.

That applies to Latin America, where normal, business-like relations are being established between the USSR and a number of countries, including Mexico, Brazil and Argentina.

The same applies to the United States of America. We are convinced that from the viewpoint of a long-term policy of principle the deterioration of relations between the USSR and the United States is not in the interests of the United States itself. The American people is hardly different from other peoples as far as the desire to live in peace is concerned. Our country has on several occasions pronounced itself—in particular at the Congresses of the Communist Party of the Soviet Union and at the USSR Supreme Soviet—in favour of developing normal relations with the United States.

The policy of the Soviet Government aimed at preserving and strengthening peace and preventing another war is endorsed by all Soviet people, since all they aspire to is a peaceful—and only peaceful—future.

At the end of this year the Soviet people will mark an important event—the sixtieth anniversary of the Union of Soviet Socialist Republics. The Land of the Soviets is invariably faithful to the peaceful behests of the founder of our State, V. I. Lenin.

As Leonid Brezhnev has recently stressed once again, "Concern for peace is paramount in the policy of the Soviet Union". This concern determines the fundamental direction of all foreign policy activities of the Soviet State, which are based on the Programme of Peace for the 1980s adopted by the 26th Congress of the CPSU.

This Programme is being implemented by the Soviet Union together with other countries of the socialist community, cemented together as they are by a common political system and world outlook, by the identity of goals and ideals.

All the activities of socialist countries convincingly prove that peace is their policy aim. Every step, every foreign policy move made by them, serve the attainment of that noble goal.

The Soviet Union has rebuffed and will continue to rebuff policies based on the cult of force. Those who come out for preventing a nuclear disaster and for strengthening peace can always count on its support and co-operation.

All our actions in the international arena will continue to be inspired by our deep-held belief in the necessity and the possibility of saving the present and succeeding generations from the scourge of war.

Expansion of Capital and the Modern Stage of the General Crisis of Capitalism

Article in the journal *World Economics and International Relations*, No. 12, December 1982

Marxist–Leninist science provides the basis for analyzing the basic trends in world development and the specific forms of international relations in the modern age.

The role played by the export of capital as one of the principal features of imperialism was shown in his time by Lenin, who made a profound analysis of capitalism in its highest, imperialist stage of development. Lenin emphasized that as capitalism developed into imperialism, the export of capital "has assumed great significance".[1]

This assessment by Lenin is also fully applicable to the export of American capital after the Second World War when it grew to unprecedented proportions and the claims of US monopoly capital to world supremacy became particularly obvious.

Numerous American loans, credits and various kinds of so-called economic and military "aid" are being used as never before for the economic and political enslavement of other countries and peoples. The scope of expansion on the part of transnational corporations is without precedent. The role of the military–industrial complex has increased enormously. US monopoly capital has become much more aggressive and is the main source of militarism and war danger in the world.

As time went on Administrations replaced one another in the White House. The political platforms of the leading bourgeois parties were

---

[1] V. I. Lenin, *Collected Works*, Vol. 27, p. 387.

revised. The order of priorities in policy were altered. But the export of capital invariably held a key place in the activities of US business and US Administrations. It is encouraged to strengthen the positions of the monopolies, the true masters of America, and to safeguard their global interests.

At the same time, the US Administration invariably uses investments abroad as a lever by which to try and steer international developments along a course fitting its political objectives. This is only natural. A government of monopolies follows a logic dictated by monopolies and shaped by their own criteria and concepts. This writer has already discussed this subject in his works *Export of American Capital* and *Expansion of the Dollar*.[1]

One can see that never before have the most expansionist forces of monopoly capital used the power of state so frankly and directly to promote their interests; never before has their political philosophy been so bluntly and arrogantly translated into policy declarations and practical actions by government leaders of the major Western powers, the United States in the first place, as it is being done today.

This aspect of US policy L. I. Brezhnev described as "adventurism, roughness and unconcealed selfishness",[2] is evoking growing indignation in many countries, the allies of the United States in particular.

Attempts to use the specific features of the modern stage of internationalization of capitalist production and capital, the specific ways and means of present-day state monopoly regulation to justify a "renaissance", of its own kind, based on ruthless exploitation, of the age of colonization of America's "Wild West" pursue the goal of imposing the philosophy of "Pax Americana" on the entire world in defiance of the will of the peoples and the process of revolutionary change in the world.

I

Now that socialism has firmly established itself on a large part of the globe and is developing steadily, that the forces which stand for a

---

[1] See: G. Andreyev, *Export of American Capital. History of the Export of US Capital as an Instrument of Economic and Political Expansion*. M., 1957; G. Andreyev, *Expansion of the Dollar, Moscow*, 1961.

[2] See: *Pravda*, 28 October 1982.

progressive transformation of society are growing in the capitalist countries, that the national liberation movement in many countries is evolving into a struggle against the entire system of exploitation and oppression, it becomes ever more obvious that imperialism has no future historically. It was with full reason, therefore, that the Leninist Party drew its all-important theoretical conclusion to the effect that imperialism had irrevocably lost its power over the greater part of mankind.

An irreversible and objective process of disintegration has afflicted capitalism from top to bottom—its government and economic system, its policy and ideology. A crisis has gripped the core of this last system of exploitation: capital as a system of social production relations, be it primary relations existing in the process of production, or *"secondary and tertiary*, or *derived*, *extrapolated* non-primary production relations in general"[1] which reveal themselves in the international sphere.

Lenin's comprehensive scientific analysis of imperialism is the clue to understanding the crisis and contradictions of capitalism at the modern stage of its development that affect the system of capitalist production relations itself, as well as individual national economies and the complex of international ties, including external economic relations.

It is a well known Marxist–Leninist maxim that capitalist society is doomed historically and that the rule of the capitalist class will inevitably collapse. "It would be impossible to put an end to the rule of capitalism if the whole course of economic development in the capitalist countries did not lead up to it", Lenin noted.[2] The social productive forces which emerged within the capitalist production relations based on private property, inevitably grow out of their shell and come in conflict with it, a conflict which cannot be resolved in bourgeois society.

The 26th Congress of the CPSU pointed to a *further aggravation of the general crisis of capitalism* and noted in this context *the historical hopelessness* of various bourgeois reforms designed to save capitalism and, accordingly, the system of international relations it brought into being.

Capitalism is obviously incapable of coping with the deep-rooted contradictions it has created. However, an incessant search is in progress

---

[1] See: K. Marx and F. Engels, *Works*, Vol. 12, p. 735 (Russian edition).
[2] V. I. Lenin, *Collected Works*, Vol. 32, p. 99.

for ever new "miracle drugs" which, even if failing to give immediate relief from the ills of capitalism, could at least hold out a promise of a "light at the end of the tunnel". Quite a few such prescriptions have been offered over the past few decades and each of them promised to put an end to severe disturbances and ills. But their uselessness both for the domestic economy and the system of international ties was sooner or later revealed by realities of life.

For instance, A. Laffer, R. Mundell, and N. Ture, advocates of the so-called "supply-side economics" have lately made attempts to give wide currency to their views. They issued "prescriptions" for invigorating the ailing US economy. This school of thought found its most ample expression in G. Gilder's book *Wealth and Poverty*.[1] That book by Gilder was promptly baptized the "desk book" of Reaganomists and the US President himself.

The theoretical baggage of the said group of experts is limited, and their scheme for overcoming difficulties is primitively straightforward. The proponents of the above concept themselves call it a compendium of earlier suggested ideas and measures of government policy "tested" in the past. That body of views on political economy and of political recommendations could hardly be called a theory or even a textbook but rather a sort of a manual for the apologists of "supply-side economics".

The illusory nature of the hopes pinned on the concept has been borne out in theory and practice. Its fallacy had been noted, long before its official proclamation, by bourgeois economists working under the former Administrations. Now it is challenged ever more often by experts of the present Administration.

It is noteworthy that even *America* magazine (November 1981) which promptly responded to it with a coverage of the new US Administration's economic views and reprinting excerpts from G. Gilder's book, failed to conceal the sceptical attitude to such views on the part of many economists and members of the US business community, whose "prosperity" the economic concepts of Reagan's Administration are supposed to secure.

As a matter of fact, it would also be an illusion to stake on renouncing "economic experiments" and reverting to the traditional Keynesian

---

[1] See: G. Gilder, *Wealth and Poverty*, New York, 1981.

methods to improve the situation. The untenability of the theoretical concepts of G. Gilder and others is to an even larger degree proved by the practical results of private business domination of the economy: the continued aggravation of economic difficulties in the USA, the enormous rate of unemployment, and so on.

In this connection, Gus Hall, General Secretary of the Communist Party, USA, emphasized that after putting an end to all the concessions inherent in Keynesian economics, Reagan's Administration is replacing it with what may be called "economics of monopolistic highway robbery".

The specific features of modern capitalism, as they were pointed out at the 24th, 25th, and 26th Congresses of the CPSU, are directly related to the characteristics of the current stage of the struggle between the two systems—capitalism and socialism, and to the unprecedented growth of anti-imperalist forces throughout the world.

At the end of the 20th century capital can fulfil its role in politics and international relations of the world capitalist system only on a contracted basis as a result of the fundamental changes in the world brought about by the Great October Socialist Revolution. The impact of those changes becomes ever more profound as time goes on. Lenin wrote in this context: "We are rightly proud to have the good fortune to *begin* the building of a Soviet state, and thereby to *usher in* a new era in world history, the era of the rule of a *new* class, a class which is oppressed in every capitalist country, but which everywhere is marching forward towards a new life, towards victory over the bourgeoisie, towards the dictatorship of the proletariat, towards the emancipation of mankind from the yoke of capitalism and from imperialist wars."[1]

Attempts to prevent the abolition of capitalist production relations by means of state monopoly regulation of the economy by facilitating the growth of transnational corporations and introducing the most up-to-date scientific and technical achievements result only in the emergence of new contradictions and an exacerbation of old ones. In the historical perspective, these attempts cannot save capitalism as a socio-political system. The formation and development of the world socialist system, the upsurge of the national liberation movement and the struggle of the

[1] V. I. Lenin, *Collected Works*, Vol. 33, p. 55.

working people in the capitalist countries for their rights invariably confirm the correctness of that Marxist–Leninist conclusion.

The significance of that conclusion for theory and practice is indisputable. Of no less importance for science and practice (especially international practice) is also the fact that capitalism, as it was pointed out at the 25th and 26th Congresses of the CPSU, has not ceased to develop and is in possession of considerable reserves. The way they are used, however, is thoroughly anti-popular in nature and fully reflects the exploitative essence of capitalism. That feature of modern capitalism is pointed out in the report of the Central Committee of the CPSU to the 26th Congress of the CPSU, which speaks of the need to "study certain new phenomena in the capitalist world, specifically the features of the present stage of capitalism's general crisis and the rapidly growing role played by the military–industrial complex and the transnational corporations."

Of course, none of the reserves available to capitalism are capable of helping capitalism as a social system avoid its doom and, even less so, of stopping the progress of human society. These reserves, however, can delay the final collapse of capitalism in a given part of the capitalist world, deform social progress in a given country and distort in the historical perspective the ways of its development, probably at a high cost to humanity.

The cost to be borne is not determined only by the losses that the peoples, primarily the labouring masses, have constantly to sustain in the process of their exploitation by capital: supermonopolized or non-monopolized, local or foreign; in principle its nature is not what matters most. A formidable danger to mankind stems from the fact that in an effort to avoid stagnation, to stimulate its development, to grow and to make profits capital resorts to any means, attaching top priority to militarism, the arms race and threats to use military force to defend its selfish class interests, especially those proclaimed as "vital interests". The arms race launched by monopoly capital has already cost a staggering price to mankind. These expenditures can grow manifold and the danger of war become even more formidable unless insurmountable barriers are put up to hold in check the ambitions of the military–industrial business.

Thus the concept of world development and international relations that reflects the interests of capital is radically at variance with the vital interests of the peoples. As the 26th Congress of the CPSU pointed out, "adventurism and readiness to gamble with the vital interests of humanity in pursuance of narrow and selfish ends—this is what has emerged in a particularly barefaced form in the policy of the most aggressive imperialist circles."

The peaceful foreign policy programme of the CPSU adopted at the 24th Congress and further developed at the 25th Congress of the CPSU, the set of proposals put forward at the 26th Congress of the CPSU and called by the peoples as the "Programme of Peace for the Eighties" are assuming growing significance. This is irrefutable proof of the fact that socialism and peace are inseparable.

Wider and more intensive use of foreign markets through export of capital is also a means of sustaining the development of capitalism and, therefore, is a reserve for its growth. The solution of their own problems through external expansion, the use of foreign markets, especially those untapped so far, has always been an attractive motive for the activities of monopolies.

Through the export of capital monopolies strengthen their control by deriving higher profits, which graphically reveals the cosmopolitan ambitions of capital. The fact that capitalism gave extra sops to part of "its own" manpower, above all in the metropolitan countries out of overseas profits changed nothing in the substance of the matter, since the export of capital invariably helped it step up the exploitation of the "privileged" labour of its home country. The founders of Marxism–Leninism emphasized the existence of an unbridgeable abyss between the capitalists and labour regardless of the position a given nation occupies in the world.

For example, the export of capital by US monopolies, in particular in the form of loans and credits, means plundering not only countries to where capital is exported, but also the people of the United States itself. The export of direct and portfolio productive investments to foreign countries facilitates the monopolies' offensive against labour rights. The export of loan capital leads to the same results: worsening conditions for the sale of labour power and growing unemployment. The export of capital through state channels entails directly or indirectly a growth of the tax burden. Additional resources are needed to render financial "assistance" to a foreign state. In particular, capitalists try to achieve that end either by intensified exploitation of workers at national enterprises at home or by taking away part of the incomes, primarily from the working people of their own country, through taxes and otherwise.

In promoting the external expansion of monopolies a share of the burden involved is shifted onto the shoulders of other sections of the population, including part of the business community, which is compelled to pay for the international operations of their more monopolized and internationalized "brethren". That, naturally, causes frictions and contradictions within the capitalist class. This was the case in the past as well, but within the framework of the so-called Reaganomics those frictions and contradictions became more acute, since the biggest monopolies which carry out major international operations receive particularly high profits.

The fact that US monopolies impose relations of inequality upon their partners of other capitalist countries is nothing new either. This was also in evidence in the past, in particular in economic relations between the United States and Latin American countries. Today, however, this has become a rule, which testifies to a more aggressive behaviour of US monopoly capital and its desire to use foreign economic relations in general, and the export of capital in particular, to prop up its shaken positions. Another new feature is that, having proclaimed "supply-side economics" as its goal, the US Administration today demands that foreign countries accept US "prescriptions", above all adopt anti-communism and anti-Sovietism in their policies as a condition for receiving US capital and technology.[1]

For all attempts to use the export of capital to strengthen the international positions of imperialism, above all those of the main exporters of capital, however, the crisis situation persists. The system of capitalist international relations is hit by steadily deepening crisis which reflects the inherent inability of the last exploitative system to find a way out of its difficulties and to resolve the contradictions of its own creation due to the immanent laws of its development.

---

[1] See: *U.S. News and World Report*, October 26, 1981, p. 20.

II

New features are evident in the present-day export of capital. Some of them have grown out of the characteristic features generally inherent in this form of imperialist expansion, while others reflect the present specifics of world development.

Firstly, one can note that the importance of the export of capital for highly developed state monopoly capitalism due to the rapid internationalization of its positions is growing and that the global ambitions of the biggest monopolies are ever more pronounced.

Before the First World War virtually the entire export of capital was carried out with resources mobilized on the home money market. Subsequently, the role of small and medium capital in the export of resources abroad diminished. Big monopolistic alliances became direct exporters. Foreign investments were concentrated in the hands of a few giant monopolies. For example, in the 1970s less than 200 US corporations possessed more than two thirds of American foreign investments. Naturally, it is characteristic not only of the United States, but of other major imperialist powers as well, where concentration of the export of capital in the hands of a few leading monopolies is also growing rapidly.

Accordingly, the scale of the export of capital and the size of foreign investments belonging to major, above all transnational, monopolies and banks have increased considerably. In the period between 1914 and the end of the Second World War foreign investments of major capitalist powers grew roughly by one third. In the post-war period foreign investments doubled practically every decade.[1] The rates of growth varied with every particular form of the export of capital. For instance, as regards direct investments, their growth has been even more rapid in the past 15 years; they doubled every 6 to 7 years.

The main share of foreign investments is concentrated in the industrialized part of the capitalist world, denying most developing states the benefits of scientific and technical progress. It is indicative that

---

[1] See: *Political Economy of Contemporary Monopoly Capitalism*, Vol. 2, Moscow, 1975, p. 73 (Russian edition).

Table 1. Distribution of US direct investments

	Total sum (mill. dollars)			Percentage		
	1950	1980	1981	1950	1980	1981
Total investments made	11788	213469	227343	100.0	100.0	100.0
In developed capitalist countries	5696	157084	167112	48.3	73.6	73.5
In developing countries	5736	52684	56109	48.7	24.7	24.7

Calculated on the basis of the "Survey of Current Business", February 1981, p. 41; August 1981, p. 32; August 1982, p. 22.

industrialized countries account for more than half of new direct investments, which means that these resources and technology remain within the zone of industrialized capitalist countries.

In 1978, for example, the net export of new direct investments from that group of countries amounted to over 30.9 thousand million dollars, and their net import, to over 20 thousand million. In the period 1978–1980 such US foreign investments annually grew at an average rate of 19.5 thousand million dollars, while foreign direct investments in the United States itself grew 10.2 thousand million dollars a year.[1] Leading Western economists note the growth of "interdependence" within a relatively narrow group of industrial capitalist countries (see Table 1). At the same time, numerous attempts are being made to use the export of capital to reconcile the interests and policies of the monopolies of various countries, including the nascent, in particular monopolized, business in the developing countries. However, these plans failed, which demonstrated the debility of capitalism, its limited potentials and resources to ensure settlements strategically advantageous to it.

The absence of requisite class unity under the aegis of Western monopolies compels imperialism to resort to "traditional" means. Along with the growing export of capital to the newly-free states to

---

[1] Doc. U.N.E/C. 10/1982/2, 16.VII.1982, p. 5.

secure the economic, political and social interests of the imperialist monopolies, the West, above all the United States, increasingly resorts to brute force and aggression to achieve its ends. The realities of life show that it is not averse to using such methods against other countries as well. In this context L. I. Brezhnev said at the 26th Congress of the CPSU: "Imperialist circles think in terms of domination and subjugation in relation to other states and peoples."

The above circumstances do not affect the aforesaid desire of the monopolies to reinforce, through the export of capital, the positions of highly developed state monopoly capitalism inside the imperialist powers and within the world capitalist economy as a whole.

Secondly, the export of capital has become considerably more aggressive. This aggressiveness is already evident in the very methods of infiltration by foreign capital under present conditions due to its inability to assure profitable investment otherwise than by flagrant violation of the fundamental rules of international relations, flouting the principles of equality and mutual benefit, undermining the foundations of the national sovereignty, freedom and independence of the peoples.

As is known, in this struggle Japanese and West European monopolies are competing ever more successfully with American capital, on the US domestic market in particular. During the 1970s the US share in world exports dropped by almost 20 per cent, which was largely due to a deterioration of the American monopolies' positions in the field of foreign investments. Competitors become particularly aggressive and ruthless, since the key role in this struggle is played by transnational corporations, of which American monopolies constitute a considerable part.

Apart from the causes originating in the centres of highly advanced state monopoly capitalism the growing aggressiveness of foreign investment policy reflects the specific situation of the less developed countries. Capitalism still retains that reserve, and the export of capital helps monopolies use it to secure the interests of state monopoly capital. However, it is becoming increasingly difficult for capitalism to put this reserve to use, due to the growth of the national liberation movement, to an ever larger number of countries opting for progressive development, including socialist orientation, to stronger all-round ties between the newly-free countries and the socialist world.

Aggressiveness is the last resort assuring the investment of capital abroad necessary for the imperialist circles. The 26th Congress of the CPSU stated: "With utter contempt for the rights and aspirations of nations, they are trying to portray the liberation struggle of the masses as 'terrorism'." Indeed, they have set out to achieve the unachievable—to put up a barrier to progressive change in the world and again to become the rulers of peoples' destinies.

This aggressiveness becomes all the more glaring as it is directly linked with the activity of the military–industrial complex, the global militaristic ambitions of the monopolies.

The policy of the Soviet Union and the fraternal socialist countries towards capitalist states is based, as before, on a struggle for lasting peace, consolidation of the principles of peaceful coexistence, reduction and, eventually elimination of the risk of outbreak of another world war. L. I. Brezhnev stated at the 26th Congress of the CPSU: "To safeguard peace—no task is more important today on the international plane for our Party, our people and for all the peoples of the world for that matter."

In their consistent struggle for peace and *détente* the countries of the socialist community along with other peace forces have scored significant successes. Their greatest achievement is their success in breaking this tragic cycle "a world war—a short period of respite—another world war" which assured for the capital a recarving of world markets and spheres of influence to fit the new balance of power.

The importance of this breakthrough for the destiny of the world and the opportunities which thus open up are evidenced by the following estimates made by the Club of Rome based on the data of the International Labour Organization. Given the present rate of population growth, by the year 2000 it will be necessary to create over one thousand million new jobs which, assuming an average cost per job at $40,000 dollars, will require trillions of dollars.[1] Even allowing for a lower cost per job in the developing countries, additional investments will nevertheless amount to a few hundred thousand million dollars. Nevertheless, this is less than the present rate of military spending.

---

[1] See: O. Giardini, *Dialogue on Wealth and Welfare: An Alternative View of World Capital Formation.* A Report to the Club of Rome. Oxford, 1980, pp. 160–161.

Hence the crucial significance of the programme of ensuring peace, promoting peaceful co-operation, limiting the arms race, and achieving disarmament put forward by the Soviet Union. For those who are unemployed, who live in misery or on the verge of death from starvation, whose number in the world totals several hundred million people today, the implementation of the Soviet initiatives is a way toward staying alive in the face of the threat of nuclear war, a way to survival.

This demonstrates fairly clearly the exploitative nature of the export of capital and its close links with the militaristic and aggressive ambitions of monopolies.

Thirdly, the relationship between the export of capital and the foreign policies of imperialist powers has become stronger, and is rather contradictory in nature, since it reflects drastic changes not only in financial–industrial capital itself, but also in the alignment of forces in the international arena, the consolidation of the forces of socialism and national liberation. The correctness of the Leninist approach to analyzing the role of capital export in imperialist policies has been fully borne out. The export of capital today means the worldwide expansion of a narrow group of industrialized capitalist countries. The USA, Great Britain, the FRG, Switzerland, Japan, the Netherlands, France and Canada account for over nine tenths of the total of 450–460 thousand million dollars in direct private investments. As we see, this group consists of the most powerful and influential countries of the capitalist world, constituting the three centres of world capitalism: the USA, Western Europe and Japan.

The above list represents the core of the group of Western countries in the United Nations, the three permanent Western members of the Security Council. The group of major capital exporters is almost completely identical with the composition of participants in the annual meetings of the leaders of Western countries who work out agreed guidelines for their policies. It includes the leading members of all the main military–political alliances, economic organizations and international agencies of the capitalist world, the basic forces which determine military and political strategy and the economic situation, the backbone of the military–industrial complex. All the principal transnational corporations belong to the above listed group of countries.

At the same time, the main capital-exporting countries which claim the role as "locomotives" of the capitalist economy constitute, in fact, a source of severe cataclysms, the focus of the insoluble contradictions of capitalist production. The 26th Congress of the Communist Party of the Soviet Union stated in this context: "The difficulties experienced by capitalism also affect its policy, including foreign policy. The struggle over the basic issues of the capitalist countries' foreign policy course has grown more bitter."

To exploit systematically the working people of various countries, the monopolies make use of the foreign policy mechanism, relying on the most aggressive and reactionary forces. Promotion of the export of capital goes hand in hand with support of military and militaristic regimes, all sorts of anti-popular groupings, the forces of racism and apartheid.

The peoples demand ever more resolutely a restructuring of international relations on a just, democratic basis. However, as L. I. Brezhnev pointed out, "imperialists, direct successors to those who subjected free peoples to slavery with fire and sword who plundered and oppressed them over many decades, do not wish to resign themselves to this. They attempt to impose upon the international community their own interpretation of the rules of international behaviour—one that would justify neo-colonialist piracy, methods of *diktat* and coercion, and would give them a free hand to suppress national liberation movements. Our positions in this regard are diametrically opposite."[1]

Deception used by the diplomacy of capitalist states is vividly reflected in a sharp contradiction between the formally declared principles and aims of their foreign policy, on the one hand, and the measures they practically carry into effect, on the other. The ruling circles of these countries, while proclaiming noble principles and objectives often conceal under a veneer of this kind their true intentions and actions on the international scene and thus hide the essence of their diplomacy alien to the peoples and the fact that it serves its aims of conquest, oppression of foreign nations, intensive exploitation of their own people, an aggressive and hegemonistic foreign policy. References to moral principles to justify an anti-popular foreign policy were widely employed by capitalist diplomacy in the past as well. Never before,

---

[1] *Pravda*, 13 May 1981.

however, were the interests of business presented so forthrightly as common national interests.

"It was the need for American corporations to expand their investments and protect their markets that led to such diverse developments as the US involvement in Vietnam, the Marshall Plan to aid Western Europe and American intervention against the left-wing regime of Salvador Allende in Chile"—these words of US historian W. Williams, on the whole, point correctly to the profound connection between vested interests and the US foreign policy.[1]

At the same time, it should be noted that the monopolies are increasingly inclined to use the international movement of capital for the purposes of imperialist policy. As was stated by L. I. Brezhnev, "the policy of peaceful coexistence charted years ago by Lenin is exercising an increasingly decisive influence on present-day international relations".

Some influential business circles in the West agree to develop cooperation with the USSR and other countries of the socialist community. Such constructive business co-operation based on the principles of non-interference, respect for national sovereignty, due regard for the partners' interests, and mutual benefit, has become a factor of contemporary international relations which exerts a restraining influence on the aggressive ambitions of monopolies and the reckless expansion of capital. This fact is of particular importance to the newly-free countries, which are interested in obtaining from abroad resources and technology to ensure their economic progress and strengthen their political independence.

Fourthly and finally, a salient aspect of the present-day export of capital is the aggravation of its exploitative nature. This is evidenced by the above-mentioned characteristics of the export of capital: its increased importance for state monopoly capitalism and the growth of its aggressiveness manifested by widespread militarism and a stronger interconnection with foreign policy and diplomacy.

The clearest indicator of increased exploitation through the export of capital is the enormous sums paid by the so-called "recipient" countries to the exporters of capital. For example, in the developing countries foreign investors annually derive profits amounting to 1/4–1/5 of the

---

[1] *U.S. News and World Report*, 25.1.1982, p. 44.

total direct investment. A new inflow of investments is far less than the sum total of profits transferred abroad, which also attests to the systematic exploitation of the relevant countries by foreign capital. As a result, the developing countries turn out to be net payers to industrialized countries rather than recipient of resources. In the crisis year 1981 profits from direct US investments in developed capitalist countries dropped, as compared with 1980, from 12.2 to 11.1 thousand million dollars, while profits from the developing countries grew from 7.5 to 7.6 thousand million.

Both direct investments and loan funds are more willingly directed to countries with a higher revenue level, which secures greater returns on such investments. For example, in 1978–1980 over 50 per cent of direct investments was concentrated in the developing countries with per capita GNP exceeding 1000 dollars a year (less developed countries with a per capita income below 400 dollars accounted for 5 per cent of such investments).

As regards loan capital, the picture is even more striking: in 1978 the most developed countries of this group received two thirds of all loans while the least developed ones received a mere 1 per cent. In the subsequent years the picture remained unchanged.

Changes in the policy of the principal private investors, i.e. transnational corporations are another indicator of growing exploitation. Direct foreign investments remain an important source of industrial financing for many developing countries. They continue to be the main

Table 2. New direct investments and profits transferred abroad (mill. dollars)

Years	New direct investments	Profits	Years	New direct investments	Profits
1967	1141	4254	1975	7683	9644
1971	2400	7192	1976	4275	11448
1972	1776	6230	1977	6875	14046
1973	4060	9374	1978	6788	16691
1974	−203	10776			

[1] Data for 62 developing countries.
Calculated on the basis of "Balance of Payments Yearbook", IMF; "Development Cooperation", OECD, for respective years.

traditional channel for TNC infiltration of these countries. Throughout the 1970s the flow of direct foreign investment from developed capitalist countries to developing countries was growing at an average annual rate of 15 per cent in nominal terms and of 4 per cent in real terms.

Investments in developing countries are made mainly through industrial TNCs, with the United States and Canada accounting for 50 per cent of all private financing in the 1970s, Western Europe for 38 per cent and Japan for 10 per cent. As a result of vigorous expansion efforts, mostly by Japanese companies which increasingly often act in alliance with US companies, the share of West European countries, which was 50 per cent in the 1960s, dropped to 38 per cent in the 1970s. The Japanese TNC group today is the most dynamic one, infiltrating the developing countries, particularly in Asia. Japanese expansion has the goal of gaining new markets and supplying national industry with raw materials and energy. Thus the most expansionist monopolies are getting the upper hand.

In the 1970s it was precisely the expanding activities of the US and Japanese groups of companies that resulted in a noticeably increased flow of private capital to Central America and the Caribbean (Mexico, Panama, Trinidad and Tobago, the Bermudas, the Bahamas and the Antilles) and Asian countries (India, Indonesia, Malaysia, Singapore). In the late 1970s they were, in terms of the volume of private investments, among the major geographical areas of TNC activities, accounting for over 50 per cent of all their investment in developing countries.

South America, which accounted for about 25 per cent of investments in the developing countries, was also an important area of TNC activities although during the 1970s the role of that region noticeably diminished. During the same period the importance of Africa and the Middle East for the TNCs also diminished (from 20 to 15 per cent and from 10 to 4 per cent, respectively). Thus, the 1970s witnessed a marked regrouping among the transnational corporations themselves.

This "innovation" in the nature of TNC's economic expansion to the developing countries brought about a substantial change in the structure of private funds. The 1970s saw the emergence of a new important source of private financing for the developing countries, i.e. transnational banks. By 1978 the total amount of loans granted through those banks, especially Eurocredits, had grown to almost 44 thousand million dollars.[1] As a result, the share of private industrial investment in the overall inflow of private funds, which accounted for 50 per cent in the 1960s, was less than one third in the 1970s. In 1979 the volume of loans extended to the developing countries exceeded the total industrial investments. As a result of all those changes the activities of the TNCs in the developing countries have become even more rapacious.

The share of production capital in the overall flow of private capital declined, since the loans granted by transnational banks are used to a substantial extent to offset the balance of payments deficit of the developing countries and for debt servicing. Payments of debts account for a growing share of the expenditures of the developing countries. The structure of imported capital has changed significantly in favour of non-productive loan capital. This means that the developing countries have less access to useful scientific and technological information, managerial and organizational know-how, which usually accompany the export of productive capital.

The growing share of loan capital results not only in the slower rate of technology transfer but, what is very important, also in more and more funds being siphoned out of the developing countries. In 1979 about 16 billion dollars was transferred from those countries to developed capitalist states in the form of profits from production investments.[2] In the same year debt servicing and interest payments for bank loans amounted to more than twice that total sum of profits. The end result of this is that capital resources are being pumped out of the developing countries at an increasing rate. Interest payments by the developing countries totalled 8 billion dollars in 1971 and 75 billion dollars in 1980.[3] Is this not indicative of the fact that loans, credits and other indirect forms of capital exports to developing countries tend to tie them in bondage? There are also other channels for siphoning out funds from the developing countries.

The magnitude of exploitation, however, is measured not only in

---

[1] Doc. U.N., E/c, 10/74, 16.V.1980, p. 13.
[2] See: *Handbook of International Trade and Development Statistics*, Supplement 1980/UNCTAD, U.N., New York, p. 250.
[3] *U.S. News and World Report*, 26.X.1981, p. 23.

quantitative terms. Mention has already been made of attempts by the state monopoly capitalism to use the export of capital in order to involve those groups of monopoly capital which do not take part in foreign economic expansion or are engaged in it on a limited scale, in the policies of leading monopolies in one form or another. Overall expansion effort also embraces capital resources of other countries, including developing countries themselves.

Such an unsavoury and anti-popular "partnership" of capital is cemented by various means of state monopoly support. Gratuitous "aid", elements of subsidizing in the traditional forms of capital exports, various methods of encouraging the export of capital whenever political, economic and social conditions in a foreign country are insufficient for it to be "self-controlled" and "spontaneous", are all used by the state monopoly capitalism to make capital expansion possible and effective despite the deepening general crisis of capitalism. Thus, economic "aid" turns out to be merely a means of protecting investments and gaining

Table 3. *Scope of economic "aid" to developing countries (1980)*

Countries	Million dollars	Percentage of GNP
1	2	3
United States	7091	0.27
France	4041	0.62
FRG	3518	0.43
Japan	3304	0.32
Great Britain	1785	0.34
Netherlands	1577	0.99
Canada	1036	0.42
Sweden	923	0.76
Italy	678	0.17
Australia	657	0.48
Belgium	575	0.48
Norway	473	0.82
Denmark	464	0.72
Switzerland	246	0.24
Austria	174	0.23

Source: *U.S. News and World Report*, 26.10.81, p. 23.

new positions for the monopolies. The "price" paid for this by various industrialized capitalist countries differs. And, of course, there is more to it than the figures listed in the table below since, besides economic aid, there also exist military "aid" and other means for satisfying the international interests of national monopolies.

While placing capital abroad with the aim of systematically appropriating the surplus value produced by the working people of foreign countries, monopolies at the same time exploit the working people of their own countries and, to a certain extent, other social strata both at home and abroad. The export of capital is the area which, like none other, shows the growing contradiction between the bigwigs of monopoly business and the rest of the capitalist society.

The study of the trends of development of the export of capital is becoming ever more important, since, on the one hand, they affect the entire system of state-monopoly capitalism and, on the other, reveal certain new phenomena in the capitalist world.

III

In this sense it is becoming particularly important to study the export of capital from the major capitalist country, the USA. The United States is now the biggest capital exporter. At present, about one half of all direct private investments of the capitalist world are American.

The American export of capital is characterized by the most reactionary features of the international politics of present-day imperialism and, above all, its subordinateness to the interests of the military-industrial complex. US imperialism would not be able to claim the role of "world policeman" if it had not at its disposal multibillion investments abroad.

It was not overnight that US capital gained those positions. Its expansion started in the last third of the 19th century, which was caused by the rapid development of capitalism not only in Britain and France, but in the USA, Germany and Japan as well. The development of interior lands in all leading capitalist countries had been basically completed. At the same time, the process of capital concentration and centralization had led to the formation of monopoly alliances and to the emergence in those states of a huge "surplus of capital" which started to flow abroad and, above all, into economically backward countries.[1]

While the export of capital had been a rare phenomenon before the last third of the 19th century, with Britain and France being virtually the only exporters of capital, a radical change took place at the end of the 19th century as a result of the above-mentioned features of the development of capitalism. The export of capital was rapidly growing with many developed capitalist countries exporting it.

The largest exporter of capital in the first decade of the 20th century was Britain, followed by France and then by the USA, Germany Holland, Belgium, Italy, and Japan. By late 1920s the USA took the lead after having gained an edge over Britain (if war loans are not to be counted, Britain was still number one) with France in the third place followed by Holland, Switzerland and Germany.

In the second half of the 1930s Britain once again overtook the USA. The Netherlands was in the third place with France only in the fourth; next came Switzerland and Belgium. The "axis" powers, Germany, Japan and Italy, were building up their foreign investments.

The late 1940s witnessed another reshuffling of the international investors: the USA took the lead having outrun Britain. Canada came third, Holland—fourth, and France—just fifth. The defeated Germany, Italy and Japan lost most of their overseas investments and found themselves "thrown out of the saddle" for a number of years as rivals of other exporters of capital.

The standings in the late 1950s were as follows: the USA, Britain, France, Canada, Switzerland, the FRG, Belgium, Holland, and Italy.

A decade later the USA was still leading in the export of capital. Britain retained its second place, France was third, and the FRG rose to the fourth place.

In the second half of the 1970s the list of foreign investors was still headed by the USA followed by Britain, the FRG, Switzerland, Japan, Holland, France (only in the seventh place), Canada, Sweden, etc. At present, the positions of the US capital are being challenged by its competitors, while the absolute value of US investments abroad continues rapidly growing. For instance, direct US investments abroad

---

[1] See: V. I. Lenin, *Collected Works*, Vol. 22, pp. 240–242.

increased by a factor of 4.5 from 1967 to 1981, i.e. from $50.4 billion to $227.3 billion. However, compared to other Western countries, the US share somewhat dwindled to less than 50 per cent in 1981. .

The USA is trying to offset this relative loss of ground by its monopolies through a more active use of political pressure, military blackmail, and by making competitors submit.

Year by year, the US book market is flooded with numerous publications on economics, history, philosophy, and foreign politics. A prominent place in those publications is given to the problem of US economic relations with other countries and to the history of those relations.

"Studies" on this problem grossly distort facts and data, for instance, those concerning relations between the USA and China in the 19th century. The expansionist policy of US capitalism in China is being misrepresented as selfless and allegedly meeting the interests of the Chinese people.

The same is true of the presentation of the history of US relations with other Asian countries, as well as with Latin America and Africa. Past instances of US brutal expansion and outright aggression against a number of countries and territories (the Philippines, Cuba, Mexico, Hawaii, etc.) are depicted as measures motivated by concern for the local populations.

The US capitalism's "historic mission" is being lauded in every possible way, while its true designs with regard to other peoples and its methods of *diktat* and blackmail are being obscured. It is known that various kinds of false slogans are being flaunted to this end, like, for example, assurances given by the Carter and Reagan administrations with respect to their commitment to "human rights" or demands of the Reagan administration that the so-called "universal favourable investment climate" should be ensured.

All this is being done in order to "establish" a connection between the practices of the US capital penetration in the economies of other countries in the past and its broad external economic expansion today by presenting both processes in a false light.

It should also be noted that the closer is the link between the direction of US capital's expansion and US foreign policy course, the more careful are the attempts to conceal this link. And this is understandable, indeed,

Table 4. *Major recipients of US economic and military "assistance" (1981, million dollars)*

Countries	Economic "assistance"	Countries	Military "assistance"
Egypt	1189	Israel	1400
Israel	785	Egypt	551
India	244	Turkey	252
Turkey	200	Greece	177
Bangladesh	155	Spain	126
Indonesia	128	The Philippines	76
Sudan	105	Portugal	53
The Philippines	92	Thailand	51

Source: *U.S. News and World Report*, 26.X.1981, p. 22.

since the aim is to deceive the peoples, including the American people as to the true nature of the policy followed now by US ruling quarters.

The export of capital in the form of loans, credits, "grants", subsidies and so on, which are extended by the United States to various countries, mostly developing ones, within the framework of economic, technical and military "aid" (in recent years it has been extended mainly through governmental channels) is depicted as "assistance" aimed at enhancing the "defence potential" of those countries, while in fact they are not threatened by anyone, except for the threat of enslavement posed by American capital.

A relatively small number of countries account for the bulk of funds channelled by the United States abroad as economic and military "assistance", of which the latter tends to grow considerably. That "assistance" is closely tied to military and strategic objectives of Washington, in particular in such areas as the Mediterranean, the Near and the Middle East and the South and the Southeast Asia (see Table 4).

It is also significant that while expansionist aspirations of the US monopoly capital and its pretentions to dominate entire areas tend to grow, there have been ever more frequent forced admissions of the fact that the possibilities for pursuing such a policy are limited. A recent study by US scholars entitled "The United States in the 1980s" admits, for instance, that in pursuing its expansionist policy which the study calls "the exercise of responsible power" (?!—A.G.) abroad, the United States has run into "definite limitations". While noting that "foreign aid cannot by itself cure poverty" (all the more so that this is not its objective!—A.G.) and that "modernization cannot be achieved quickly", W. Campbell, director of the Hoover Institute, writes: "It has been recognized that the United States cannot export democracy (?!—A.G.) to the rest of the world (?!—A.G.)."[1] In the wake of Vietnam, he continues, the extent to which the US can influence world development in the desired way have been markedly limited. Longing for the time in the past when the United States felt free to demand obedience of all countries, the authors of the study note with obvious regret that even an overt use of arms (as was the case in Vietnam) is not producing the effect desired by Washington.

What the analysis of the data pertaining to the US external economic expansion reveals above all is that essentially the US monopoly capital has been and remains an enemy of the independence and sovereignty of other countries and peoples whom it views as objects of exploitation and plunder.

The reactionary nature of the export of capital has found its most graphic expression in the monopoly capital's policy designed to erode the unity of the world socialist community. A vivid example of this is their policy of provocations against Poland and attempts to use errors in the socio-economic policy committed in that country in the past to their own advantage. This example proves that capitalism is making use of every opportunity to secure its own class interests.

The deepening of the general crisis of capitalism has aggravated as never before the contradictions of the present-day capitalist production and of the entire system of international capitalist relations.

Imperialist apologists are particularly angered by the fact that some segments of the American business community, including affiliates abroad, are seeking ways of co-operation with socialist countries and expressing their readiness to establish and develop various forms of economic, scientific and technical relations with them.

The facts also show that US West European partners have largely

---

[1] *The United States in the 1980's*, Ed. by P. Duignau and A. Rabuschko, Stanford (Calif.), 1980, p. VII.

failed to follow Washington's policy of economic and other "sanctions" against the Soviet Union. What is more, West European business community has repeatedly taken its own initiatives to further expand the economic co-operation with the USSR. Even those who swallowed the US "bait" were later compelled to recognize that the "sanctions" against the Soviet Union were ineffective.

The discriminatory policy of the current US administration aimed at disrupting economic co-operation between countries with different social systems is inevitably doomed to failure.[1]

It is appropriate to recall the words of V. I. Lenin concerning the development of co-operation between Soviet Russia and the West in the first years following the Great October Socialist Revolution. V. I. Lenin put it this way: "Why are they acting against their own inclinations and in contradiction to what they are constantly asserting in their press? . . . They call us criminals, and all the same they help us. And so it turns out they are bound up with us economically."[2] And then V. I. Lenin makes a major conclusion: "It turns out . . . that our calculations, made on a grand scale, are more correct than theirs. . . . We see that their forecast of economic development was wrong and ours was right. We have made a start, and we must now exert all our efforts to continue this development without interuption. We must make it our primary concern, giving it all our attention."[3]

The present conditions differ, certainly, from those existing 60 years ago although today as well the reactionary forces, as is known, are ready to write off all their failures blaming the Soviet Union and its policy. However, wide public and business community of the developed capitalist countries, above all those in Western Europe, are more aware today of the opportunities and benefits of developing relations with the USSR. They can rely on the vast experience that has already been accumulated.

* * *

---

[1] It is indicative that, for example, M. Friedman, a recognized "guru" of the economic platform of the present US administration, has noted the futility of such a diplomacy. He described the economic "sanctions" against the USSR as "a confession of impotence" (see *Newsweek*, 21.1.1980, p. 48).

[2] V. I. Lenin, *Collected Works*, Vol. 33, pp. 153–154.

[3] V. I. Lenin, *Collected Works*, Vol. 33, p. 154.

"From the initial days of Soviet power our state has always expressed its readiness for frank and honest co-operation with all countries that reciprocate. Differences in social systems should not get in its way—and are no hindrance in cases where goodwill is expressed by both sides"—said Yuri Y. Andropov, General Secretary of the CPSU Central Committee, at the Plenary Meeting of the CPSU Central Committee in November 1982.

US monopolies failed to realize their expansionist designs in the past. They will, certainly, be unable to realize such designs in the future as well. The world is not following the road mapped out by US monopolies and American big business, by those in Washington who are at the helm of the foreign policy of that country. The world is developing according to the objective laws discovered by Marxist–Leninist science. The future belongs to socialism.

For Peace on Earth

Article in the journal *Communist*, No. 18, December 1982

Our people, all the forces of peace and progress are celebrating the 60th anniversary of the formation of the Union of Soviet Socialist Republics.

The establishment of the USSR was an historic event in the life of the Russian people. It was also an event of immense international significance, a major milestone in the struggle of the masses of working people for revolutionary renovation of the world. The entire history of the USSR convincingly shows what peaks of true equality, monolithic cohesion, and fraternal friendship can be reached by relations among the peoples, based on the principle of proletarian, socialist internationalism.

The fraternal union of the equal socialist republics, which emerged six decades ago—on December 30, 1922, as a result of the expression of the will of our country's peoples, even more strengthened the international positions of the Soviet state created by the Great October Revolution, and enhanced its authority on the world scene. The necessity for this stable state union was dictated by the objective course of social development, by the tasks of building a new society.

The path traversed by the Soviet state is marked by the outstanding accomplishments in all the directions of socialist and communist construction. There is in this also a great service of the Soviet foreign policy, the guidelines and fundamental principles of which were evolved and laid into the foundation of the Soviet state's international activity by V. I. Lenin, the leader of the proletarian revolution.

Soviet foreign policy has absorbed the best democratic traditions which shaped up during the long history in relations among the peoples, in relationships among states. At the same time, the character of this policy logically ensues from the very essence of the socialist system which, as it has been convincingly confirmed by life, gives birth to altogether new international relations free of discrimination, domination and subordination that characterize the preceding social and economic structures.

The path which the Soviet Union has traversed over the past sixty years was not simple and smooth. The CPSU and the Soviet state pursue their political line in a complicated international situation. But the USSR has been consistently marching forward, following the charted course and being sure that it has made a correct choice.

I

The process of the shaping of Soviet foreign policy was determined by the historical circumstances of its emergence on the boundary of two epochs—mankind's transition from capitalism to socialism and communism. With the emergence of a new social system as a result of the triumph of the Great October Socialist Revolution, no tendencies of the world's development could any longer remain uninfluenced by this mighty revolutionary-transforming factor. Since that time the ideas and practice of socialism have influenced every country or group of countries, and every ideological-political trend. ". . . From the very beginning of the October Revolution, foreign policy and international relations have been the main questions facing us" (V. I. Lenin, *Collected Works*, Vol. 28, p. 151). The task of ensuring necessary international conditions for consolidation of the revolutionary gains and for establishment of normal, friendly relations with other countries and peoples acquired paramount importance.

On October 26 (November 8), 1917, the 2nd All-Russia Congress of Soviets adopted the Decree on Peace which was the first foreign-policy act of the Soviet state. In this Decree the Soviet government called upon all the peoples and governments of belligerent countries to put an end to the world war, and to conclude a just, democratic peace. In the Decree on Peace the Soviet state declared proletarian internationalism in relations with the peoples struggling against imperialism and colonialism, and peaceful coexistence in relations with the capitalist states to be the principles of its foreign policy. Operating simultaneously and in interconnection, these principles constantly determine the essence of the international line of the CPSU and of the Soviet state. The Great

October Socialist Revolution, the establishment of Soviet power, and its first powerful impulses towards peace found a broad-based support of the masses of working people in many countries.

The reaction of the imperialist circles was altogether different. It was the result of the class instinct, of the desire to hamper the revolutionary process, and of the narrow-mindedness in the understanding of the objective laws of historical development. The Soviet state displayed its preparedness to start negotiations with the capitalist states and to conclude equal treaties, but it encountered a wall of alienation and hostile conspiracies. The imperialist powers launched an armed intervention against it. History has shown that this course of imperialism was its first major strategic error in relations with the Soviet state.

The peoples of the Soviet state withstood with honour the ordeals forced upon them by the imperialists, having rebuffed the onslaught of the interventionists and of the forces of internal counter-revolution. Our state strengthened its international positions consistently, step by step, working for and achieving establishment of new, truly equal relations with foreign states. The relations of Soviet Russia with the countries of the East developed successfully. Equal treaties with our southern neighbours—Iran, Afghanistan and Turkey—were concluded in 1921. November 1921 saw the signing of an agreement with Mongolia, an agreement which laid a stable foundation of friendship between the peoples of the two countries. Peace treaties were also concluded with Finland (1920) and Poland (1921). A treaty with Germany was signed in Rapallo, Italy, in April 1922, and it dealt a serious blow at the imperialist policy of isolating Soviet Russia.

In 1922 the Soviet state took part in its first international conference which was held in Genoa. Lenin formulated our political platform at that conference with utmost clarity: ensuring stable peace and economic co-operation among the peoples, and establishing trade relations between the Soviet state and the capitalist countries. It is also deeply symbolic that at the Genoa conference our country raised in practice for the first time ever the question of a universal arms reduction.

After the formation of the USSR—the world's first single, federal, multinational state of workers and peasants, the Party and the government launched wide activity in the international arena on many planes. The growth of our country's international prestige resulted in a

P.N. K

breakthrough of the diplomatic blockade, when the bourgeois states had to officially recognize the Soviet Union. In 1924–25, thirteen states, among them Britain, Italy, France, Norway, Sweden, Austria, China, Japan and Mexico, established diplomatic relations with the USSR. During that period the Soviet Union concluded a number of important trade treaties with the capitalist countries. In this way a ramified structure of the USSR's political and economic relations with the outer world began to take shape.

Since the late 1920s the development of the Soviet state and the shaping of its international relations took place in the context of the deepening general crisis of capitalism. In the early 1930s, the sharp heightening of imperialist antagonisms led to the emergence of dangerous hotbeds of war first in Asia, where the Japanese militarists launched an aggression against China, and then in the heart of Europe as a result of the establishment of a fascist dictatorship in Germany.

The Soviet Union did all possible to curb the aggressors. Our country gave active assistance to the peoples of China, Spain and other countries which became victims of the foreign intervention. A befitting rebuff was given to the Japanese militarists in the Lake Khasan area and on the Khalkhin Gol river.

A broad programme of peace, based on the concept of its collective defence, was the proposal advanced by the USSR in those years for establishing an effective system of collective security in Europe and concluding a regional Pacific pact. Our country also bent its efforts toward signing individual mutual help agreements with capitalist states for joint rebuff to the most dangerous aggressor—Hitler's Germany.

But the obstructionist policy of these states prevented the erection of a firm shield from the impending Nazi threat at that time. The Western countries' ruling circles struck a deal with Hitler at Munich in the hope that they would channel fascist aggression eastward, against the Soviet Union. The peoples of Britain, France and other West European states had to pay a heavy price for that short-sighted policy. Events took a turn in which those who had helped to restore the positions of German monopoly capital and revive militarism in Germany and incited the Hitlerite aggressors against the USSR, were themselves subjected to their attack in the first place.

As for the general plan to let the German Nazis destroy the Soviet

Union, it was another major strategic error of the imperialist forces in the evaluation of the strength and viability of the socialist system and the might of the Soviet state.

Life eventually forced the ruling circles of the Western powers to co-operate with the USSR. Within the anti-fascist coalition, our country arranged broad political, military and other co-operation with the other members of the coalition to ensure victory over the common enemy and prepare a post-war peaceful settlement.

The coalition of states and peoples that won victory in the Second World War over the bloc of aggressive powers—Germany, Japan and their allies—was a new event in international relations. In the great battle against fascism, which tried to impose an order of the vandals and hangmen on the world, the peoples of countries with differing social systems fought shoulder to shoulder. The co-operation of the participants of this alliance was quite logical and had an enormous progressive significance for all mankind.

The victory over Hitler's Germany and militarist Japan did not come the easy way. But the Soviet people, who made a decisive contribution to this victory, successfully defended their socialist Homeland and fulfilled their international duty. The defeat of Nazi Germany and its satellites had a tremendous impact on the further course of world events. The peoples of Poland, Czechoslovakia, Yugoslavia, Bulgaria, Hungary, Rumania, Albania, the German Democratic Republic and the peoples of China, Vietnam and North Korea received an opportunity to choose the socialist road of development. From now on the capitalist encirclement was broken once and for all. A community of socialist states appeared on the international scene. The world socialist system came into being.

The positions of progressive, democratic and peaceloving forces grew stronger throughout the world; the prestige and political influence of communist parties increased everywhere. The workers' movement in the countries of capitalism achieved considerable successes.

An active struggle of the peoples of colonies and dependent countries for their liberation was launched. The period of the disintegration of colonial empires set in, and young sovereign states of Africa, Asia and Latin America began to appear on their ruins. Most of these states became the allies of the socialist countries in the struggle for peace, freedom and national independence.

"In the course of the 20th century", stressed L. I. Brezhnev, "our country twice stood at the origins of major changes in the face of the world.

"Such was the case in 1917 when the victory of the October Revolution heralded mankind's entry into a new historical epoch. Such was the case in 1945 when the defeat of fascism, the decisive part in which was played by the Soviet Union, raised a powerful wave of social and political changes that swept across the planet and led to a strengthening of peace forces in the world."

In the post-war years objective conditions arose for broader and more stable co-operation among states, regardless of the distinctions in their social systems, in the name of safeguarding durable peace. They reflected the strong desire of the peoples of the world to prevent a repetition of the tragedy that mankind had gone through as a result of the aggression unleashed by German fascism and militarist Japan. However, through the fault of the forces of imperialism, above all the US, these conditions were not taken advantage of. Moreover, the Cold War started by the imperialist circles of the USA, accompanied by the arms race, especially in terms of nuclear arms, and local conflicts now in one, now in another area of the world, led to a grave complication of international relations.

Everything indicated that imperialist circles had not drawn the proper conclusions from the lessons of history. Their attempts to place obstacles in the way of the development and consolidation of the world socialist system, of the growth of the national liberation and revolutionary movements was another major strategic error in assessing the world alignment of forces and in approaching the formation of their relations with our country, its allies and friends.

In face of the imperialist powers' fomenting of international tension, whipping up of the arms race and creation of the aggressive NATO bloc and other military alliances under the aegis of these powers, the Soviet Union and other socialist states were compelled to take the necessary steps to strengthen their defence capability. At the same time, the USSR even in the period of the Cold War consistently advocated a healthier international climate and demanded a dismantling of military bases on foreign territories that were created primarily by the United States in dozens of countries and were directed against the Soviet Union.

In the 1950s and the 1960s our country continued its indefatigable campaign to promote peace and international co-operation, counter the imperialist policy of suppressing the sovereignty of nations, curb the arms race and bring about disarmament and, above all, ensure the prohibition of nuclear weapons. These efforts brought about a number of significant achievements. In 1963 there was concluded the Treaty on the Prohibition of Nuclear Weapon Tests in the Atmosphere, in Outer Space and Under Water. In 1968, prepared on the USSR's initiative, another important international document, the Treaty on the Non-Proliferation of Nuclear Weapons, was signed. Representatives of over 100 states affixed their signatures to both these treaties.

Great political response in the world was evoked by the Soviet proposal submitted to the UN in 1960 for granting independence to the colonial countries and peoples; this initiative marked an important contribution to the struggle for national and social liberation. Drawn up in the spirit of Soviet proposals and solemnly adopted by the UN, the Declaration on this question gave a powerful impetus to the process of decolonization. A considerable number of new independent states appeared. This was a historic achievement in the struggle of the colonial and dependent peoples for freedom and national sovereignty. The great service of our socialist state, which raised in the UN as an urgent item the question of putting an end to the disgraceful colonial system, will never fade in history.

It took the ruling circles of the Western powers a lot of time to realize that their attempts to retard the onward march of the USSR and the socialist world as a whole did not produce the desired results. They became ever more convinced that the Soviet Union and other socialist countries, overcoming the obstacles and difficulties on their road, continued to confidently move ahead, building up their economic potential, strengthening their defensive might and improving their international ties in many fields.

II

By the beginning of the 1970s the change in the international situation in favour of the forces of peace, democracy, national and social progress became obvious.

The more far-sighted and realistically minded bourgeois statesmen and political leaders, who could not ignore this process, were coming to better realize that there was no, nor could there be any reasonable alternative to the peaceful coexistence with the socialist states.

Under the circumstances, the policy of peaceful coexistence and mutually advantageous co-operation which had been consistently pursued by the Soviet Union since Lenin's times, was gaining vigorous support of the public at large and a growing understanding in the leading circles of the capitalist countries.

This largely promoted the normalization of relations between the USSR and other socialist countries, on the one hand, and a number of capitalist states, on the other, in the 1970s, and eventually facilitated a turn from the Cold War to the development of *détente* and the consolidation of the foundations of universal peace. "International *détente* has become possible", noted Leonid Brezhnev, "because a new alignment of forces took shape in the international arena. The leaders of the bourgeois world can no longer seriously hope to solve the historical dispute between capitalism and socialism by force of arms."

Taking into account all factors in the development of the international situation, the CPSU made a scientifically sound conclusion about the emergence of objective opportunities for a radical improvement in the world's political climate, and for the remodelling of the entire system of state-to-state relations on the basis of the principle of peace coexistence.

Being confident that it was possible to build a solid edifice of peace, and being profoundly interested in this, our country advanced a broad complex of measures covering all spheres of the struggle for peace, freedom and independence of nations. Taken in their totality, these measures were set forth in the Peace Programme adopted by the 24th Congress of the CPSU (1971). It contained concrete and realistic proposals on the solution of the most pressing problems pertaining to the task of strengthening peace and developing peaceful co-operation among states.

A serious positive shift took place in Soviet–American relations which began to be filled with new content. The two sides held summits and many other meetings and talks primarily concerning the problems of nuclear-missile weapons and their limitations. A document on the foundations of mutual relations between the USSR and the USA was signed in May 1972. It sealed the commitment of the sides to proceed from the common conviction that in the nuclear age there was no other foundation for maintaining bilateral relations than peaceful coexistence. The sides concluded a Soviet–American Treaty on the Limitation of Anti-Ballistic Missile Systems (1972), and an interim agreement on certain measures in the field of limiting strategic offensive weapons— SALT I (1972), an Agreement on the Prevention of Nuclear War (1973) and a number of other agreements covering various spheres of bilateral co-operation.

Positive shifts took place in Europe under the impact of the foreign policy of the Soviet Union and other socialist countries. There appeared a series of treaties which brought interstate relations in Europe in line with the realities of its post-war development. Relations between the USSR, Czechoslovakia, Poland, and the GDR, on the one hand, and West Germany, on the other, were normalized on the basis of corresponding treaties, and a quadripartite agreement on West Berlin was signed. The German Democratic Republic received broad international recognition. The Vienna talks on mutual reduction of armed forces and armaments in Central Europe began.

The Conference on European Security and Co-operation became an event of exceptional importance. It reaffirmed the inviolability of post-war frontiers and elaborated a code of principles governing the interrelations of 35 participating states, and mapped out the prospects of peaceful long-term co-operation among them.

An end to imperialist aggression in Indo-China came in the same period as well. The peoples of Vietnam, Laos and Kampuchea managed to score major success in their national liberation struggle. The revolution triumphed in Ethiopia. The peoples of Angola, Mozambique and a number of other countries gained independence as a result of the collapse of the last Portuguese colonial empire.

The Programme of Further Struggle for Peace and International Co-operation, for Freedom and Independence of Nations (1976), adopted by the 25th CPSU Congress became an organic continuation and development of the Peace Programme. The Congress put at the top of the list of foreign policy priorities the tasks of bridling the arms race and effecting a transition to real disarmament, asserting the principle of the non-use of force in the practice of international relations, and concentrating the efforts of peace-loving states on the elimination of the hotbeds of war in different regions of the globe.

The tackling of these tasks encountered fierce resistance on the part of the more aggressive imperialist quarters. The confrontation between the two opposing courses in world politics became markedly exacerbated by the end of the 1970s. In these conditions, the Soviet Union and other socialist community countries continued to further the cause of *détente*, displaying the necessary vigilance and giving a befitting rebuff to the intrigues of aggressive forces.

International relations of this period are marked by several positive actions of considerable importance. This applies to the conclusion of the Soviet–French Agreement on the Prevention of an Accidental or Unsanctioned Use of Nuclear Weapons (1976), the signing of the Soviet–British Agreement on the Prevention of Accidental Nuclear War (1977), the coming into force of the Convention on the Prohibition of the Development, Production and Stockpiling of Bacteriological (Biological) and Toxin Weapons and Their Destruction (1975), and the conclusion of the International Convention on the Prohibition of Military or Any Other Hostile Use of Environmental Modification Techniques (1977).

Special mention should be made of the signing in 1979 of the Soviet–American treaty on the limitation of strategic offensive armaments (SALT II) which would become an effective obstacle in the way of further accumulation of the most destructive and costly types of weapons. One may say that the whole world was looking forward to its entry into force. Washington, however, chose another road—that of frustrating its ratification.

The changes in the world arena which took place in the 1970s, especially in their former half, reaffirmed that differences in the social system, in ideology or world outlook are not an insurmountable obstacle for states to maintain normal, constructive ties which facilitate the positive development of the world situation in common interests. *Détente* is a unique phenomenon in international relations. It expresses the fundamental aspirations of the peoples in the Soviet Union and all other states, and reflects their will for peace. So, all countries should display concern and utmost responsibility for *détente*, and show their understanding of the fact that the *détente* process serves to guarantee man's overriding right—the right to live.

This is exactly what the Soviet Union does, overcoming in its work for *détente* and peaceful coexistence the obstacles of bias, mistrust and hostility, erected by certain forces in the West. The Soviet Union is doing all it can to contribute by practical action to the curbing of the arms race, and the strengthening of security on the basis of promoting mutual understanding and development of state-to-state peaceful co-operation.

III

The Leninist strategy of peace, upheld by our Party and the State, has had to be implemented in the context of a strained international situation in the early 1980s. This situation has been aggravated, first and foremost, by the action of the most aggressive forces of imperialism, above all, of the US which has launched an attempt at opposing the policy of *détente* and the achievements in strengthening the positions of socialism, in advancing the national liberation movement and in promoting peace by its own policy of stepping up military preparations, interfering in the internal affairs of other peoples, and whipping up international tensions.

The imperialist forces, bent on upsetting the present military balance between NATO and the Warsaw Treaty and between the US and the USSR, to their own advantage, have launched an unprecedented arms buildup. They have been putting forward, one after another, their aggressive doctrines for the prosecution of nuclear wars—quick and protracted, limited and general. Besides, they have declared vast areas of the world to be a "sphere of the vital interests" of the US.

Imperial ambitions show themselves up through the increasingly gross intervention in the affairs of other nations and peoples, the fanning of the hotbeds of tension and conflicts, and proliferating acts of self-will in international affairs. This policy has been particularly manifest in the Middle East where it means encouraging and directly backing Israel's aggression against Arab countries and peoples, making possible such acts as Tel Aviv's recent criminal action in Lebanon and genocide against the Palestinians.

In the prevailing circumstances, the Soviet Union continues to make unflagging efforts and to use all of its political and moral potential to forestall the further deterioration of the international situation and preserve peace on Earth. Realistic ways towards lessening the threat of war, promoting *détente* and developing broad co-operation of nations with differing social systems have been indicated by the Peace Programme for the 1980s, adopted by the 26th Congress of the CPSU. It has been summed up in the CPSU Central Committee's Report to the Congress as follows: "To safeguard peace—no task is more important now on the international plane for our Party, for our people and, for that matter, for all the peoples of the world." This document is a direct follow-up to, and a creative elaboration of the foreign policy programmes of the 24th and 25th Congresses of the CPSU as applied to the most burning and the most pressing problems of international affairs today. The Peace Programme for the 1980s, supplemented since the Congress with new initiatives, is a wide range of interconnected constructive measures covering both nuclear and conventional types of weapons and relating to the situation in Europe, in the Middle East and in the Far East. These are political and military measures. All of these proposals have one goal and one common ambition of ours that unites them—to do everything possible to save the nations from the threat of nuclear war.

The CPSU proceeds from the assumption that there are potent forces in action to safeguard peace, this greatest value of common interest to humanity. The struggle for the noble ideals of peace today is a joint effort of the countries of the socialist community, the international Communist, working-class and national liberation movement.

The high tide of anti-war movement is mounting everywhere today. This movement, represented both by large-scale spontaneous action by the mass of the people and conscious activities of various political parties and organizations, has become so tangible a factor and assumed so wide a scale as to be producing a telling effect on the international situation. This cannot be ignored even in those capitals where the official quarters are still dominated by militarist trends and obsessed with the policy from "a position of strength".

The Soviet Union also considers that the potential of *détente* is far from being used up. *Détente* retains its power of attraction and it is necessary for this process to continue. Many of the most far-sighted spokesmen of political quarters of Western countries have also been speaking out for it to be kept up.

The Soviet Union, *unshakeably* convinced of the historical justice of the forces of peace and certain of their selfless readiness to do everything to bar the way to war-like ventures, is pressing for the implementation of the Peace Programme for the 1980s which has been winning the under-standing and support of all the peace-seeking nations and all anti-war forces.

Acting as they do as the leading factor in the battle to keep the peace, the countries of the socialist community have been contributing towards resolving a problem of world-wide importance, indeed. At the same time, they are doing everything within their power to bring about an indispensable external environment for successful construction of the new type of society. The countries of the socialist community link their present and future up with peaceful development.

Close co-operation of the sister nations in the furtherance of the cause of peace and socialism is a clear manifestation of the life-asserting force of the new type of relationship among nations—sovereign and equal, welded together by the community of their basic interests and priorities, their Marxist–Leninist ideology, and united by the bond of comradely solidarity and mutual assistance and their all-round co-operation.

The countries forming the socialist community keep drawing closer to-gether. The 26th Congress of the CPSU has declared the continued deepen-ing of socialist integration under long-term goal-oriented programmes to be a top priority. They are to help resolve the most urgent and vitally important problems of their national economies. These programmes are now being translated into practice. The object is to make the next two 5-year plans a period of intensive industrial as well as scientific and technological co-operation of the socialist countries. Another one is to complement plan co-ordination with that of their economic policies in general. Steady headway is being made in improving bilateral and multilateral co-operation in the ideological, scientific and cultural areas.

"Experience indicates", said the CPSU Central Committee in its Resolution on the 60th Anniversary of the Formation of the Union of Soviet Socialist Republics, "that loyalty to the principles of Marxism–Leninism and socialist internationalism and close co-operation of the fraternal parties in every area make it possible to combine properly the common and national interests of the socialist states, successfully resolve the contradictions and difficulties arising in the course of this development, and for every nation and for the entire socialist community to advance confidently. The Council for Mutual Economic Assistance and the Warsaw Treaty Organization are dependably serving this purpose."

The early 1980s have seen an unprecedented hostile campaign organized by certain Western quarters against the socialist countries. There has been a lot of provocative sabre-rattling attempts at exercising political pressure as well as subversive acts and ideological subversion. Washington is not giving up its plans to launch what amounts, in point of fact, to a trade and economic war against the socialist community, although it has come to grief more than once in this enterprise.

The USSR and other socialist countries have no intention of fencing themselves off from mutually beneficial links, including economic links, with capitalist states. But they cannot, naturally, fail to draw appropriate conclusions for themselves in the face of all manner of manoeuvrings of those who resort to a policy of sanctions and boycott and to attempts at interfering in internal affairs.

The course of life has more than once proved the total futility of the hopes to make the socialist states depart from the principles of their peace-building foreign policy, complicate the solution of the economic and social problems they have before them, and shatter the foundations of their social system. Any attempt at interfering in the affairs of these countries, setting them apart, or pushing them off their peace course are as foredoomed as they have always been. There are indications to show that the imperialist forces resorting to such stratagems in their policies are making yet another blunder in their relations with the socialist countries.

Now about our relations with such a socialist country as the People's Republic of China. The improvement of these relations could promote a safer peace in Asia and elsewhere. The Soviet Union is prepared to do and is doing everything for these relations to develop favourably and return to normalcy. And we see that of late the PRC has positively responded to this approach of ours.

As before, the strategy of Soviet foreign policy, underlying the Peace

Programme for the '80s, remains curbing the arms race, promoting disarmament, and averting the danger of a new war.

The Soviet Union has declared more than once that there is no type of weapons which it would not be prepared to limit or reduce on a reciprocal basis. And if the stockpiling of weapons continues and is even intensified, if the rates of the arms race exceed the curbs clamped on them by the relevant accords, and the existing agreements in this field are called in question, this is a direct result of the militaristic course of the NATO bloc.

The USSR confirms by deeds its consistent policy of principle in this direction. This country's unilateral commitment not to be the first to use nuclear weapons is an action of historic importance. Indeed, this means facilitating a turn from the dangers of the nuclear age to a safer and more lasting peace and hindering the intrigues of those who are trying "to accustom" mankind to the idea of a nuclear conflict being admissible and even acceptable.

We call on all nuclear powers, which have not yet done this, to assume such a commitment. This would help considerably to lessen the danger of nuclear war breaking out.

The Soviet Union stands for all states to undertake not to use force or threat of force in relations between them in general. To set the question on a practical footing, in 1976 this country proposed concluding a world treaty on the non-use of force in international relations. The relevant draft treaty was submitted for consideration by the United Nations. The great majority of the UN member-states met this initiative with understanding and approval. We intend to work further for its implementation.

At the second special session of the UN General Assembly on disarmament, the Soviet Union put forward a comprehensive programme of measures aimed at curbing the arms race. This programme generalizes both the positions of principle of this country and its main specific proposals. They cover all major aspects of limiting the arms race and promoting disarmament, from nuclear and chemical weapons to conventional arms and the naval activities of states. This programme was favourably received by the overwhelming majority of the UN member-states.

The Soviet Union exerted great efforts to start talks with the USA on the limitation and reduction of strategic arms. Soviet and American representatives currently meet at the negotiating table in Geneva. This is a positive fact. However, we cannot fail to note that our partners do not yet show the desire to come to terms.

The USA's approach betrays its obvious desire to win concessions from the Soviet Union to the detriment of the latter's security interests. One cannot otherwise assess the fact that out of the strategic arsenals of the USSR and of the USA, Washington snatches out, arbitrarily, only the ground-based missiles, which make the backbone of this country's strategic potential, and proposes cutting them down. As for the hardware in which the USA shows preponderance—missiles installed on submarines, strategic bombers, and cruise missiles—America would like to leave them outside the negotiations. With things standing as they are, it is difficult, of course, to count on progress in the negotiations.

The Soviet–US negotiations to limit nuclear arms in Europe are also under way in Geneva. However, here too, the United States displays a lopsided approach. It is suggested that the Soviet Union scrap its ground-based missiles, including those we have commanded for over 20 years. As for NATO's medium-range nuclear potential, America believes that it should be preserved and even increased. The bias and illogicality of such a stand are obvious and the Soviet Union cannot, naturally, agree with it. At these negotiations the Soviet Union makes proposals leading to mutually acceptable accords.

The Soviet Union backs its sincere desire to limit nuclear arms in Europe and to continue the relevant negotiations also by appropriate unilateral measures. We have stopped the further deployment of medium-range missiles in the European part of the country. More than that, the USSR is cutting down some of these weapons and does not install east of the Urals more medium-range missiles capable of reaching Western Europe.

On the whole, the Soviet–US negotiations in Geneva proceed with difficulty because of the obstacles regularly created by Washington's position. Clearly feigned are attempts to present the situation at the negotiations in rosy colour. Judging by everything, such "optimism" is designed to confuse world public opinion, calm down the allies concerned over the prospects of the above negotiations, and gain time to implement militaristic plans.

The Vienna talks on the mutual reduction of armed forces and armaments in Central Europe continue to mark time. At these negotiations too, the difficulty is in the unwillingness of our Western partners to come to terms on the basis of justice and equality.

We firmly believe that the main principle of the negotiations to limit the arms race and promote disarmament should be one of equality and equal security, from which the Soviet Union shall not depart.

If our partners accepted this basic principle, the negotiations would proceed confidently. However, if the negotiations were used to camouflage further military beefing up, this would further complicate the situation. Foul play should have no place here. Neither side should seek advantage to the detriment of the security of its opposite number. This should make the real logic of the talks on very serious problems affecting the destinies of world peace.

I also want to make it clear that this country, proceeding from the existing military equilibrium between NATO and the Warsaw Treaty, between the USA and the Soviet Union, is not after military preponderance either in Europe or on a global scale. However, we shall not recognize the right of others to military supremacy either. It is clear, at the same time, that it is necessary to lower the high level of today's equilibrium. The Soviet Union is doing everything possible for this, although, understandably, not everything depends on us.

If the Madrid meeting of the states which participated in the all-European countries decided to call a conference on confidence-building measures and disarmament in Europe, this would be of great importance for strengthening security in the continent. Such a decision would become a new and powerful impetus to the development of the all-European process started by the Conference on Security and Co-operation in Europe. The Soviet Union resolutely stands for the progress of this process; for these purposes, this country is doing everything it can for the successful completion of the Madrid meeting.

Great importance would also attach to the implementation of the latest initiative of the countries of the socialist community, their joint proposal to the effect that the leading bodies of NATO and the Warsaw Treaty should make statements about not spreading the sphere of action of these alliances to Asia, Africa and Latin America.

At the 37th session of the UN General Assembly, the Soviet Union came out with a major initiative by proposing to put on its agenda the question about the immediate cessation and banning of the tests of nuclear weapons. The basic provisions of a treaty on the complete and general prohibition of nuclear weapons tests were also submitted for the consideration of the Assembly. This document records all that has been achieved in the course of many years of discussing a ban on nuclear weapons tests, and reflects the additional considerations of many states, particularly as regards control over the observance of the future treaty. The full ending of nuclear weapons tests would become a serious obstacle for the development of new types and systems of nuclear weaponry and for the emergence of new nuclear states.

To stop another channel of nuclear danger, the USSR also proposes putting the question of multiplying efforts to eliminate the threat of nuclear war and to ensure a safe development of nuclear energy on the agenda of the 37th session of the UN General Assembly. We suggested that the General Assembly should declare the destruction of peaceful nuclear projects even by means of conventional weapons tantamount to an attack with the use of nuclear weapons, i.e. that it should identify it with the actions which the United Nations has qualified as the gravest crime against mankind.

It was stressed in the Main Report of the CPSU Central Committee to the 26th Party Congress that in recent years military conflicts broke out now in one, now in another region of the world, not infrequently threatening to overgrow into a big fire; that extinguishing them was anything but easy; and that it was necessary to prevent the emergence of seats of such conflicts. Promoting the solution of conflict situations makes a major direction of our policy. In tackling this task, the USSR acts under the Peace Programme for the '80s and complements it with new initiatives.

The Soviet Union is demonstrating a simplistic and dogmatic approach to a conflict situation. However, it has become axiomatic that whenever a serious hotbed of tension appears in one or another region, it is traced to the imperialist ways of those who disregard the legitimate interests of other countries and peoples and try to interfere in their domestic affairs and enforce their will on them. This policy is conducted by the US ruling quarters, which are deliberately steering towards the aggravation of the situation in a number of regions of the world. A

"rapid deployment force", to discharge obviously policeman's functions, has been formed. As a result, dangerous conflict situations and
"hot points" arise in various parts of the world, particularly in the
Middle East, the South Atlantic, Central America and the Caribbean.

Israel's intervention in Lebanon serves as an example of the tragic
consequences which the imperialist policy of retaining its positions by
force may have. There is no denying the fact that Israel risked the
aggression because it has a "strategic consensus" with the United States.
Although in Lebanon, Israel and its patrons suffered a serious political
and moral defeat, the breeding ground of tension they created there
continues to pose a great threat. The situation is fraught with new
conflicts.

The statements made by the US administration on the Middle East
settlement leave no doubt about Washington's continued opposition to
an independent Palestinian state. Flouting the UN resolutions, the
United States ignores the Palestine Liberation Organization as an
indispensable participant in the settlement process, studiously omits any
mention of the problem of Israel's pullout from all occupied Arab
territories and is preoccupied with the security of only one Middle East
state, Israel, to the exclusion of the other states and peoples of the
region. There is no doubt either that the United States is seeking to play
a decisive role in Middle East affairs.

The experience of the past few years serves to show that the US policy
predicated upon the Camp David separate deal has not brought about
and could not bring about a settlement in the Middle East. Moreover, it
further complicated the situation in the region. Now Washington is
trying once again to prevent a genuine settlement of the Middle East
problem.

The Soviet Union is firmly at one with the Arab peoples. Israel must
get out of Lebanon and return to the Arabs all Arab lands it seized. The
principles of the Middle East settlement formulated by the Soviet Union
are of special importance in the current situation. These include: the
strict observance of the principle of inadmissibility of the seizure of
foreign lands by aggression; the implementation of the right of the Arab
people of Palestine to create an independent state on the West Bank of
the Jordan and in the Gaza Strip; the return to the Arabs of the eastern
sector of Jerusalem; ensuring the right of all the countries of the Middle

East to safe and independent existence and development, the ending of the state of war and the establishment of peace between the Arab states and Israel: international guarantees of the settlement. This could be achieved by the collective efforts of all the sides concerned, including the PLO, the legitimate representatives of the Arab people of Palestine. An international conference is the best way of working out decisions leading to a lasting peace in the Middle East. The Soviet position on the Middle East settlement is consistent with the view expressed recently at the Arab summit meeting at Fez.

The conflict between Iran and Iraq is also fraught with grave consequences. The Soviet Union is convinced that the bloody war which has been going on for more than two years is senseless from the point of view of the fundamental interests of the peoples of both countries. It only plays into the hands of the imperialist forces.

The situation around Afghanistan, that is, understandably, the external aspects of the problem, also remains unsettled. The reasons for this are clear: the enemies of the Afghan people keep trying to prevent the building of a new, truly democratic life in that country, interfering in its internal affairs and conducting armed intervention from the outside against Afghanistan, a sovereign non-aligned state. A realistic opportunity to ensure a political settlement on Afghanistan is provided by the well-known proposals of the government of the Democratic Republic of Afghanistan. The Soviet Union fully supports them. The main condition for a full settlement is the cessation of the armed intervention from the outside. The Soviet Union looks favourably on the contacts established in Geneva between Afghanistan and Pakistan, who are now exchanging views on the problem.

The Soviet Union is in favour of the plan to make South-East Asia a zone of peace and stability. The peoples of Vietnam, Laos and Kampuchea have chosen their way of social development and the forces that are trying to prevent them from deciding their destiny themselves are running against the spirit of the time and the objective laws of history. The proposals made by the three countries of Indo-China to promote dialogue and improve their relations with the neighbouring countries open up new opportunities for bringing about substantial changes for the better in the situation in South-East Asia.

The strengthening of international security in Asia is facilitated by the peaceloving foreign policy pursued by India, a great Asian country. We are bound with that country by the bonds of close friendship and fruitful co-operation and the common cause of safeguarding peace and freedom of the peoples.

In the south of Africa, with the connivance of the United States and other Western powers, the racist regime of South Africa is waging an undeclared war against Angola and some other states. It ignores the UN decisions on granting independence to Namibia. A breeding ground of tension remains in that region as a result. The aggressive actions against the newly-independent countries in the south of Africa must be halted. The people of Namibia must be given the right to free existence in an independent state of their own.

The Soviet Union believes that urgent international problems can and must be solved peacefully at the negotiating table. The Soviet Union is prepared to co-operate, on a constructive and reciprocal basis, with all countries in Europe, Asia, Africa and Latin America in the struggle for peace, the improvement of the situation and the development of normal and good relations between states.

The same applies to the Soviet policy *vis-à-vis* the United States. We are not to blame for the current tension in relations with the United States. The Soviet Union continues to believe that our relations with the United States can be normalized and bettered on the basis of peaceful coexistence, provided, of course, Washington is prepared to play the ball. We hope that common sense will eventually prevail in Washington.

The Soviet Union's activities in the international arena have always been in the focus of attention of the CPSU, its Central Committee and the Politbureau of the Central Committee which formulate and direct the Soviet foreign policy on the basis of an in-depth Marxist–Leninist analysis of the international situation, taking into account the alignment of forces in the world and the laws and factors that determine the main trends and prospects of the world's development. This ensures the effectiveness and continuity in the implementation of the tasks that face the Party and the country in international affairs.

"Soviet foreign policy has been and continues to be determined by the decisions of the 24th, 25th and 26th congresses of our party", Yuri Andropov, General Secretary of the Central Committee of the CPSU, said in his address at the November Plenum of the Central Committee of the CPSU. "The invariable aims of our foreign policy are to ensure a lasting peace and to defend the right of the peoples to independence and social progress. In the struggle for these aims the leadership of the party and the state will be acting consistently and thoughtfully in line with its principles." That statement was made with a full sense of responsibility and at the most authoritative level.

The Leninist line of Soviet foreign policy is unanimously approved and supported by all Soviet communists and the Soviet people as a whole.

The recent celebrations of the 60th anniversary of the USSR once again demonstrated the unity of the Soviet people. They also showed that all Soviet citizens, regardless of their nationality or occupation, hold dear the interests of their country and its future.

The Soviet Union celebrated its anniversary by new achievements in all areas of communist construction. The Party's Leninist nationalities policy, the turning in a short space of time of Russia's erstwhile backward provinces into the flowering socialist republics and the establishment of equitable relations between the Soviet nations, both big and small, have become an inspiring example in the struggle of the peoples for national independence and their sovereign right to choose their social and political system themselves.

Sixty years after its founding the Soviet Union appears to the world as a peaceloving socialist state, an integral part of the community of the socialist nations and a great world power without which no major international problem can be solved.

In celebrating this anniversary the peaceloving Soviet people justly takes pride in the great authority their country commands in the struggle for the maintenance and strengthening of peace among nations. Relying on its economic and defence potential, the Soviet Union will continue to do everything to ensure effective defence for the work and peaceful life of Soviet people and our friends in the socialist countries.

"In the complicated international situation when the forces of imperialism are trying to push the peoples onto the road of hostility and military confrontation, the party and the state will firmly uphold the vital interests of our homeland and maintain great vigilance and readiness to give a crushing rebuff to any attempt at aggression", Yuri Andropov said. "They will redouble their efforts in the struggle for the security of the peoples and strengthen co-operation with all the peace forces of the world. We are always ready for honest, equal and mutually beneficial co-operation with any state that is willing to co-operate."

The peoples fighting against the threat of nuclear war and all the champions of peace and socialism are looking to our country with confidence and hope. Much credit for the authority which the Soviet Union commands today goes to its foreign policy of peace.

The Main Features of Export of US Capital Today

Article in the journal *World Economics and International Relations*, No. 4, April 1983

At the present stage of the general crisis of capitalism when the growing economic instability of capitalism has become clearly evident, when the cataclysmic character of the development of imperialist powers has intensified and dozens of young states of Asia, Africa and Latin America have come on the international political scene and attached first priority in their home and foreign policies to implementing decolonization in the economic sphere, the United States has begun to attach special significance to securing its leadership in the capitalist world, relying on increasing the expansion of capital.

Karl Marx stated in his "Capital" that with sufficient profit rate "capital becomes bold", and with an increase in the profit rate consistently "agrees to any application", "becomes excited", "is positively ready to rush headlong", "tramples underfoot all human laws" and, finally, "there is no crime it would not risk to perpetrate even on pain of the gallows".[1]

The export of capital which earns enormous profits for the US monopolies removes, as it seems, all moral and other barriers (including those erected by the bourgeois itself), all standards of international intercourse, if they interfere with obtaining superprofits and enrichment at the expense of the peoples of other countries.

US capital, just as before, is making use of all available means,

---

[1] See K. Marx and F. Engels, *Works*, Vol. 23, p. 770.

including military means, to secure advantageous spheres and conditions for its functioning. That was the case in Indo-China where the American military provoked a prolonged and sanguinary war. This is the case today in Central America where direct intervention in the internal affairs of El Salvador is continuing, and encroachments on the independence of Nicaragua are repeated again and again. A tense situation is in evidence in the Middle East which is created by the Israeli aggressors with direct connivance on the part of the US ruling quarters. Trouble spots are to be found in some other regions of the world as well. Quite often one can see there without much effort the striving of US imperialism to secure stable economic, political and military positions for itself so as to derive superprofits, at the expense of its rivals in particular.

As was pointed out in the report of the CPSU Central Committee to the 24th Party Congress, "neither the integration processes nor the class-motivated interests of the imperialists in pooling their efforts for struggle against world socialism have removed the contradictions between imperialist states. Towards the beginning of the 'seventies the main centres of imperialist rivalry had become clearly manifest: these are the United States, Western Europe . . . Japan. Economic and political competitive struggle is growing ever stiffer among them. The bans imposed by US official authorities on the import of ever greater numbers of commodities from Europe and Japan, the attempts of European countries to limit their exploitation by American capital—these are just a few of the manifestations of this struggle."

The change in the positions of US imperialism in its economic rivalry against Western Europe and Japan, the loss by US imperialism of its complete hegemony in the sphere of international trade and other economic spheres leads to an increase in the aggressive character of the export of US capital. This manifests itself in crude violations of the fundamental rules of international intercourse, in flouting the elementary principles of equality, in undermining the foundations of national sovereignty, the freedom and independence of nations.

In the international policy of US imperialism the export of capital has a significant part to play. A high degree of monopolization is characteristic of this sphere of its external economic activity. Suffice it to say that in the early 'seventies more than 70 per cent of all capital investments belonged to 187 corporations. In the same years the American companies in possession of assets of over 250 million dollars each (which accounted for less than 0.07 per cent of the total number of US companies) received almost 84 per cent of all profit returns on overseas operations.

Among the factors which have a determining influence on the intensified export of capital to other countries one can single out the continuing growth of the concentration and centralization of production and capital in the United States, the increasing impact of scientific and technological progress, the exacerbation of the inter-imperialist struggle for markets, the sources of raw materials and the spheres of capital investments.

The United States remains, as before, the main capitalist power, retains its leadership in key branches of the economy (especially in those requiring a high scientific level), and enjoy the highest standards of labour productivity and is the biggest exporter of capital. Nevertheless, the countries of Western Europe and Japan are ahead of the United States in rates of growth of both main capital assets, capital investments in the economy and the gross national product, as well as industrial production. The sharp decline in the growth rates of the productivity of labour in the last few years is causing concern within the business community. The position of the United States abroad has been greatly undermined.

In the 'seventies the United States stepped up its activity in the struggle for economic recarving of the world according to the availability of "capital and strength", which reflected the striving of the ruling quarters to regain the positions they had lost in the sphere of world economic relations.

All these factors tend to intensify the competitive struggle between the United States and other power centres—Western Europe and Japan, result in outbreaks of "trade wars", the enactment and stiffening of protectionist measures. However, although Western Europe and Japan are much superior to the United States as regards their involvement in the world trade turnover, they are inferior to it for the scale of production abroad on the basis of exported capital. In the mid-seventies the relation of the cost of products of overseas subsidiary companies of the United States to its gross national product was equal to 30.3 per cent, whereas for the countries of Western Europe this indicator was 24.8 per cent and for Japan 11.5 per cent.[1]

It is interesting to compare the relation of overseas production and national commodity export: in the United States it changed from 2.7 : 1 in 1960 to 5.3 : 1 in 1979; in the countries of Western Europe, from 0.7 : 1 to 1.3 : 1, and in Japan from 0.1 : 1 to 1.4 : 1. These data show the degree of the real presence of capital of the three centres of imperialism on foreign markets.

On the whole, the 'seventies introduced essential corrections into the alignment of forces between the main centres of modern capitalism. It is necessary to point out the specific features of the first half of the 'seventies: while one could observe a definite displacement of the United States from its monopoly positions in a number of sectors of the capitalist economy as a result of the development of Western Europe and Japan which was gaining momentum, the latter half of that decade was characterized by a certain stabilization of the US position and a deceleration of the growth rates of the economy of Western Europe and Japan. After the increase in the number of members of the Common Market the United States is opposed by a wider economic group which is comparable to the United States in the volume of GNP, is largely superior to it for the share of these countries in world capitalist trade, the production of a number of commodities (steel, motor vehicles), as well as in the growth rates of industrial production as a whole.

The crisis of the capitalist currency and financial relations was a painful blow to the United States. This crisis ruined the Brettonwood system which secured for the dollar the role of the key currency in the capitalist world. Nevertheless the dollar remains as before the chief currency in the capitalist world, although it has surrendered some of its positions.

Soviet economists have proved that the opinion concerning the relatively small significance of foreign economic relations for the United States with its enormous home market, highly developed scientific and production potential and rich resources is not true to fact. It has been shown in one of their works that the "gradual accumulation of

---

[1] *Zapadnaya Evropa v Sovremennom Mire (Western Europe in the Modern World)*, Vol. 2, Moscow, 1979, p. 24.

quantitative elements of dependence led in that period to a qualitative change in the relationships between the American and world economies, the progressively growing dependence of the US economy on foreign economic relations as the key prerequisite for securing an extended character of the reproductive process in the country".[1]

The main manifestation of these shifts was the increase in the 'seventies of the dependence of the US economy on the import of raw materials, primarily energy carriers, the expansion of foreign trade operations, a marked increase in overseas capital investments.

As a result the United States significantly stepped up its activity on the world economic scene within the framework of which it sought to live up to its self-styled role as the political leader of the capitalist countries, to take advantage of its scientific and technological superiority over the states of Western Europe and Japan and to involve the young states of Asia, Africa and Latin America into the orbit of its influence. The power of its scientific and technological potential which combined with the external expansion of American corporations was, in effect, the chief trumpcard of the United States in the increasingly acute inter-imperialist rivalry. In relation to the developing countries the United States staked on the use of a complex of measures, in which investment expansion was combined with many means of pressure on sovereign states, including economic sanctions, interference in foreign internal affairs, blockade, boycott, support for anti-popular forces, reactionary regimes, racism and apartheid.

The United States had come to the turn of the 'seventies in a situation of stiff economic rivalry against its NATO allies, a deterioration of the US political positions on the international scene, and the disgraceful finale of the US aggression in Indo-China.

It was found that the Atlantic allies of the United States at times pursued a policy discrepant with American policy in certain respects. Acute manifestations of contradictions between the United States and Western Europe, the rapid economic progress of Japan which began to compete with the United States on the world markets

---

[1] *Soedinennye Shtaty: Vneshneekonomicheskaya Strategia (US Foreign Economic Strategy)*, Moscow, 1976, p. 27.

forced Washington to revise the priorities of its foreign and economic policies.

The export of capital, direct investments first and foremost, are the main means of implementing the chief strategic task of the United States in the field of external economic policy: its attempt to unite all capitalist states under the aegis of US monopoly capital, to lift all restrictions on the activities of subsidiary companies and branches, to secure full freedom for re-investment of capital within the framework of this system, or, to use more exact terms, to transfer profits to the United States without any obstacles and to pump out financial resources from other countries.

However, in the last few years the United States has been waging its struggle to preserve its economic and political positions with the aid of the export of capital in conditions of growing external expansion on the part of the West European states and Japan.

The share of the United States in the annual increment of direct foreign investments of the developed capitalist states gradually declined although the absolute volume of the annual American capital exports increased (see Table 1).

Table 1. Export of capital from developed capitalist countries for direct investment abroad

	1966	1970	1975	1976	1977	1978	1979
Total (mill. dollars)	7,429	12,059	25,066	24,366	25,816	35,126	47,183
USA	72.9	62.9	56.9	47.7	47.3	46.7	51.7
Canada	0.1	2.5	3.1	2.3	2.9	6.6	3.9
Western Europe including:	25.02	30.7	32.4	41.1	42.5	39.4	37.6
The FRG	4.8	7.2	8.0	10.1	10.7	10.3	9.8
Great Britain	10.4	10.9	9.7	15.6	12.8	13.1	12.3
Italy	1.3	0.9	1.4	0.6	2.1	0.5	1.2
The Netherlands	3.5	4.3	5.3	4.0	6.3	5.2	4.9
France	3.1	3.1	4.1	5.0	4.7	5.8	4.3
Japan	1.4	3.0	7.0	8.2	6.4	6.7	6.1

Source: "Salient Features and Trends in Foreign Direct Investments". United Nations Centre on Transnational Corporations, ST/CTC 14, 1981, p. 70.

The Seizure of Bridgeheads

Taking a look at the history of American infiltration of the countries of Western Europe it may be noted that the present positions of US capital in this region were predetermined by the intensive expansion launched by the United States here after the Second World War with the aid of political, economic, and other measures, undisguised threats and intimidation of its NATO partners with an imaginary "Soviet menace" and "communist infiltration". The general specific features of the expansion of American capital also played a part here.[1]

The main object of expansion is, as before, Great Britain, and the sources of the present position of US monopolies go back to The Lease–Lend Act, the American–British financial agreement of 1945 and other international acts of US monopoly capital. As far back as the early 'sixties direct investments of the United States held important positions in a number of branches of the British economy, primarily in the manufacturing and oil industries. By that time American direct investments in Great Britain were greater almost by 300 million dollars than US direct investments in the five other highly advanced European states (Belgium, France, the FRG, the Netherlands, and Italy). Such is the economic result of NATO partnership with the United States and the dependence on trans-Atlantic monopoly capital to which Great Britain has come. This dependence systematically increased and contributed to the creation, in the opinion of American businessmen, of the "favourable climate" for direct investments.

In the countries of continental Europe the infiltration on the part of American capital was not so rapid. However, in this region, too, it is consolidating its positions, building up its direct investments gradually, step by step, with the aid of economic, political, diplomatic and other measures.

The class co-operation between monopolies of the United States and the FRG is a well known fact although many of its details are concealed,

---

[1] For greater detail see: A. A. Gromyko, *External Expansion of Capital*, Moscow, 1982, Chapter 6; A. A. Gromyko, Expansion of Capital and the Present Stage of the General Crisis of Capitalism (*World Economics and International Relations*, No. 12, 1982).

as before, from the public at large. History repeats itself in some respects and reminds one in certain features of the period between the First and the Second World Wars when millions of dollars were invested into rebuilding the war machine of German imperialism.

The inflow of American capital into the West German economy, primarily into heavy industry, which is of military significance, largely explains the fact that many industrial giants of West Germany were not only put into operation but radically modernized, in particular, the plants of Krupp, "IG Farberindustry" and others. This also largely accounts for the fact that West Germany has become a formidable rival of other West European countries on the international market in many types of commodities of industry, the military industry in particular.

One can witness a repetition of what took place after the First World War when foreign loans infused into German industry helped renew its productive apparatus and placed in a difficult situation a number of branches of French and British industries incapable of competing against Germany on the international market.

American companies operated just as vigorously in France where US direct private investments in the early 'sixties exceeded 0.7 thousand million dollars and ran to 1.8 thousand million dollars in 1966.

American companies actively infiltrated the Italian economy. Under pressure from the United States which was bent on the idea of converting Italy into its dependable military-strategic bridgehead, the door was flung wide open for American monopolies to invade the Italian economy. The main branches in which US capital was invested were the oil, electrical engineering and chemical industries which accounted for over two thirds of all investments.

US monopolies also regarded Austria, the Netherlands, Denmark and other small countries of Western Europe as advantageous areas for capital investments.

To ease their penetration into the West European countries the US monopolists intensively took advantage of their economic and political difficulties. This is exemplified by the Netherlands which had lost such a source of enrichment in Indonesia, and US corporations immediately turned this fact to their benefit, investing capital in the Dutch economy and setting up dozens of subsidiary companies in the Netherlands.

The US press frankly admits that the American monopolies have an interest in the Netherlands in view of the possibility of conducting from this bridgehead commerce with practically the whole of Western Europe. Many Dutch enterprises are connected through a network of canals, railways and motorways both with the oceanic ports and a number of countries in Central Europe, primarily those of the Common Market.

The character and scope of capital infiltration of Japan inevitably generates grave contradictions between the two countries. The fact that the Japanese bourgeoisie advances to the foreground current tasks and temporary economic benefits rather than the country's vital needs by no means mitigates the contradictions between Japan and the United States which are growing and will inevitably get worse.

There is no doubt that as the realization that economic dependence on the United States contradicts the country's vital national interests grows in Japan, the resistance to the policy now being pursued by Japan's ruling quarters to the detriment of its vital interests will steadily grow.

In the mid-sixties the total sum of US direct private investments was 0.8 thousand million dollars, of which 89 per cent was in the manufacturing and oil industries. Needless, to say, the aforesaid data are far from complete, since the penetration of capital takes a variety of forms and does not boil down to direct investments alone. The construction of military bases and numerous projects is an important means of the expansion of American capital in Japan. The withdrawal of profits from Japan just as from other countries where American capital is invested is implemented in predatory forms. This is largely due to the fact that in the technological respect a number of industries of Japan (the oil, aircraft, and some other industries) are particularly dependent on US capital.

The experience in obtaining tax privileges gained by US capitalists is widely applied in Japan with the connivance and encouragement on the part of its ruling quarters. Its national legislation affords foreign nationals great privileges with regard to income. Moreover, American capital has secured for itself extremely advantageous terms of taxation in Japan, which are much more advantageous than even in some developing countries.

The US authorities encourage in every way the establishment and activity in Japan of various organizations and societies facilitating the infiltration of the country by American capital. Many of them are an inheritance of the early post-war years when the US military command ruled the country without any control whatsoever.

American capital investments are made primarily in large enterprises, mostly in heavy and war industry, as well as in branches serving them. The US monopolists are seeking to establish their control over the main areas of the economy. This refers primarily to private capital as the main channel of US direct investments in Japan.

It would be relevant to recall a significant statement made by Dean Acheson, the former Assistant Secretary of State and later Secretary of State of the United States, made exactly two years after the Second World War. He claimed that the task facing the United States in that situation was one of promoting the reconstruction of the two great workshops of Europe and Asia—Germany and Japan—on which the final restoration of both continents largely depends. Indeed, the history of the post-war expansion of US capital demonstrates that US imperialism has played a decisive part in the rapid economic growth of these states. By its profound infiltration of the economy of its overseas partners it contributed to the formation of new power centres of modern capitalism and retains important economic levers for keeping these countries within the orbit of its influence.

However, the quoted statement is significant, of course, not because it speaks of the significance of American investments in Japan and Germany and the need "to promote" the reconstruction of these countries which are called "workshops of Europe and Asia" with a pretention of geographical determinism. The investments of the United States in Japan and the countries of Western Europe are subordinated above all to the interests of American monopolies and their policy rather than to the interests of the peoples of these countries.

The Offensive Maintained

Relying on the bridgeheads it captured US capital launched active expansion in the countries of Western Europe. The forms of its expansion are not limited to direct private investments, but portfolio investments and the export of loan capital are also growing rapidly. However, for the purpose of authenticity and comparability of data I will dwell precisely on direct investments.

From 1966 American investments grew at the most intensive rate in the countries of Western Europe and increased 530 per cent between 1966 and 1981. In 1981 West European investments accounted for 60.6 per cent of all US direct investments in the developed capitalist countries. Thus, the significance of this region as an area of investments substantially increased (in 1966 Western Europe accounted for 45 per cent US investments in the capitalist countries). The bulk of American capital is invested in branches of the manufacturing industry although there was a certain decrease in their proportion from 55 per cent in 1966 to 45 per cent in 1981. Investments in the oil industry of the West European countries show a stable growth: their share is from 24.7 to 22.2 per cent of all American investments in this region.

In 1977 a total of 10,262 subsidiaries of US corporations operated in Western Europe, about 8000 of their number operated in the EEC countries. The total volume of their assets ran to a gigantic sum—394 thousand million dollars. These enterprises employed more than 3.1 million persons, the gross profits amounted to 293 thousand million dollars, the net income to 10.1 thousand million dollars, and the repatriated profits 7.2 thousand million dollars.

Great Britain holds pride of place in the West European investments of US private capital. In 1981 American capital investments topped the 30 thousand million dollar mark. In the latter half of the 'seventies investments in that country began to exceed the sum of American capital investments in the FRG and France.

The sectoral structure of American capital investments in Great Britain indicates that in 1981 44.5 per cent of investments (13.4 thousand million dollars) was in the manufacturing industry. Out of this sum 3.3 thousand million dollars was in engineering, and 2.2 thousand million dollars was in the chemical industry. US corporations directed 26.9 per cent of investments (8.1 thousand million dollars) into the oil industry and over 2 thousand million dollars into commerce.

American direct investments are rapidly growing in the FRG. Although the share of this country in the total sum of West European investments of the United States has practically remained unchanged, there has been an absolute increment in investments from 3.1 thousand million dollars in 1966 to 16.1 thousand million dollars in 1981, which is a 420 per cent growth. The greater part of investments (64 per cent) is made in the manufacturing industry. In the oil industry the sum of direct investments in 1981 amounted to 3.3 thousand million dollars, whereas capital investments in commerce, banking and insurance ran to 2.3 thousand million dollars.

France is the third biggest partner of the United States in Western Europe with regard to the volume of American capital invested in its economy. In 1981 direct investments of American corporations in France exceeded 9 thousand million dollars, whereas in 1966 this indicator had been equal to a mere 1.8 thousand million dollars. In 1981 the share of France in the total sum of direct West European investments of the United States was 9 per cent (as compared with 11 per cent in 1966). The sectoral distribution of American capital investments in France is similar to that in Great Britain and the FRG: the share of investments in the manufacturing industry, especially in the chemical industry and engineering, is quite large (3.3 thousand million dollars in 1981).

The growth of direct investments in the Netherlands is worthy of note. Between 1966 and 1981 American investments increased here almost ten times and ran to 8.8 thousand million dollars. The United States has large investments in Belgium and Italy (6.3 and 5.4 thousand million dollars respectively).

Direct investments of the United States in Western Europe have a dual impact on the economies of the recipient countries. On the one hand, one can witness the further development of their economic and scientific and technological potential, on the other hand, the expansion of American capital retards the progress of national industry.

Besides the important political and strategic tasks which US imperialism achieves with the aid of the foreign economic expansion of its corporations, the export of capital brings it fairly large profits. Taking a look at the distribution of incomes derived from individual countries of Western Europe, according to data for 1981 the biggest profits were derived by US corporations from Great Britain (5.4 thousand million dollars, of which 53.7 per cent—2.9 thousand million—came from investments in the oil industry). Great Britain is followed by

Switzerland—1.9 thousand million (1.6 thousand million from investments in commerce and insurance), the Netherlands where the profits exceeded 1.2 thousand million dollars (including almost 1 thousand million dollars from the oil industry). In the FRG American business derived slightly over one thousand million dollars (1.9 thousand million dollars in 1980).

Noteworthy is the fact that in the 'sixties US investments in the oil industry of the countries of Western Europe were unprofitable but later (particularly after 1973–1974) the profits derived from these branches began to rise and amounted to 5.3 thousand million dollars in 1981. The increase in American profits from the oil industry of Western Europe in the latter half of the 'seventies coincides chronologically with the "revolution in oil prices".

The apologists of US expansion maintain that in spite of certain inconveniences most of the European countries desire to have as many American enterprises as possible. What is more, in their opinion, American corporations in Western Europe are at an auction where European governments compete for a better deal.[1]

In fact, the infiltration of US capital is accompanied by a sharp exacerbation of inter-imperialist contradictions, leads to the domination of American corporations, the increasing dependence upon them in the scientific and technological fields.

From 1966 to 1981 direct private investments of the United States in Canada increased from 17 to 47 thousand million dollars. Throughout the history of American–Canadian relations they have been characterized by Canada's unequal status. Operating with the aid of private monopoly expansion the United States has in fact gained a controlling interest in Canada's key industries and made the Canadian economy dependent on its technology. The scope of American infiltration of the Canadian economy is so great that the American and Canadian economies are actually interlocked, the Canadian partner invariably being assigned the role of the exploited party. Nevertheless, in political life the ties between the two countries are called by no other name than "special relations".

Despite a substantial decrease of Canada's proportion in US direct

---

[1] See W. R. Burgess and S. R. Huntley, *Europe and America*, New York, 1970, p. 47.

foreign investments in the period from 1966–1981 (from 31.1 to 20.7) per cent), this country as before holds first place in the volume of direct investment of American capital. Its role is especially significant as a sphere of American capital investment in the manufacturing and oil industries: 19.7 thousand million and 10.7 thousand million dollars out of 47 thousand million dollars, or 42 and 23 per cent respectively.

The domination of American capital has led, particularly in the last few years, to grave contradictions in relations between the two countries. The essence of these problems was frankly described by the Canadian Minister of Foreign Affairs, who declared that the indicators of foreign property in Canada were at a level which, as he was confident, the United States would not tolerate within its own territory. For instance, according to the latest data available for 1978 foreign investments in the United States accounted for 5 per cent of the capital in the extractive industry and 3 per cent in the manufacturing industry. The relevant data for Canada were 37 and 47 per cent respectively.[1]

In 1974 a special agency for inspection of foreign capital investments (FIRA) was set up in Canada. Its activities caused sharp dissatisfaction of the business community and government of the United States, because it restricted the uncontrolled investment decisions of American corporations.

However, these measures failed in the final analysis to produce an appreciable impact on the scope and character of American investments. According to data for August 1981, the Canadian government gave its approval in 90.5 per cent of all requests from American investors for the relevant permission. Nevertheless, the activities of FIRA were one of the main "disputed issues" and, as a consequence of these contradictions, growing tensions have been in evidence in the political relations between the two countries in the last few years.

Another problem which also has as its base the domination of the Canadian economy by American capital is the development of the energy sector of the Canadian economy. American–Canadian contradictions are also growing in the motor industry and in the field of currency, financial and monetary regulation.

Investments in Canada ensure very high profits for American

---

[1] *Statements and Speeches*, No. 81/24, p. 4.

corporations. Whereas in 1966 the profits of American companies ran to about 1.3 thousand million dollars, the figure for 1981 was 4.1 thousand million dollars, which was a 220 per cent growth.

US direct investments in Japan are still relatively small. In 1981 Japan accounted for a mere 3 per cent of all direct investments of the United States and for 4.1 per cent of American direct investments in the developed capitalist countries.

The positions US monopoly capital had gained before the Second World War largely facilitated its further infiltration of the Japanese economy. A certain analogy suggests itself with Western Germany where the old-standing relations between American and German financial and industrial concerns are extensively used by American monopoly groups to infiltrate the German economy. As Japan is being turned into one of the "centres of economic power" of modern capitalism (not without assistance from the United States) the American monopolies have come to regard the development of relations with Japan and securing their "effective presence" there as one of the key directions of their policy. In 1977 a total of 903 subsidiaries of American companies operated in Japan. These companies possessed assets of a total of 55.7 thousand million dollars and employed over 390,000 persons.

One of the chief forms of US capital investments is the ownership of share stocks of mixed companies. For instance, the subsidiaries in which 50 per cent of the capital and more is owned by American corporations, account for one half of US direct investments (2.3 thousand million dollars of the total 4.6 thousand million dollars in 1977). However, in a number of industries the US positions are strong because they were gained as far back as the period of the occupation of Japan. According to estimates, American capital is in control of up to 40 per cent of the production and marketing of petroleum products. For Japan which meets its demand for oil by imports practically completely the problem of supply from foreign sources is especially acute. The key positions in this area have been seized by big monopolies—giants of the US oil business—"Caltex", "Exsson", "Mobil", "Gulf Oil". In 1979 they accounted for 39 per cent and in 1980 for 35 per cent of Japanese oil imports. Large American companies are also operating in radioelectronics and engineering. Despite the existence of a series of obstacles (currency legislation, restriction of spheres of investment, and others) subsidiaries of American companies experience no difficulties in their relations with Japan's government authorities.

American companies in Japan on the whole prefer to repatriate their profits as distinct from Western Europe where reinvestments and repatriated profits are roughly equal, whereas in Canada the former are substantially larger than the volume of profits transferred to the United States.

The crisis in the capitalist economy inevitably exacerbates the struggle within the imperialist camp for sales markets and the spheres of capital investment. The forms used to dispose of difficulties in marketing commodities on other than the American market on the part of the ruling quarters (loans, credits, subsidies, "gifts", etc.) fail to remove the root of evil whatever the scope of their application. The chief evil is the arms race and the militarization of the economy of the capitalist states. The burden of war production stimulated by Washington is shifted onto the shoulders of the working strata of the population of the capitalist countries, the United States itself in particular. The antipopular, parasitic character of capital's activities on the international scene manifests itself especially glaringly in this field.

Exploitation of the Developing Countries

The export of capital brings into focus many cardinal problems involved in relations between the developing countries and monopoly capital behind which stands official policy. Among these problems are the unequal international division of labour imposed on the newly independent countries and the control retained by foreign, primarily American monopolies over the key sectors of their economies, as well as the repatriation of profits to the metropolitan countries although today they are called as former ones. The main obstacle in the way of asserting the independence and progress of nations is US capitalism and its policy.

Flouting the sovereignty of the states of Asia, Africa and Latin America, US imperialism gradually built up the scope of economic expansion in the early decades after the end of the Second World War.

The neocolonialist content of US foreign policy finally shaped during these years. The latter half of the 'forties, the 'fifties, and the early 'sixties were characterized by the US intensive infiltration of the developing countries and seizure of the main sources of their mineral wealth. This period may be described with full reason as a period of peculiar "colonization" by US capital of the economy of the developing countries, when "bridgeheads" were built for unimpeded draining of material and financial resources from the developing countries to the United States, as was planned by American strategists. In the mid-sixties the United States accounted for over one half of the export of capital from the developed capitalist states to the developing countries.

The aims of American foreign policy have remained essentially unchanged. However, the United States was compelled to adapt to the process of change in the world, to the changing conditions of the functioning of capital in the developing countries. The class content of American foreign policy was manifested primarily by an ambition to oppose the onward progress of the world social system and the construction of socialism in young states of Asia, Africa and Latin America.

Lenin pointed out in his time that "The deepest roots of both home and home policies . . . are determined by the economic interests and the economic position of the classes in power".[1] The policy of the United States in relation to the developing countries is an important part of the struggle waged by imperialism against the social renovation of the world.

The first few steps in this direction were made in the early 'sixties when the Administration of John Kennedy adopted the so-called "new approach".

Such a turn in US policy had been predetermined by the disintegration of the colonial system as a result of which imperialism lost its direct military and political control over the majority of young states. The United States found itself confronted by the need to introduce substantial amendments into the practice of its economic relations with the newly independent countries and developing relations with them on a long-term strategic basis. In a situation of rising national liberation

---

[1] V. I. Lenin, *Collected Works*, Vol. 36, p. 327.

struggle of the peoples and intensification of its anti-imperialist and sometimes anti-American orientation the policy of prodding the developing countries towards the capitalist way of development, "direction" of this process relying on sophisticated forms of economic coercion, the stake on the neocolonialist regearing of their economies to the needs of developed capitalism became the pivotal direction of the policy pursued by the United States and its NATO partners to secure the safety of their "rear" in the contest against world socialism. The American side made quite a few declarations on the beginning of an allegedly "new stage" in relations with the developing countries, but their meaning invariably boiled down to one and the same thing: to absolve themselves of the responsibility for the backwardness of these countries and to channel their development into a route advantageous to US monopolies.

Regardless of change in the situation on the foreign political scene the export of private capital remains as before the main instrument for implementing US policy on the world arena. This became particularly strikingly manifest in the latter half of the 'sixties. As the General Secretary of the Communist Party, USA, Gus Hall, pointed out, American imperialism is beginning a new offensive for the purpose of establishing still greater financial hegemony over all countries which are its debtors. It is demanding their financial and economic subordination, threatening to terminate its loans and refuse to grant them new credits.

One can also witness a new attempt to use supplies of food and other agricultural products as a tool for hegemony, especially in relations with the developing countries.

The total volume of direct investments annually coming from the United States to the developing countries grew from 5.3 thousand million in 1965 to 31.1 thousand million in 1979, that is, almost six-fold. At the same time substantial changes occurred in the structure of exported capital. Noteworthy is the increase in the flow of private direct investments from 1.3 thousand million to 8.1 thousand million dollars. Whereas in 1965 the funds set aside by the US Administration accounted for 63 per cent of the total volume of capital exports to the developing countries, towards the beginning of the 'eighties the export of private capital began to predominate and accounted for 69 per cent of the total sum.

The intensification of the export of American private capital in the 'seventies was associated with a sharp exacerbation of inter-imperialist rivalry, the increase in the economic instability in the Western countries where the production recession and the growth of unemployment were closely interlocked with such grave upheavals of the world capitalist economy as the raw materials, energy and currency crises. In that situation the aggressiveness of US capital on the international scene grew to a still greater extent along with its characteristic ambition to guarantee access to the sources of raw materials in the developing countries, to secure markets for its manufactured products, to widen and protect local markets against competitors and, of course, increase profits.

The escalation of the export of American capital to the newly liberated countries was accompanied also by a change in methods of financing investments. In the period of the 'fifties and early 'sixties the increment in US investments was secured mainly by new investments while from the mid-sixties there was an increase in the share of reinvested profits. For instance, in 1967 the increment in US direct investments in the developing countries, which was equal to one thousand million dollars, consisted of new investments by 71 per cent. In 1980 reinvestments accounted for 54 per cent of the total sum of US direct investments in these countries.

Thus, American capital investments in the developing countries increasing the latter's economic dependence are effected to an ever greater extent in fact from their own resources.

Retaining direct investments as the principal form of investment of capital in the developing countries the United States also resorts to diversification of the forms of export. It uses, in particular, increases in portfolio investments and export credits. The share of portfolio investments in the export of private capital to the developing countries grew over the 'seventies from 19.1 to 24.3 per cent, the share of private export credits from 2.7 to 32 per cent, while direct private investments reduced from 58 to 38 per cent.

The increase in the share of portfolio investments and export credits in the total sum of private capital investments is evidence of the sharply intensified activity of American monopolies which supply directly or through the channels of the European market up to two-thirds of the credits delivered to the young national states from private sources. According to estimates of the US Federal Reserve System, the dominating companies here are the "big six"—the Bank of America, Citycorp, Chase Manhattan Bank, Morgan Guarantee Trust, Manufacturers Hanover and Chemical Bank.

The expansionist activities of American banks rest on their growing power, the predominance of the dollar in international payments exchange and European currency deals, the presence of the United States at all international and regional financial centres, including Panama, Singapore, and the Middle Eastern countries, the penetration of American capital into the credit systems of the majority of former colonies and semi-colonies.

In the last fifteen years American corporations as a whole accounted for over one half of the inflow of new direct investments from the capitalist countries to the developing states. This is by no means accidental. There is every reason to maintain that the increase of the expansion of US private capital in the developing countries from the mid-sixties has had a purposeful character and is one of the strategic tasks of US foreign policy.

The structure of US direct investments in the developing countries has undergone no substantial changes over the last few years. The Latin American countries, which are the main object of the expansion of American private capital accounted in 1981 for 69.3 per cent of all direct US investments in the developing countries (72 per cent in 1955). The share of Asia was 23.2 per cent in the same year (19 per cent in 1955), the share of Africa 7.5 per cent (9 per cent in 1955). From 1975 to 1979 the export of US direct capital investments to these countries amounted to 14.9 thousand million dollars, almost 52 per cent of that sum went to Latin America.

The United States more and more often faces a situation where it can no longer rely on "gunboat diplomacy", pressure and dictation to suppress the national liberation movement and to impose on young states a policy advantageous to itself. What is more, the developing countries, relying on political and economic support from world socialism, have repeatedly forced US imperialism to make concessions, deliver its strikes at the system of international exploitation established by the United States with the aid of transnational corporations. This demonstrated the untenability of both the programme of bourgeois reforms in the developing countries put forward by the John Kennedy Administration and the futility of the more rigid line pursued by President Lyndon Johnson. The United States had to revise again the arsenal of tactical means of its policy.

A little over a decade later the sphere of economic international relations underwent a series of sweeping changes. The economic instability in the developed capitalist countries, primarily in the United States, was growing and provided the basis for a stiffening of imperialist contradictions, for greater dependence of the imperialist countries on the fluctuation of the world commodity markets, the import of the main kinds of mineral raw materials, particularly crude oil. In a number of the developing countries the process of ousting American private capital from the key sectors of the economy got under way. US President Richard Nixon declared in this context that US relations with less developed countries should no longer be built exclusively on a basis of relief programmes. The United States sought to plan an all-embracing and co-ordinated policy in the field of development covering all aspects of its economic relations with less developed countries. . . . US aims in the field of trade, investments and the monetary reform might be threatened if it failed to draw poor countries into participation in a more open world economic system and thus this country would be denied the chance to make progress to meet their hopes for development.[1]

Disregarding the rhetoric contained in the statement one will clearly see the main idea of the US President: the developing countries must become a component part of the world capitalist economy, while the United States is using for this purpose a "comprehensive" approach to impose its will upon them, including both "aid" and foreign trade relations, on the one hand, and the export of capital on the other.

In the 'seventies the United States embarked on a more active policy of economic expansion making, at the same time, some tactical corrections. It pursued, on the one hand, the object of reducing the degree of "involvement" of the United States in rendering "aid" to the so-called second-rate countries and concentrating the main efforts on the key states, on the other. Simultaneously appropriations for govern-

---

[1] See: "International Economic Report of the President", Washington, 1974, pp. 19, 20.

ment "aid" were reduced and the conditions for stimulating the activity of private capital improved.[1]

The organizational structure was also reorganized to a certain extent: "aid" for purposes of economic development was differentiated from aid for "security". In practical terms this "reorganization" gave a free hand to advocates of active intervention in the affairs of foreign nations, with the use of military means and investments in particular.

Simultaneously, in the 'seventies the US Administration undertook a series of measures to widen assistance to the export of private capital to the developing countries. Among these measures was primarily the establishment in 1970 of a corporation to handle private foreign investments, the cancellation of the programme of compulsory restrictions and control of the export of private capital (1974), the incorporation in the Trade Act of 1974 of a series of provisions discriminating against the developing countries pursuing a policy of nationalizing American assets.

It is important to emphasize that from the second half of the 'seventies the rate of increment in direct US investments in the developing countries began to surpass the corresponding indicator of capital investments in the economy of the developed capitalist countries. Besides, the main reason, that is, the fear that the US positions may be seriously undermined by the national liberation struggle, one can identify a group of factors which entailed intensified escalation in American direct investments in the developing countries.

First, the economic crisis of 1974–1975 which combined with an exacerbation of the raw materials and especially energy problems and lent acuity to the problem of "dependability" of the sources of raw materials and fuel and the need to reinforce American positions there.

Second, one could witness the impact of certain factors associated with the general character of the economic development of the United

---

[1] Such reduction was dictated to a certain extent by the domestic economic problems of the United States, in particular, by the chronic negative balance of payments and the enormous deficit of the federal budget. At the same time, the expansion of the export of private capital on the short-term plane led to an increase in the negative balance of payments of the United States, although later these losses, as evidenced by estimates of Soviet economists, are offset by the reverse transfer of profits within 5 to 6 years (for greater detail see: G. G. Chibrikov, *The Socio-Economic Effects of the Export of Capital*, Moscow, 1971).

States itself, in particular the efforts of American corporations to relocate individual fields of energy- or material-intensive productive operations (the so-called "polluting" branches of industry) to the areas of location of the relevant resources. The relocation of some sectors of the manufacturing industry, for instance, the assembly of manufactured goods from imported components and similar items to countries with a cheap labour market in the 'seventies was also associated with the aforesaid factors.

Third, the expansion of the scope of US economic infiltration of the developing countries was influenced by the stiffening imperialist rivalry for sales markets and the sources of raw materials, the progress of which showed that in the 'seventies the United States gradually lost its influence in a number of developing countries as a result of the active infiltration of their economies by Western European and Japanese capital. For instance, even in the Latin American countries the share of direct US investments in the total volume of invested foreign capital diminished in the period from 1971 to 1975: in Brazil from 38 to 32 per cent, in Mexico, from 81 to 69 per cent, in Colombia from 56 to 48 per cent.

The geographic distribution of US direct investments in 24 developing countries which accounted for 92 to 87 per cent of the total volume of US direct investments in the period 1977–1981 shows the selective character of the distribution of capital in this region. Significantly, monopolies concentrate their investments in countries which have from their point of view more or less stable political regimes, rich natural resources, a sufficiently large home market, and a certain level of development of local industry.

The main countries where American capital is invested are the countries and territories of Latin America and the Caribbean basin, such as Brazil, Mexico, Panama, Argentina, Venezuela, Peru, the Bermudas and the Bahamas. In 1981 they accounted for about 70 per cent of the total sum of US direct investments in the developing countries; at the same time their sectoral "specialization" can be easily seen. The vast majority (66 per cent) of US capital investments in the economies of Brazil, Mexico, Argentina, and Venezuela was concentrated in the manufacturing industry, whereas in the Bermudas and the Bahamas as well as in Panama most investments were in commercial, credit and financial, and insurance companies (14.4 thousand million out of 17.1 thousand million dollars).

US capital investments in Latin America were made and are being made today both through companies fully owned by American monopolies and through mixed companies. For instance, in Mexico 56 per cent of American subsidiaries fully belonged to a maternal (American) company, while the rest were in mixed ownership, but only in 15 per cent of the subsidiaries American interests were in the minority. At any rate the monopolies are seeking to retard the progress of those branches of industry in the Latin American countries with the aid of which the latter could build up their own developed economy. The monopolies intend to relocate to these countries the "lower sectors" of their manufacturing industry, which often runs counter to the national plans of industrialization.

Table 2. Direct US private investments in developed capitalist countries (mill. dollars)

	1966	1977	1978	1979	1980	1981
Austria	—	—	—	0.4	0.5	0.6
Belgium	0.7[1]	4.2[1]	4.7[1]	5.9	6.3	6.3
Great Britain	5.7	17.4	20.4	23.5	28.6	30.1
Greece	—	—	—	0.4	0.3	0.2
Denmark	0.2	0.7	0.9	1.1	1.3	1.4
Ireland	—	1.2	1.6	1.8	2.3	2.6
Spain	0.4	2.2	2.1	2.7	2.7	2.9
Italy	1.0	3.0	3.6	4.4	5.4	5.4
Canada	17.0	35.4	37.3	40.2	45.0	47.0
Luxemburg	—	—	—	0.5	0.7	0.6
The Netherlands	0.9	4.0	4.7	6.9	8.1	8.8
Norway	0.2	1.6	1.6	1.3	1.7	2.3
Portugal	—	—	—	0.2	0.3	0.3
France	1.8	6.1	6.8	8.0	9.3	9.1
The FRG	3.1	11.0	12.7	13.5	15.4	16.1
Switzerland	1.2	6.2	7.4	9.7	11.3	12.4
Sweden	0.4	1.2	1.2	1.4	1.5	1.4
Japan	0.8	4.1	5.0	6.2	6.2	6.8

[1] Including Luxemburg.

Source: *Surgery of Current Business*, October 1968, p. 24; August 1978, p. 28; August 1979, Part I, p. 26; August 1981, p. 31; August 1982, pp. 21–22.

Table 3. Direct investments in the developing countries, in percentages

	1966	1970	1975	1976	1977	1978	1979
The USA	49.7	51.2	69.0	39.9	51.2	50.3	59.2
Canada	1.5	1.7	2.9	5.5	4.1	4.1	1.3
Western Europe including:	43.7	37.1	25.5	39.8	36.1	33.1	33.6
Great Britain	7.9	9.2	7.6	12.2	12.9	10.5	11.2
Italy	1.9	3.3	1.4	2.7	1.7	0.6	3.4
The Netherlands	4.8	5.0	2.2	3.1	5.1	4.0	1.2
France	15.7	6.4	2.6	3.1	2.8	3.7	5.0
The FRG	6.8	8.6	7.8	9.8	8.9	9.2	6.1
Japan	4.5	7.1	2.1	13.9	7.6	11.8	5.1

Source: *Salient Features and Trends in Foreign Direct Investments*, p. 85.

The bulk of US investments in the manufacturing industry of Brazil is in such branches as the chemical and general engineering, electrical engineering, electromechanical and electronics industries, as well as the manufacture of transport equipment. The structure of US investments in Mexico, Argentina, and Venezuela looks roughly the same. US companies are practically in full control of Brazil's motor industry, and hold in their hands 80 per cent of the pharmaceutical industry, about 50 per cent of the chemical industry, 47 per cent of aluminium production, and 50 per cent of engineering. In Mexico the four biggest financial groups of the United States—those of Morgan, Rockefeller, Citycorp, and the Bank of America—have controlling interest in two thirds of the assets of all American companies operating in its manufacturing industry. It should be pointed out that US corporations are actively consolidating their positions in the manufacturing industries of other Latin American countries as well: in 1979 alone these industries accounted for 87 per cent of the influx of net capital from the United States to the manufacturing industry of all developing countries and, accordingly, for 66 per cent of reinvestments.

The 'seventies saw an increase in US direct investments in Asia, primarily in areas of South East Asia. However, the distribution of US capital in the countries and areas of this region also indicates the selective character of investment decisions. The list of 25 largest areas of investment of this capital includes Hong Kong, Indonesia, Malaysia, Singapore, Thailand, Taiwan, the Philippines, and South Korea. In 1980 they accounted for 15.5 per cent of US direct investments in the developing countries. It should be noted that the region of South East Asia has always been the focus of attention of the US government and business community. The US Administration has always attached crucial significance to the key strategic position of this region, to an expansion of the network of war bases there, while American business has been attracted by a favourable investment climate, rich deposits of minerals, and cheap manpower.

In the post-war period US policy was directed to suppressing the national liberation movement and was distinguished by its aggressiveness, military and political interference in the affairs of Indo-China so as to impose regimes subservient to the United States by force of arms. However, the finale of the war against the Vietnamese people waged for long years showed that any attempt to dictate let alone force a foreign will on other nations by a resort to arms is hopeless and inevitably doomed to failure. In the mid-seventies the US positions in this region were seriously undermined.

It would seem that the radical change of the situation in Indo-China created favourable prerequisites for organizing peaceful co-operation in Asia, economic co-operation in particular. However, the United States responded to this change by a sharp escalation of its political and economic expansion. Direct investments of American Companies in Hong Kong, Indonesia, Malaysia, Singapore, Thailand, Taiwan and the Philippines increased from 1966 to 1977 from 0.9 thousand million dollars to 4.6 thousand million dollars, and in 1981 they amounted to 9.7 thousand million dollars. As a result, their proportion in the total volume of US direct investments in the developing countries and territories increased from 6 per cent in 1966 to 17.3 per cent in 1981.

In the late 'seventies 361 subsidiaries of US companies with assets running to about 11 thousand million dollars operated in Hong Kong, where American companies invested greater funds than in the other developing countries of Asia. The bulk of these funds (75 per cent) was in the banking business.

The 'seventies saw a considerable increase in investments in the manufacturing industry. The biggest investments were made in the

Philippines (0.6 thousand million dollars in 1981), US capital holding dominating positions in oil refining, the chemical and pharmaceutical industries. In Singapore and on Taiwan American companies invested 0.6 and 0.3 thousand million dollars respectively, primarily in assembly factories of the electronics and engineering industries. A growth of such investments has been in evidence in Indonesia and South Korea.

In its economic strategy in relation to the young national states the United States increasingly orients itself on extending its ties with the more developed countries to which they assign the role of an auxiliary link in the economic mechanism of the United States itself. Whereas in 1966 US direct investments in the manufacturing industry of the developing countries constituted a little over one fourth of all direct investments of American companies in these countries, the figure for 1977 was as large as 36 per cent. By infiltrating ever more deeply the manufacturing industry of the developing countries the United States pursues the object of perpetuating the technological dependence of these countries, revising and renewing the forms and methods of its expansion.

Since the advent of the Ronald Reagan Administration to power a further shift to the right has been in evidence in the foreign, including economic, policy of the United States. The present Administration identifies its internal and foreign policy goals with the interests of Big Business and has lifted all restrictions on expansion of US private capitalist business to the developing countries. According to plans of Washington strategists the young states must be exposed to still greater exploitation and oppression.

In the 'seventies American companies lost some of their positions in a number of countries in the national liberation zone. In those circumstances capitalism resorted to its old trick of depicting its selfish aims as common national interests. As a result the conception of "vital interests", naturally, American ones, came on the scene. As bourgeois researchers are compelled to admit, US foreign policy is directly aimed at securing guarantees of private property, the freedom of markets and profits for "internationally operating US businessmen". The conception of "vital interests" is based on protection of real and potential profits safeguarded by the full power of political, economic, and military means.

At the same time, the US monopolies had to make some concessions. This is illustrated especially graphically by the example of investments in oil extraction in the region of the Middle East, as well as in North Africa.

After the Second World War the capitalist oil market was seized by the international oil cartel which incorporated the "Big Five" of giant American oil corporations. Although towards the mid-seventies at least forty American companies were operating in the Middle East, the "Big Five" extracted about 60 per cent of the oil production of the region and remained the main tool of expansion of the United States.

The national liberation movement in the countries of this region was aimed at ousting American monopolies. In the complex of measures used against US capital the revision of unequal concession agreements, the nationalization of the property of American companies and the increase of oil prices proved the most important ones in respect of their economic and political implications. These are the main interconnected links in the chain of measures taken by the oil-producing countries in the 'seventies to protect their interests.

The socio-political heterogeneity of the oil-exporting countries, the Arab countries in particular, was expressed in a variety of forms and methods used for the nationalization of the property of American oil companies. For all their differences, however, the struggle of the oil-producing countries for their economic independence yielded the best results precisely along the path of nationalization. Already towards 1975 the companies of the developing countries owned 62 per cent of the world's capitalist oil production (12 per cent in 1972), while the share of the International Oil Cartel decreased from 73 to 30 per cent.[1]

In the West, primarily in the United States, a propaganda campaign was launched and has been continuing to this day. Its initiators are accusing the Arab countries of all energy and other difficulties experienced by the capitalist economy.

It is well known, however, that the oil-producing countries only defended their economic interests, restoring their rights flouted by imperialism. To allege the opposite means to turn the hard facts upside down. Indeed, the present oil situation in the West is the result of a

---

[1] A. E. Primakov, The Oil Transnational Companies and the Oil Producing Countries: Evolution of Relations (*The USA: Economics, Politics, Ideology*, No. 11, 1981, pp. 17–18).

definite policy and of the predatory exploitation of the natural wealth of the oil-producing countries for decades on end. Israel's policy of annexation of Arab lands and its unwillingness to withdraw from them is another factor responsible for this situation. In this politics and economics are closely interlocked and cannot be separated from one another.

In the 'seventies when a shortage of fuel and energy raw materials became evident in a number of capitalist countries the catchy term "oil crisis" was put into circulation. However, mankind is not threatened with catastrophe in energy supply, which is a concensus of all experts. Science has not yet said its last word in developing new energy sources. The causes of this crisis are social and political rather than natural. The best evidence of that is the fact that the socialist world has practically encountered no energy crisis. This is why the USSR and other fraternal socialist countries are supporting those states which see the way out of this crisis in consistent restriction of the activities of foreign oil companies who bear the main burden of responsibility for this crisis. No sober-minded politician can recognize as legitimate actions aimed at safeguarding the sovereignty of states over their natural resources, at securing respect for their territorial integrity and independence.

The new system of price formation secured for the oil-producing countries a rich source for financing their own economy. Suffice it to say that in 1972 the oil income of the Arab oil-producing countries alone amounted to roughly 7.5 thousand million dollars, whereas the figure for the end of 1975 was 57 thousand million dollars. In 1980 the total volume of funds accumulated by the member countries of OPEC reached, according to some estimates, 350 thousand million dollars. As a result the oil-exporting countries have gained funds to buy up American companies. This by no means signifies that there is no inflow of direct investments from the United States to the Middle East. On the contrary, as a result of certain statistic tricks a veil of camouflage has been drawn over not only the remaining positions of the US oil business following nationalization, but also new investments. In the period 1975–1979 the volume of private capital exported from the United States for direct investment in the Middle East exceeded 5.1 thousand million dollars and, upon addition of reinvested profit, 6 thousand million dollars.

Table 4. Sectoral distribution of US direct private investments in the developing countries (mill. dollars)

	1966				1981			
	Total	Mining ind.	Oil ind.	Manufact. ind.	Total	Mining ind.	Oil ind.	Manufact. ind.
Argentina	1035	–	–	656	2735	69	483	1570
The Bahamas	–	–	–	–	2987	–	289	39
The Bermudas	–	–	–	–	10,353	–	609	15
Brazil	1247	58	69	846	8253	152	422	5420
Venezuela	2615	–	1862	291	2175	–	126	1156
Hong Kong	–	–	–	–	2655	–	267	470
Indonesia	–	–	277	–	1861	–	1499	140
Colombia	571	–	–	190	1178	–	318	574
Malaysia	–	–	–	–	849	3	497	244
Mexico	1248	108	42	802	6962	77	189	5140
Panama	792	19	153	28	3671	–	601	302
Peru	548	291	29	93	1928	–	–	106
Singapore	–	–	–	–	1791	–	798	594
Thailand	–	–	–	–	551	10	406	24
The Philippines	579	–	–	180	1294	–	251	554
Chile	844	494	–	51	834	–	98	112
South Korea	–	–	–	–	778	–	315	163

Source: *Survey of Current Business*, October 1964, p. 24; August 1982, p. 22.

In the 'seventies the mechanism of extraction by American companies of profits from operations with oil of the Middle Eastern countries underwent a radical restructuring. In those years the Arab countries substantially increased the rates of income tax and "royalty". The income tax on the profits of American and other foreign companies was raised from 50 to 85 per cent from 1970 to 1974.

The first half of the 'seventies should be regarded as a boundary line where, on the one hand, the escalation of US direct investments in the Middle East reached a peak (about 3 thousand million dollars in 1974) and, on the other hand, it resulted in a drastic decrease in the scope of capital invested by US companies following the nationalization of the property of foreign oil companies. The biggest American oil corporations lost their main positions in the oil-producing industries of Iraq, Kuwait, Saudi Arabia, Qatar and Bahrein, which was an important result of the 'seventies.

The nationalization of the property of American oil companies was accompanied by generous compensation paid to their owners, whose size was determined by mutual agreement. Thus, the reduction of the role of companies as direct investors of capital in oil extraction did not entail a substantial reduction of the scope of US activity in the oil economy of the developing countries, although nationalization did solve the fundamentally important problem of ownership of the oil produced. Moreover, in the latter half of the 'seventies the United States stepped up its activities in the Middle East, taking advantage of the continuing dependence of the countries of the region on foreign oil corporations in the field of transportation and marketing, the acute shortage of qualified engineering and managerial personnel, as well as the plans of certain countries to establish a ramified national economy. Acting often as shareholders jointly with the state or with private national capital American corporations have substantially widened their business activity in the oil industry.

The developing countries remain, as before, the source of enormous profits for foreign oil companies. On the other hand the host countries suffer losses in consequence of relations of inequality. The annual losses of the developing countries as a result of the transfer of profits by foreign monopolies, manipulation of purchase prices and sales in the trade between firms of Western monopolies, exorbitant prices paid for licenses, transportation, the "brain drain", depreciation of currency returns, as a result of galloping inflation in the West, and so on and so forth, which exceed, according to estimates, 100 thousand million dollars a year.

In the period 1966–1981 the developing countries accounted for one third to over a half of all profits from direct investments transferred to the United States. It should be added to this that the total volume of profits reinvested by American companies in the developing countries from 1966 to 1981 surpassed 29 thousand million dollars. US direct investments in these countries which constituted 28.9 per cent in 1966 and 24.7 per cent in 1981 of the total volume of US direct foreign investments bring American corporations about one half of all repatriated profits. This example strikingly illustrates the special interest of the United States in safeguarding its so-called "vital interests" in the developing countries and shows the part played by US imperialism as the principal financial exploiter of the developing countries. It is not the vital interests of the United States but sweat and blood that stand behind the super profits of imperialist monopolies plundering foreign oil wealth.

The great income from US direct investments in the developing countries is associated with a number of causes, in particular the high degree of exploitation of labour at foreign enterprises as well as the use of cheap manpower. For instance, the consortium of American oil corporations met more than 80 per cent of its demand for manpower by employing local inhabitants. The monthly average earnings here in 1969 were less than the average wages in the US oil industry by a factor of 2.3 and in 1971 by a factor of 2.1. This clearly illustrates the nature of the US oil business which is profitable for the monopolies and exploitative for the peoples of the developing countries.

The dynamics of the rate of profits from US direct private investments in the developing countries from 1966 to 1980 tended to increase throughout that period. It grew from 17 per cent in 1966 to 22 per cent in 1980, and in individual years reached 30 to 40 per cent.

Thus, the decrease in the profitability (per barrel of oil produced) of operations of American companies in the oil industry of the developing countries as a result of nationalization, the stiffening of the financial terms of agreements, etc., were more than generously compensated by the growth of oil prices. Having lost some of their positions at the stage of oil extraction US companies at the same time retained control of other links of the "oil chain" and increased their profit by hiking prices of petroleum end products and operations in oil transportation.

Accurate calculations give the lie to the allegations of the present US Administration to the effect that American private capital investments assist to a "transfer of resources" from the United States to the developing countries. In fact, the latter's resources are drained to the United States. It is not accidental, therefore, that profits from direct foreign investments in the developing countries are an important item of revenue in the US balance of payments.

Apologists of Big Business go out of their way to emphasize the "positive contribution" of the oil corporations to the economy of the oil-producing countries, the role of returns received through the channels of these companies as the "financial basis of development". However, facts concerning the correlations of American investments and profits in the developing countries completely disprove fabrications of American propaganda.

The expansion of capital on a growing scale with the aid of international monetary and credit organizations is another important distinction. From the very beginning of their foundation the International Monetary Fund and the International Bank for Reconstruction and Development were used as an instrument for putting political and economic pressure on the less developed countries. These organizations have become to a considerable extent the political foundation of the present-day monetary and financial system of imperialism controlled by the United States.

Of late the Western powers, especially the United States has shown a tendency to invest the International Monetary Fund with broad functions of control over the economic, monetary and financial policies of the member countries of the Fund.

The demands made by the International Monetary Fund as a condition for granting credits increasingly acquire a multiple character, affecting the budgetary, money and credit, currency, foreign trade and general economic policies. These demands usually include restriction on the volume of internal credits, a rise in taxes, a freeze on wages, devaluation of national currencies, which results in a slowing of the rates of growth of the economy, a rise in prices, an increase in unemployment, and a reduction in the working people's standards of living.

Indicative in this respect was the 36th joint session of the International Monetary Fund and the International Bank for Reconstruction and Development held in Washington in 1981. It was attended by representatives of the member countries of these organizations: the Ministers of Finance, managers of central banks, staff members of the secretariats of international organizations.

The developing countries put forward at the session a number of concrete demands addressed to the International Monetary Fund and the International Bank for Reconstruction and Development, which, however, came up against active opposition from the Western states, the United States first and foremost. The US President Ronald Reagan's speech at the session frankly demonstrated the unwillingness of the US Administration to reckon with the interests of the young independent states. US representatives, who were given active support by the new President of the IBRD O. Klausen, insistently recommended the developing countries to "adjust" their economic mechanism by vigorous encouragement of private enterprise, primarily foreign business, to the detriment of the state sector. These conditions were to be decisive for a decision to grant loans by the bank.

On the eve of the session a special group of the US Congress set up for analyzing the activities of leading financial institutions of the West published a report. The conclusions made in the report, which were officially supported by the ex-Secretary of State Alexander Haig and the Secretary of the Treasury Donald Reagan contain, in particular, recommendations to use the political and financial influence of the United States to establish a more rigid control in development banks, appeals for a sharp reduction of the programme of granting long-term loans to the poorest countries at low interest rates, and terminating financing countries with an average per capita income through international organizations.

Summing up the results of the session, the IBRD President O. Klausen expressed himself in favour of providing funds for the purposes of development of the developing countries and emphasized the need for expanding the role of the private sector. He pointed out that one of his duties in the future would be to work for a substantial increase in the rate of private financing. At the same time, Klausen emphasized that potential debtors would have to revise their economic policy, to reduce government spending, to contribute to the development of the private sector, and to promote export trade.

For his part, the chairman of the group of developing countries, which consists of 24 states, declared in his statement reviewing the results of the session that some developing countries might even withdraw from the IBRD, unless calls for a further reduction of funds granted to them were stopped.

Many of the developing countries are beginning to realize ever more clearly that the ruling quarters of the United States regard the IMF and the IBRD as tools for implementing their policy and a means for maintaining its transnational corporations.

The results of the last session prove convincingly once again that both leading financial organizations of the capitalist world are hit by a severe crisis. It is not unlikely that under growing pressure from the developing countries the leaders of the Fund and the Bank will be compelled either to revise the present methods and forms of activity of the IMF and IBRD or give greater attention to the demands of the developing countries.

Commenting on the deliberations of the session, foreign news agencies pointed out the stubborn unwillingness of industrially developed capitalist states to listen to the demands of the developing states. A concentrated expression of the position of the capitalist powers on the issue of widening the framework of "aid" to the developing states is the US stand: unless these countries introduce order into their economic and financial affairs no assistance can bring progress.

This is another evidence of the unwillingness of the ruling circles of US Big Business to reckon with the needs of the developing countries and to make substantial changes in the monetary and financial system of capitalism, taking account of their interests. At the same time, the developing countries show growing discontent with the activities of these organizations, primarily the attempts of the United States and the West as a whole to convert financial institutions into a tool for collective neocolonialism.

*   *   *

The present stage of the expansion of US capital may be described as follows: never before have the most rapacious circles of monopoly capitalism tried so bluntly to subordinate the entire process of world development to their selfish interests. In his time Marx wrote with his characteristic sarcasm that whenever it is a question of property his "sacred duty" compels the capitalist "to support the viewpoint of the ABC book as the only correct one for all ages and all degrees of development".[1] Somebody would like to make the American "imperialist ABC book", a desk book for all mankind.

This anti-historical approach is disproved by the logic of social development, of which the most influential and constructive component is the theory and practice of Marxism–Leninism. The General Secretary of the CPSU Central Committee Yuri Andropov writes in this context: "Open to whatever is best and progressive in modern science and culture it is in the focus of the world's spiritual life today and commands the minds of millions upon millions of people. This is the ideological creed of an ascending class liberating all humanity. This is a philosophy of social optimism, a philosophy of today and tomorrow."[2] Capital has no such future either at home or abroad, in theory or in practice.

---

[1] K. Marx and F. Engels, *Works*, Vol. 23, p. 726.
[2] *Communist*, No. 3, 1983, p. 23.

Statement at a Press Conference

Moscow, 2 April 1983

Ladies and gentlemen,
I would like to speak on some questions of the international situation
and the foreign policy of the Soviet Union.

This press conference was in a way prompted by statements made by
the American President, mainly the latest of these. In them he touched
upon a number of important issues of the international situation, the
policy of the United States of America and the policy of the Soviet
Union. In almost none of his speeches does the President miss the
opportunity to speak about the policy of the Soviet Union. Some other
questions that need to be elucidated have also accumulated.

What above all attracts attention in the recent speeches of the US
President and in his statement of March 30 and, I would say, in his
April 1 statement, if one has European time in mind? The President said
that in its foreign policy the United States, and to be more precise, the
present US Administration is guided by lofty moral values, pursues the
aim of guarding and protecting the rights of peoples and that of
adequately defending the interests of the United States of America
regardless of what corner of the world these interests lie in.

But of course, the US President had and has his own understanding of
the first, the second and the third. Lofty moral values cannot be
defended by a state which is engaged in preparing for war, above all a
nuclear war. If one asks whether it is possible to defend lofty moral
values and at the same time to engage in preparations for a nuclear war
in whose flames hundreds and hundreds of millions of people would die,
every honest person will answer in the negative. A government engaged
in preparations for a nuclear war, which, as many politicians and almost
all scientists rightly say, would be a catastrophe for civilization on Earth,
has no right to speak about defending lofty moral values in connection
with its foreign policy activities.

212

Apropos defence of American interests. It would be a good thing if this meant defence of the legitimate interests of the United States of America, the defence of what really belongs to the US. But on the whole few people can be found in the world today who are not familiar with the way the formula "the defence of American interests" is understood in Washington. It appears that any corner of the world where Washington believes suitable conditions have been created for the US to secure some moral, political, and especially military-strategic gains for itself, is proclaimed an area of American interests. Declarations are made that these should be defended with the utmost strength, including the force of arms. If one is to speak about all the specific facts, it would take a very long time.

Let each person think, for instance, about the Persian Gulf zone and adjoining waters. He will get a sufficiently convincing answer to the question as to how Washington understands "American interests", human rights and the rights of peoples.

The Soviet people, our country and its leadership have never objected to the foreign policy of each state being imbued with the idea of protecting the rights of peoples and, consequently, protecting human rights. Since the days of Lenin this demand for defending the rights of peoples' human rights, has been an integral part of Soviet foreign policy. But we also know how this formula, which is a good one in itself, is exploited when politics is dominated by other interests. We know how the genuine content of this formula of protecting the rights of peoples' human rights, is emasculated and replaced by other demands, those suiting the views of a particular power—its political, military-strategic and, last but not least, economic views.

What would I like to say here about our foreign policy? The foreign policy of the Soviet Union has been determined by the congresses of our party, the ruling party, the Communist Party of the Soviet Union, and by decisions of its Central Committee. It finds its expression in many actions, including the major ones which, I think are known to all. It finds its expression in the speeches of Soviet leaders and, above all, in the speeches of the General Secretary of the CPSU Central Committee Yuri Andropov on specific issues, with concrete proposals. I think you remember those speeches.

Soviet foreign policy is a policy of peace, a policy of friendship between peoples. It is a policy of non-interference in the internal affairs of other states. It is a policy aimed at easing tensions and defusing the tense international situation. Our policy aims at reversing the insane arms race. It is necessary, above all, to find ways to limit and reduce arms, and then to find ways to destroy arms.

In the West it is now for some reason not customary to speak and write about the Soviet proposal for general and complete disarmament. I should like to emphasize that after the end of the Second World War the Soviet Union submitted two proposals which will be inscribed in golden letters in the annals of history and, it may be said, have already been.

The first proposal is that an international convention be concluded on prohibiting the use of nuclear weapons for all time. The second—the Soviet Union put forward a programme of general and complete disarmament. When it became clear that other states had the intention of delaying the solution of disarmament questions on various pretexts— the need to specify the proportions, how to approach the reduction of armaments of particular types, how to combine all that—that is, when on the pretext of complexity they started thwarting the solution of these issues, the Soviet Union proposed: "Let us stop arguing, let us work for general and complete disarmament." Then our partners began to say how could general and complete disarmament be effected if there was no confidence that it was really being effected. In other words, they raised the question of verification, believing that a squeeze could be put on the Soviet Union here and it could be made to feel uncomfortable, so to say.

In response the Soviet Union proposed general and complete verification—general and complete disarmament combined with general and complete verification. This proposal of ours remains in force to this day. I repeat, in the West it is not customary to write about that, and it is a pity. It is more or less clear, though, why they do not want to write about it. For it is difficult to speak of the significance of general and complete disarmament, of general and complete verification and at the same time to conduct a policy of war preparations, to continue the arms race at full steam, to inflate military budgets.

I have recalled two major Soviet initiatives. Now I should like to emphasize that in the recent period too the Soviet Union has proposed steps which nobody has a right to ignore without fully admitting his unconditional, open—I repeat, open—adherence to a militarist policy. What are these steps?

First. The Soviet Union has unilaterally assumed an obligation not to be the first to use nuclear weapons. It did not wait for the consent of other powers to that. This was a resolute and bold step. I think everyone present here will probably agree with this. The Soviet Union takes upon itself an obligation not to be the first to use nuclear weapons, while the other nuclear powers did not even move a finger to advance in that direction. Yes, this is a bold and peaceloving step of ours. In the West they are not at all keen to speak of this. That is wrong.

Second. The Soviet Union and its friends and allies in the Warsaw Treaty decided at a meeting of the Political Consultative Committee to propose to the NATO countries that a treaty be concluded. On what? On the non-use of nuclear weapons and the non-use of conventional weapons, that is to say, on the non-use of any force at all in relations between the states of NATO and the Warsaw Treaty. Why was the proposal made in this form? Because there was a lot of demagogy in the West that the Soviet Union allegedly might launch an attack on a state or a group of states not necessarily with nuclear weapons but with conventional weapons. I repeat, this was, of course, demagogy. But those fabrications could mislead all informed people who are not conversant with foreign policy matters.

The proposals put forward by the Warsaw Treaty member countries undercut such arguments. We are prepared to sit at the negotiating table with the NATO countries even today and to discuss this issue, or, better still, to sign an appropriate document with reciprocal commitments not to use force against one another.

How do the countries of the North Atlantic alliance respond to this proposal of ours? Most answer us in the sense that the proposal is being studied. So much time has already passed and it is still being studied.

Not so long ago I visited the Federal Republic of Germany. Chancellor Kohl and Foreign Minister Genscher also stated that the proposal was being studied. The governments of other countries also say this. The American leaders are reacting somewhat differently. Although officially they do not give a final negative answer and are refraining from doing this, we get the impression that this is tactical consideration. From the occasional hints that are made one may conclude that this proposal is not to Washington's liking. It is regrettable if that is so.

I would like to express the hope that this proposal of the Warsaw Treaty countries will be met with understanding. If there are any questions to be put to us, we are ready to get together and examine them. Perhaps they will be removed or taken into account. Perhaps some amendments may be suggested? We are prepared to discuss them together. It may be that they—or some of them—will be accepted. Perhaps there is a proposal on improving some wording about the commitments of the sides? We are prepared to exchange opinions on this point as well. As a result of an exchange of opinions a common language on the treaty may eventually be found.

Comrades and gentlemen,

There are both the former and the latter here. If there is a will for peace, there can be no convincing arguments against the conclusion of such a treaty. Just think: it is a proposal for abolishing war and the use of force by one state against another or by one group of states against another group. Can there be any reasonable objections to this proposal if people want to live in peace? No, there can be no reasonable objections to it.

We appeal to the governments and, naturally, to the peoples to give serious consideration to the proposal we are talking about, a proposal which reflects the will of the peoples of the socialist states. This proposal, we are confident, will also be inscribed in golden letters in the history of international relations.

Some questions of nuclear arms have now moved to the forefront, questions of nuclear arms in the global sense, that is to say, of strategic armaments, and of nuclear weapons on the European plane, that is, of medium-range weapons.

These questions are now the focal point of international life. They are literally the daily concern of the peoples, political and public figures in Europe, in the US, in Canada and in other countries. The peoples and politicians understand what these questions are, what their impact is, what the possible solution or non-solution of these questions is and what follows therefrom.

I want to dwell on questions of nuclear weapons in Europe in connection with the talks now taking place between the Soviet Union and the United States. What is our view of their immediate prospects and of the present-day situation in this regard? To begin with, we would like to stress the fallacy of the claims made in Washington that, generally speaking, serious talks are being conducted in Geneva—that there is presumably no cause for alarm there, and the only thing to do is to pressure the Soviet Union and to strike a tougher posture, and then everything will be all right. They even claim: "The more pressure we put on the Soviet Union, the better the chances of agreement." This line is manifest in the specific proposals tabled at the talks.

The statements made in Washington contain many untruths, false assertions, misrepresentations and much juggling as regards factual data. It is necessary to examine the assertion which has been formulated particularly explicitly in the latest statements of the US President and his proposals with regard to medium-range missiles are a road to agreement, to peace.

This is wrong: they are not a road to peace and agreement. The gulf between agreement and these proposals will be even wider. Does everyone know that the President is leaving out whole components which are enormous both in importance and in scope? This relates to aviation, to nuclear delivery aircraft. They are not to be found in the statements and discourses of the American President. Neither politicians nor military leaders have the right to exclude this component from talks and agreements. What difference does it make to people what they die from—a nuclear warhead delivered by a missile or a nuclear warhead delivered by a plane? What was dropped on Hiroshima and Nagasaki was dropped from planes. And today planes can deliver even more horrendous weapons. How is it possible to exclude this entire component?

The delegations in Geneva have attempted to discuss this question. They tried to approach it. Nothing, however, came of that discussion. Why so? Because the US representatives had instructions not to agree on that question. I shall cite an example.

They say: you see, medium-range planes can deliver not only nuclear weapons. They may serve a military and peaceful purpose. And for this reason, it is alleged, they cannot be included among nuclear weapons delivery vehicles. This would be the same as if someone described the most powerful and formidable ballistic missile say, a land-based one, like this: it can deliver a nuclear warhead, but it can also be used for meteorological purposes, so it is better not to include it among those that deliver nuclear warheads. Absurdity? Yes, total absurdity. But it is essentially this position that is stated by official representatives expressing the opinion of the US government.

Next. The United States has aircraft carriers and carrier-borne aviation. According to widely known data, at least six American aircraft carriers are especially fond of Europe. They are staying in the waters of Europe, in the Mediterranean, or near Europe—beyond the line which separates European waters from non-European waters and which they can cross in a matter of minutes. They are a tremendous force. Each aircraft carrier has about forty planes capable of carrying nuclear weapons.

Should we, the Soviet Union, close our eyes to this and not include the carrier-borne aircraft in the count? This is absurd. The intentions of a government which proposes we should close our eyes and not see this, are not serious. Therefore, any proposal which excludes a whole, we would say, dreadful component of the nuclear weapons delivery vehicles, such aircraft, from the count, is not serious. And it is impossible to look for agreement on this basis.

The second important element of the picture. It must be known in order to avoid confusion. So many words are spoken and statements made without any knowledge of the specific facts. One must know a minimum. Otherwise, I repeat, one can get confused even without wishing it.

Britain and France have nuclear systems—missiles, nuclear missiles. The Soviet Union suggests that these be counted in the course of the talks. It is impossible to close our eyes to them, to believe they are non-existent and to seek agreement only on the American systems. For these missiles are a part of the common forces of the North Atlantic alliance. Many statements have been made on this score. There are hundreds— thousands if you want—of statements, most solemn ones, to the effect that the nuclear forces of Britain and France are an inseparable part of the nuclear forces of NATO as a whole. It is suggested that we seek agreements while leaving these nuclear forces aside. This is not a serious proposal. Imagine that a terrible tragedy has occurred and that, say, a nuclear-tipped British missile is in flight. Will it carry the tag "I am British"? And if it delivers its charge people will die just as they would die from any other missile. Or imagine a French missile flying. Perhaps it will also carry a tag saying "I am French, I should not be included in the count"? It is an absurdity. People will be killed by that missile as by any other. That is why these missiles, the British and French alike, must be included in the total count. This is the only approach well-grounded from the political, military-strategic, scientific and technical points of view, however you regard it—the only correct approach. It seems that everything is perfectly clear here. However, the US stand has so far not been changing, and it has not altered, judging by the latest statements of the US President.

Furthermore, and this is also explicit in the above statements, the demand is made that if any reduction in European missiles is to be discussed, you should bear in mind that it is not enough to reduce and abolish these missiles in Europe. One must eliminate missiles of this class in Asia too. A tall order! One must say that this, and this alone, makes agreement possible. Why should Asia be dragged into this?

We envisage the possibility—this was mentioned by Yuri Andropov in making the well-known relevant proposal—that we might withdraw part of our missiles from Europe, from the European zone, to Asia, if an agreement were reached. This is our business and our right. And we are prepared to install them at sites from which they will not reach Western Europe. We have stated this at the talks and the US Administration know it. I repeat what we have said: we shall withdraw them to sites from which these missiles will not reach West European countries. But we are told: no, this is not enough. The arguments of the US Administration and the President personally boil down to the demand that these missiles should be eliminated too. This demand alone precludes agreement.

These missiles pose no threat to European countries. But why are they needed? The Soviet Union needs them to ensure its security. It is common knowledge that a circle of American military bases surrounds the Soviet Union. Japan and the waters around it are stuffed with nuclear weapons and carriers for them. The island of Okinawa is a huge base of nuclear weapons. South Korea is a huge base or, rather, a complex of bases of nuclear weapons. The Indian Ocean, especially the Diego Garcia base, is bristling with nuclear weapons which can reach the Soviet Union. The Persian Gulf and adjoining waters are bristling with nuclear weapons. And, please note, I ask you to concentrate your attention: what is at issue is medium-range weapons. All these weapons can reach Soviet territory. Moreover—and if someone is not conversant with what I say, it will be especially interesting for him to know that— these weapons have within their range the whole of Siberia, the whole of the Asian part of the Soviet Union, even its northernmost part—the Taimyr Peninsula. And reference here is being made only to medium-range weapons. I do not mean here the US strategic arms which exist and are deployed in the same areas that have been mentioned. Strategic arms are regulated by another agreement, an interim agreement, while it operates. The sides have agreed to extend the operation of that agreement. Consequently, only medium-range weapons are being taken into account. And so it is these weapons that keep within their range the whole of the Asian territory of the Soviet Union. Doesn't the Soviet Union have a right, for the purposes of defence, to have something to match those weapons? It does have such a right.

They do not speak about all this publicly in the West, they do not tell the truth to the people. We are confident that if the people had been told the truth on the first, on the second, and on the third questions, then people who are uninformed today would have changed their opinion— and most certainly not in favour of the US Administration which is ignoring facts. But they simply do not talk about these facts; neither in the press, nor on the radio or over television are the facts mentioned, they are being hushed up. If you take the United States, there people hear from dawn till late at night only one and the same thing: the Soviet Union is a threat, it does not want to conclude agreements, it tables proposals which do not meet the US line. And this instead of providing people with factual material to ponder over. No such material is provided. This may sound harsh, but one cannot help saying that in general it is deceptive propaganda that is being fed to the people, and that the picture that is being formed in these countries in the minds of the people, who are little informed through no fault of their own, is a totally distorted one.

As for the claim that the more pressure is put on the Soviet Union, the better are the chances of an agreement, it is also totally unserious. In a measure, it is, perhaps, explained by a lack of knowledge about the Soviet Union, a lack of knowledge, if you wish about our character.

In short, the US proposal is not a serious one. It is not designed to open up opportunities for an agreement with the Soviet Union. This is what we think. This is why we call, but do not know how people in Washington will react, for the adopting of a more objective approach to this question, renouncing lop-sidedness, taking into account all the factors, taking into account the legitimate security interests of the Soviet Union and adopting a line for reaching agreement, for bringing positions closer.

The line currently maintained at the talks in Geneva by the United States is not a line for rapprochement. It is a line of moving away from agreement, a line of complicating the situation, of whipping up the arms race even further, of worsening relations with the Soviet Union even further, securing an even faster growth of military budgets and containing the forces which favour finding a common language with the Soviet Union and resolving the problems of disarmament, to a greater degree.

By the way, once in a while it is alleged in Washington, above all by the Administration's spokesmen, that the movement in the United States for a nuclear freeze has been inspired by the Soviet Union or is perhaps guided from the Soviet Union. In any case we must most emphatically point to the absurdity of such speculation, the absurdity of such statements. This movement is a spontaneous American movement. This movement is based on a desire to facilitate efforts to find a common language with the Soviet Union and to contain the forces preparing for war, the militarist forces. The Soviet Union does not have anything to do with this, and we ourselves can only voice solidarity with this movement because we also think war must be averted and one must seek agreement and accords on these issues. And neither the movement nor ourselves can be accused of having a common centre, for which the Soviet Union or the leaders of this movement should bear responsibility. Let us hope that these reproaches will be short-lived, that they will be dispelled and that people who realize, one may say, instinctively what does and what does not match the interests of the American nation, will in an even more effective way, in an even louder voice make their presence known and felt in the political life of the United States of America.

Thus, we may say in conclusion, having in mind the latest statement, mainly those by the US President, that the "interim option", as the

President has called his idea, is unacceptable, unacceptable for the following reasons.

First, it does not take into account the British and French medium-range nuclear systems, including 162 missiles.

Secondly, it does not take account of the many hundreds of American nuclear-capable planes based in Western Europe and on aircraft carriers.

Thirdly, the Soviet medium-range missiles in the Asian part of the USSR would also be subject to liquidation, although they do not have any relation to Europe.

On the whole, while at present NATO has a 1.5:1 superiority in medium-range nuclear warheads in Europe, in the event of the "interim option", as it is called by the President, being implemented, NATO would have almost 2.5 times as many such warheads as the Soviet Union.

This is in concise form our attitude to what is called the "interim proposal" of the American Administration. By the way, we do not doubt that Washington did not expect any different reaction from us.

Before concluding my statement, I would like to draw the attention of those present to two circumstances without which, probably, the picture would be incomplete—anyway in terms of an understanding of the situation as a whole by people who supply information to the population, to people today, and will supply it tomorrow and the day after tomorrow. It would be useful for everyone always to remember that our weapons, meaning medium-range weapons in Europe, cannot reach the territory of the United States. Such a task is not even set. As for the American weapons planned for deployment in Europe, each missile can reach the territory of the Soviet Union. This is a geographic factor. Whom does it favour? It favours the United States to the prejudice of the Soviet Union. But we do not ask for any compensation and we are not raising this question, although we could do so if we were working out the balance scrupulously and accurately.

Furthermore, a missile is a missile. Missiles fly. Well, the time it takes a US missile to reach Soviet territory from West European territory is about one-sixth or one-seventh of the flight time of a missile from the territory of the Soviet Union to reach the US, in the event of a nuclear tragedy that would affect the whole of mankind. Consequently, from this viewpoint, too, if one takes a scrupulous and a more accurate attitude to building a corresponding equation, the Soviet Union, in order to preserve the principle of equality, would also have a right to raise the question of compensation. We do not, however, raise this question, we, as it were, put this factor outside the brackets. Why so? We do this in the interests of facilitating the way to agreement. Besides, we take into account the fact that, if an agreement were reached, then, apparently, steps would be taken in the direction of further, more radical cuts, and maybe, who knows, to the point of the total destruction of nuclear missiles. And so I also ask that this circumstance be borne in mind.

Here we are displaying flexibility and, if you wish, even magnanimity, in the interests of agreement, bearing in mind, as I have already said, the objective for which all must strive—peace, the total destruction of nuclear weapons and the use of nuclear energy only for peaceful aims and only for the benefit of mankind.

Our policy on questions of both medium-range and strategic weapons, if one goes beyond the framework of Europe, is to preserve at all costs the equality, the principle of equality and equal security, that has evolved over many years. One may say that life itself has led to the principle of equality. This is not just the result of office work.

US policy aims at breaking, destroying this principle. We shall do everything—with an agreement reached or without it—in order to preserve this principle. If it were violated as a result of the actions of the US government and those of other NATO countries, then the Soviet Union would certainly—and there can be no two ways about it and no doubts in the mind of anyone—adopt such measures as are required to protect its legitimate interests so that this principle could continue to operate. And we will do it. For this, we have enough material and intellectual possibilities—there can be no doubt on this score. And we think that, properly speaking, those who bear the blame for the present situation also know this.

Andrei Gromyko then answered questions from correspondents.

Question: It looks as if Washington is still counting on the USSR becoming "more tractable" as the end of the year draws nearer, when it is planned to start deploying the US missiles in Europe.

Answer : This is an incorrect and profoundly erroneous viewpoint. It shows a predilection for looking at the tactical side of things, which means that those who express themselves in that way give little thought to the substance of the matter at hand. This just cannot be the case. On the contrary, the US and the Soviet Union would be even farther from agreement than they are now. If an agreement is to be reached, it is necessary to take into account the legitimate interests of both sides, to observe the principle of equality. The media will be rendering a real service if they tell the truth about this.

Question : What will be the response of the Soviet Union if the Americans go ahead and deploy Pershing and Cruise missiles, and will not the deployment of these missiles be in a way similar to the Caribbean crisis of 1962?
Answer : I have already said in my statement that if the missiles were deployed and the reaching of agreement were disrupted, the Soviet Union would do its best to see that in the material—and in other—respects its interests were safeguarded. We will not allow the equality or balance, call it what you will, to be upset. We will not allow it. And our words will be matched by deeds. We have possibilities for this. We have repeatedly demonstrated this. But it will be the least desirable, a forced measure on our part. It is our first, preferred position to solve the issue on the basis of agreement with the United States, with NATO.

Question : The Soviet Union is upholding the principle of equality and equal security. But the American side is talking about the principle of "equal rights and limits". What is the difference here?
Answer : If you were to ask the US representatives at the talks about the meaning of the formula of "equal rights and limits", they would not give you an answer. They would make an incoherent statement, because they themselves do not know exactly what it is. One can guess that of central importance here is the question of the British and French missiles. By resorting to this formula they hope to steer clear of this question. This follows from occasional remarks made, and from the logic, so to say, of the negotiations. But this formula has been worked out with the specific aim of befogging the issue. The mathematically precise formula—which is also precise politically and acceptable in the military-strategic

respect—is equality and equal security, and consideration of all factors. This is a simple, but scientifically substantiated formula.

Question: You recently said that it would be a mistake for the Western public to think that the talks in Geneva will continue even after the start of the deployment of the new missiles. Does this mean that the Soviet Union will discontinue the talks as soon as the first American missile has been deployed?

Answer: I must say that this will be an extremely negative development both for Europe and for the world as a whole. And the situation would be such that we would have to examine it most carefully, with account taken of all circumstances, and I emphasize, of all circumstances, and take a corresponding decision.

Question: In his recent speeches President Reagan described the Soviet Union as an "evil empire" and the "focus of evil". What do you think of these pronouncements?

Answer: Yes, we know that the American President is fond of formulations of this kind. One day he organizes or predicts a "crusade", and next day he proclaims the Soviet Union, the socialist countries a "focus of evil". But in general he is not the first in history to have recourse to such methods.

There were some who even predicted the collapse of socialism. But socialism is still advancing along the chosen path, advancing and gaining strength. The President's predictions will not add to the authority of American foreign policy, let alone shake socialism or our foreign policy in even the slightest measure. It is our conviction that since World War II the star of the Soviet Union, our banner and the banner of our foreign policy have never shone so brightly for the whole world—in the North, in the South, in the West and in the East—as they do today.

Would the elimination of colonialism have been at all possible without the Soviet Union and without our victory in the war against the fascist aggressors? No, it would not. No knowledgeable, thinking and sensible person would say so.

We firmly believe that what has been accomplished by socialism, by the socialist states, and first and foremost by the Soviet Union, is a rock-hard basis for the future. It well serves our people, who are making good progress in fulfilling their plans. It serves as a fine example for mankind as a whole. We do not interfere in the internal affairs of other states—it is one of the principles of our foreign policy. But an example is an example. One cannot annihilate it even if one comes with a cross.

You know, the strong words and insults which the people in Washington are so fond of using do not broaden the possibilities of US foreign policy but only show what threshold of decency Washington has now accepted in dealing with other states, particularly with the Soviet Union. This is not the way to do business.

Suppose responsible representatives of the United States and the Soviet Union were to meet at the negotiating table and start exchanges of this kind. One side would try to prove that the other is a "focus of evil" while the other, of course, would counter and try to give as good as it gets. What sort of negotiations would they be?

If anyone today were to compile catalogues of evildoing, I assure you that the one for the United States would be very long. We get appeals for protection of their legitimate interests from those who are injured by the United States and whose territories—territories of dozens of countries—are declared by the United States to be a zone of its vital interests, practically its backyard or pond. It is we who get appeals from them. So are they appealing to a "focus of evil"? Nothing of the kind. Was it a "focus of evil" that tabled at the United Nations the proposal that colonialism, the colonial system, be abolished? No, it was a socialist state, the Soviet Union, that tabled it.

Was it a "focus of evil" that proposed way back in 1946 the signing of an international convention to declare nuclear weapons incompatible with human conscience, according to which nuclear weapons should be banned and nuclear energy put to peaceful uses, for the benefit of mankind? Was it a "focus of evil"? No, it was the Soviet socialist state.

Is it a "focus of evil" that now calls for reducing the military budgets and undertaking a commitment not to use force in relations among states, that is, for preventing war and building international relations on the basis of peace? No, it is a state which is the vehicle of a policy of peace and friendship among nations. We do not impose our ideology on anyone. Our ideology is a reflection of what is objectively taking place in human society. Our policy is an open book and everyone can read it.

If I should continue in this vein, someone might say that this is propaganda. But there is propaganda and propaganda. You, all of you present here, perhaps will not agree to being called mere propagandists, but to some extent you are propagandists because you supply information to people. But there is information and information. Information misleading people and information opening their eyes. The latter is truthful information. And the strength of our policy lies in truth. That is why the exercises of the President or anyone else in sticking labels like a "focus of evil" and choosing other derogatory words of this kind are futile. And they will not last. Perhaps such rhetoric may dazzle someone standing or sitting next to the President but it will fade for sure.

We are proud of the role played by the Soviet state and we know that most of the countries of the world duly appreciate it. We are also proud that in the great battle of the peoples for peace and against nuclear war there are many who think like us, and in this sense they are our allies, if you wish.

Question : What lies behind the US proposal about a "global" limitation of medium-range missiles?
Answer : You are probably referring to the US proposal or demand regarding liquidation of missiles in the Asian part of the Soviet Union. I have already spoken on that subject. The US has proposed that the Soviet Union should liquidate medium-range missiles not only in the European part but also in the Asian part of the country. Now if all of this is translated into concrete terms, it would mean that the US would then have almost two and half times more warheads. Why do I say warheads, not missiles? Because warheads are a more precise, mathematically more accurate expression of the yield of nuclear weapons.

Question : As I gather from your answer to one of the questions, you actually entertain no hope at all for the possibility of reaching agreement on medium-range missiles before the end of the year. Do I understand this correctly?

And another thing I would like to ask you: does your recent appointment as First Vice-Chairman of the Council of Ministers of the USSR mean that you will now give less time to foreign affairs, and what will be your additional responsibilities in this connection?

Answer : I would answer the first question as follows: if the position of the United States of America remains as it has been announced by the President, then there are no chances for an agreement. That is why it would be good if the US Administration should adopt a more objective position, one that meets the need to preserve the principle of equality and equal security and fully take into account the legitimate interests of the Soviet Union and of all Warsaw Treaty countries.

As for your second question, it concerns me personally and I could decline to answer it, but I will say this: I doubt very much that there will be less work in the Ministry of Foreign Affairs. I rather think, there will be more work, and of a greater scope, concerned, to put it briefly with co-ordination of foreign policy activity.

Question : Do you think an improvement in Soviet–American relations is possible despite the US position? Do you believe that agreement can be reached between the USSR and the US at all within the next few years?

Answer : You have asked me a very easy question. (Animation in the audience.) I will only say one thing: we would like relations between the United States and the Soviet Union to improve. Numerous statements have been made on our part to this effect from the rostrums of Party congresses, the Supreme Soviet of the USSR and the plenary meetings of the Central Committee. Yuri Andropov has also spoken on this subject on more than one occasion. I repeat, we would like it. But to all appearances, the American Administration does not want to improve relations with the Soviet Union. It wants the Soviet Union to make fundamental concessions to the detriment of its legitimate interests. That will never do. That is why we call upon the United States to take a more objective approach to questions of Soviet–American relations and to understand that normal or, even better, good relations between the US and the Soviet Union would meet not only the interests of the international situation as a whole, but also the interests of the American people. We have already said on more than one occasion that this would meet the interests of the Soviet people.

To preclude the possibility of war, primarily nuclear war, it is necessary first and foremost to change for the better the character of the relations between the Soviet Union and the US. We are for this. The US

Administration does not want it. It is worth recalling that there was a time when we were allies in the war and therefore found a common basis for co-operation, although at that time too we were states with different social systems and ideologies, we believe that our two powers with their huge military potentials can normalize relations between them. We firmly believe that the peoples of both countries, the Soviet Union and the United States, could only breathe more freely as a result.

Question : Could you tell us about the nature of the proposals which are reported to have been made to the Chinese side last month to facilitate the normalization of Sino–Soviet relations?
Answer : I will give a very general outline. China and the Soviet Union have begun consultations. These consultations concern many questions. They have not yet gone far enough to reach definite conclusions, particularly on major questions. The sides have agreed to continue consultations. The atmosphere at the consultations is on the whole normal. The consultations will be continued. We believe it a good thing that they have begun, a good thing that they will continue. Time will show what comes out of them. We are for normal relations with China.

Question : Washington continues to claim that the Soviet Union does not honour the unilateral moratorium it has announced on the deployment of medium-range missiles in the European part of the territory of the USSR. What could you say on this score?
Answer : My answer will be short. These are misleading statements. The Soviet Union matches its words with deeds. This holds true for the case in hand as well.

Question : Yuri Andropov has said that there are solutions which will not impinge upon the interests of either side. Your position, however does not seem very flexible. Will the Soviet Union agree to any new missile deployment?
Answer : We have stated our opinion in the course of the talks. We have heard the opinion of the United States of America. I have dwelt upon the basic lines of both our and the American policy in these talks. What is now known about American policy precludes the possibility of agreement. We do not know what will happen tomorrow. But the prospect, as

far as it can be judged, does not look very good, if only because the American position already today proceeds from the assumption that the missiles are to be deployed according to the plan. The missiles must be deployed, they repeat every day, every hour. We would like to see changes for the better in the US stand. But so far there are no signs of this.

Question: According to President Reagan, the US regards effective verification as one of the principles basic to any arms control agreements. What is the Soviet Union's position of principle on this question?
Answer: I would like to stress most emphatically that for the Soviet Union verification has never been an obstacle to the implementation of agreements, or to negotiations aimed at reaching agreement, although we have heard from the other side very many demagogic statements on this score, especially outside the framework of the talks. Where verification is necessary, we are for verification, and where there is no need for special verification—well, then it means it need not be carried out and there is no need for it.

Here I should like to stress, and many people may not know this, that, since the matter concerns several treaties—among others, the SALT II treaty, which as a result of the actions of the American side, has not been ratified and has not entered into force, much has been based on bilateral national verification. Bilateral in the sense that each side, or more precisely, both sides acted in this question in their own way. Bilateral does not mean "joint". It means that each side has used its national technical means. And there has been no serious criticism. It has suited both sides.

It is sometimes said nowadays that there are doubts (incidentally, it has never been directly stated that there have indeed been violations) concerning the observance of some commitments or other assumed by the Soviet Union. Well, as regards doubts, we have also on more than one occasion expressed our doubts to the US government. By way of proof I will cite one case.

We noticed all of a sudden that certain objects had been hidden from observation in the United States for some time. We raised this issue. We were told: indeed, they had been hidden—because of the weather. A month passed, then another and more. So certain objects are hidden, but they are not supposed to be hidden—they are supposed to be seen by our devices. Such was the agreement reached. We again raised the issue. We were told: you know, it has been raining, we have to hide them. Well, of course we asked half seriously, half ironically: but when are your rains going to stop? It has been raining for several months now. Is a second deluge about to come, or what?

It was an American trick, of course. But on the whole we treated the matter calmly. There were other cases, but we do not want to exploit them for propaganda purposes. Something of this kind may happen. But nothing serious has happened on our side, and we do not intend to allow anything to happen. It is not our way in implementing a policy to put something down in a treaty and then to act differently. It would be a good thing if the United States acted in a similar manner.

Question: How do you assess the present situation in the Middle East? How do you assess Washington's reaction to the Soviet government's statement concerning Israel's aggressive designs against Syria? Have there been any contacts lately between the USSR and the US on the situation in that region?

Answer: There have been no regular contacts between the USSR and the US on this issue. If there are contacts, usually they take the form of mutual representations. Sometimes there are electric sparks. It would be better, of course, to conduct matters in a different manner, in a calmer way. But one has to speak the truth, which may be unpleasant, and in a rather sharp way. How can one speak gently about what is now taking place in the Middle East, in particular in Lebanon? What nerves and frame of mind must people have in order not to perceive in a most forceful and vigorous manner and with much alarm what is taking place there?

There was a time when in connection with Israel's aggressive action in Lebanon statements were made in Washington that the United States would not send its troops to Lebanon. Some time passed and other statements were made: indeed, the United States might send troops, but only for a limited period of time, if it were asked to do so. Some more time passed and contingents of American troops appeared in Lebanon. Again official statements were issued by the US Administration: indeed, there are American troops in Lebanon and Washington has no intention for the time being to withdraw them and is not scheduling any date for their withdrawal. And with its contingents Washington has already firmly established its presence in Lebanon. Or it is said: indeed, the American military contingents will leave Lebanon, but Israel, too must withdraw from there as well as all other foreign troops. But Israel says: we have no intention of leaving. Then Washington says that since Israel is not planning to leave, it is not planning to do so either. It is not difficult for these two partners to agree on a division of roles between them. Every outside observer who thinks objectively will make a correct conclusion that in reality there is a collusion there.

The Soviet Union is for the withdrawal of all foreign troops from the territory of Lebanon. All of them. Syria is also for this. But Israel wants to consolidate its hold on a part of Lebanon: actually there is a desire to tear Lebanon as a state apart.

Take the neighbouring region, a huge region encompassing 19 countries. These states are of special interest to the United States. The strategic interests of the United States, as it is declared in Washington, extend to these states. Even a special American command has been set up for this region. Among the aims pursued by Washington there is the aim of interfering even when internal events take place in these countries that do not accord with American interests. The Middle East is included in this zone.

If we are to approach this with the norms of objectiveness and decency, what kind of rights, what lofty morals, what lofty moral principles will we find? Any time some internal social changes take place in these countries, Washington arrogates to itself the right to interfere, including by its armed forces. What do you call it? I would not like to use too strong words.

We sympathize with the Arab cause and are for peace in the Middle East; we are also for Israel existing as a state. No one can reproach us for having changed out position with regard to Israel as a state. When the question of the future of Palestine was being considered, the Soviet Union voted in favour of the establishment of an Israeli state side by side with a Palestinian one. This continues to be our position today as well. We do not share the point of view of extremist Arab circles which are in favour of abolishing Israel. This is an unrealistic and unfair view. But Israel should be a peaceable state; it should have good relations with its neighbours. We are for such a state of Israel. Regrettably, everything Israel has been doing for many years now merely undercuts the political and historic foundation which was generally upheld by all those who were for the establishment of Israel as an independent state. When we voted for the establishment of Israel, we voted for a peaceable Israel and not for an aggressive Israeli state. We would like to see healthy and realistic tendencies prevail at long last in the politics, in the political and social life of Israel, tendencies in favour of Israel living in peace with its neighbours.

We support the Arabs; we support their just cause. We support the Palestinians and believe that they have the right to establish their independent Palestinian Arab state, even if it is not to be a large one.

Question: As is known, last February the Soviet delegation at the Vienna talks on mutual reduction of armed forces and armaments in Central Europe tabled, on behalf of the socialist countries, a package of concrete proposals aimed at breaking the deadlock at the Vienna talks. What has the reaction of the other participating countries been and what are the prospects of the Vienna talks?

Answer: The prospects are rather bad. One feels that Washington, London and the other Western participants, our partners in the talks, do not give serious attention to them and that their positions are solidly frozen. We approached the matter from different angles on several occasions, put forward proposals concerning the overall strength of troops. We suggested a way of making it easier to reach agreement by brushing aside all secondary considerations. Regrettably, the Western participants have not shown much interest in this, although no official answer has yet been given. In general, certain Western capitals have rather often resorted to this method lately. No progress has yet been made at these talks, just as at the talks on chemical weapons and at other talks which have been initiated, and there has been no movement forward regarding the talks which should have started. The reason is that our partners do not want to conduct talks.

We reproach the Western countries on the matter of ending nuclear weapons tests, particularly the US Administration which refuses to reach agreement on this question or even to conduct talks on it. Strange as it might seem, even the Madrid forum has not yet ended. And, given even a slightly objective approach, it should have ended long ago, because the basic political framework for it was defined by the Helsinki Final Act. Those specific questions which arise and have arisen should be tackled within the framework of this basic document, and given goodwill, they should be resolved. It is to be hoped that this forum will eventually end with positive results. We trust that this will be so.

At a meeting in the Kremlin with the President of Finland, Mauno Koivisto, June 1983.

At a presentation of the award of the Order of Lenin to the First Secretary of the Central Committee of the Hungarian Communist Party, Janos Kadar, Moscow, July 1983.

Moscow, the Kremlin, 1983.

A. A. and L. D. Gromyko (Crimea).

A. A. and L. D. Gromyko with their children and grandchildren (Crimea).

Bust of A. A. Gromyko, twice decorated Hero of Soviet Labour, in his hometown, Gomel. Family and relatives at the unveiling of the bust.

A. A. and L. D. Gromyko with their daughter and granddaughter (Crimea).

With the family at the dacha in the Moscow region.

Lenin and Soviet Foreign Policy

Article in the journal *Communist*, No. 6, April 1983

Generations change in this, 20th century, but the giant figure of V. I. Lenin, who has illumined mankind with the light of his ideas, grows ever more majestic. The colossal energy and scope of his activity—theoretical and practical, in the world revolutionary movement, in the domestic and foreign policies of the Soviet state—extend beyond the common perceptions about human genius.

It is impossible to overestimate the services of Lenin, a brilliant thinker and a true follower of Karl Marx and Friedrich Engels, in the creative development of all component parts of Marxism, which he raised to a new, higher level, and in the consistent application of this teaching in the new historical conditions. Leninism is the Marxism of the epoch of imperialism, proletarian revolutions and the disintegration of the colonial system, the epoch of mankind's transition from capitalism to socialism. "Outside and without Leninism, Marxism in our time is simply inconceivable," notes General Secretary of the CPSU Central Committee Y. V. Andropov.

Leader of the Russian and international proletariat Lenin and the Bolshevik Communist Party founded by him spearheaded the victorious Great October Socialist Revolution, which has radically changed the social and political face of the world. The Land of Soviets, of which Lenin was the founder, became the first state of workers and peasants in mankind's history.

Thereby scientific socialism had been fused with the living practice of millions upon millions of working people. An era of grandiose acquisitions of the working class and accomplishments of the popular masses was ushered in. It is precisely such a fusion of theory and practice that was always characteristic of Lenin.

Lenin's thoughts and actions are an inexhaustible source of inspiration for the Soviet communists, the fraternal communist parties, the international working-class movement, the forces of national liberation and all people of good will in their struggle for peace, social progress and a peaceful future of the nations.

In history there is no other personality that has ever enjoyed such boundless respect and affection of the working masses in our country and outside it. Even those who do not share his ideas pay a tribute of recognition to Lenin's genius. Our class enemies also cannot but reckon with his thought.

Lenin's theoretical legacy is inexhaustible in the full sense of the word. It is contained in his writings, in his speeches and reports, in his conversations, letters, theses and other numerous documents, each phrase and each word of which are a potent and sharp-edged weapon of our Party, the Soviet people and all forces working to advance socialism, democracy and peace.

Upholding and enriching Marx's teaching, Lenin did titanic work in the field of philosophy. With inherent depth and compelling logic he showed the viability of Marxist theory as reflecting the objective laws of social development and affirmed the conclusion about its inevitable triumph and so about the inevitability of the victory of the working class and labouring masses.

In his fundamental work "Materialism and Empirio-Criticism" Lenin substantiated and developed further the theses of dialectical and historical materialism, comprehensively analysed the main issue of philosophy—the attitude of consciousness to being, of thinking to matter—and the basic principles and major categories of Marxist philosophical science, especially its theory of cognition, and convincingly proved how great is the significance of the method of materialist dialectics, which he called the "soul of Marxism", for scientific progress. He gave strong rebuff to the campaign "against the philosophy of Marxism" (see *Collected Works*, Vol. 14, p. 19), exposed the various theoretical conceptions of an avowedly bourgeois nature and revealed the invalidity and reactionary character of all manner of revisionist trends that demagnetized the will to fight for a proletarian, socialist revolution. As no one before him, Lenin sharply raised the issue of the principle of partisanship in philosophy, demanding of the Marxists an irreconcilable attitude to every variety of idealism and metaphysics.

This work of Lenin's was written at a complicated period which followed the defeat of the first Russian revolution of 1905–1907, when among a part of the Party's membership there had appeared defeatist sentiments, ideological and political waverings that gave rise, in particular, to confused, pseudoscientific philosophical theories. Lenin's book from principled positions, in a well-argumented way rebuked those views, which had nothing in common with the Marxist world outlook, and ideologically armed the Bolshevik Party on the eve of forthcoming revolutionary battles. In our days, too, it effectively serves the struggle of the communists against bourgeois philosophy and revisionism.

Lenin worked out a scientific theory of imperialism, which he explored in many writings, above all his outstanding work "Imperialism, the Highest Stage of Capitalism". This work continues the analysis of the capitalist mode of production given in Marx's "Capital", and discloses the laws governing economic and political development in the conditions of imperialism, the highest and last stage of capitalism, the "eve of the social revolution of the proletariat".

Lenin's theory of imperialism is a remarkable scientific discovery permitting us to understand the basic features of the present stage of world development and international relations. But Soviet foreign policy and the world communist movement have adopted it. Marked by depth and accuracy, Lenin's characterizations of the main contingents of imperialism—US, German, British, French and so forth—continue to help us to work out a differentiated policy in regard to such capitalist states as the USA, the Federal Republic of Germany, Britain, France, Italy and Japan.

There have been many attempts to limit the significance of Lenin's teaching and the practical experience of the CPSU to the boundaries of our country and to present matters so as if Leninism is a purely Russian phenomenon. But the entire course of historical development again and again bears out its international, worldwide relevance.

Such is, for example, Lenin's thesis about the alliance of the working class and the peasantry, marked by the leadership role of the proletariat. In his capital study "The Development of Capitalism in Russia" and other works Lenin on enormous factual evidence theoretically substantiated the identity of the basic interests of the working class and the peasantry. This thesis played an invaluable role in the efforts of the Party to mobilize revolutionary forces in the country before and after the revolution, as well as in the enrichment of Marxist theory.

Lenin's conclusion about the necessity of a working class–peasantry alliance and its realization in practice in the Land of Soviets are of intransient value not just for our domestic policy. They are also exceptionally important for the fraternal parties of other socialist countries and for those states that have embarked on the path of thorough-going social change even if they are not yet engaged in socialist construction in the true sense of the word.

The foundation and highest principle of the working class–peasantry alliance is the dictatorship of the proletariat. The winning of proletarian dictatorship, the idea of which Lenin considered one of the most important in the Marxist doctrine of the state, constitutes the main content of a socialist revolution and is an indispensable condition of its victory.

Marx wrote about his "Capital" that "it is unquestionably the most terrible shell that has ever been shot at the head of the bourgeois" (K. Marx and F. Engels, *Works*, Russian ed., Vol. 31, p. 453). Well, aptly said!

Lenin's works on the dictatorship of the proletariat carried an equally perilous charge for the bourgeoisie. His classical "The State and Revolution", written on the very eve of Great October, substantiates a conclusion that the top priority of the working class in a revolution as regards the state is to break the bourgeois state machine and to establish proletarian dictatorship. Lenin outlines the main ways for the development of socialist statehood: extension of democracy and the enlistment of the broad masses of people in the running of the state. The book contains scathing criticism of anarchism and opportunism, which distorted the teaching of Marxism about the state and emptied its revolutionary content chiefly by the negation of proletarian dictatorship. Lenin's words that "a Marxist is solely someone who *extends* the recognition of the class struggle to the recognition of the *dictatorship of the proletariat. . . .* This is the touchstone on which the *real* understanding and recognition of Marxism should be tested" (*Collected Works*, Vol. 25, p. 412) remain as pertinent today as they were over six decades ago.

The Bolshevik Party erected the edifice of the Soviet socialist state on a firm theoretical foundation laid by Lenin, who generalized the experience of class battles before the October Revolution and during it, the experience of the first years of proletarian dictatorship in our country. The CPSU, relying on this foundation, is perfecting and strengthening the Soviet state and socialist democracy.

The practice of the USSR and other fraternal countries of socialism confirms that in the course of the building of a new society the content of socialist democracy grows richer and the forms of the exercise of the people's rule become more varied. Socialist statehood also undergoes qualitative changes, the most important of which is the evolution of the state of proletarian dictatorship into an all-people's state. "This is a shift of enormous significance for the political system of socialism," points out Y. V. Andropov. "It found reflection in the Constitution of the USSR approved by the entire people in 1977, which provides a legislative basis for the further development of socialist democracy."

Our country is now in the stage of perfecting developed socialism. The elaboration of the concept of developed socialism, reflecting the main features of contemporary Soviet society, was ranked by the 26th Congress of the CPSU as first among the accomplishments of recent years in the field of Marxist–Leninist theory. Proceeding from this concept, our Party determines its strategy and tactics for the immediate and more distant future.

One could go on listing the works of Lenin, which played a great role in the development of Marxist theory and illumined the way not only for socialist construction in our country, but also for our international policy.

The change of the social system in such a vast country as Russia as a result of the October Revolution, led to a powerful upheaval of the entire imperialist-established world order. But even the more far-sighted representatives of the bourgeoisie failed at that time to realize in full the profundity of this upheaval. Nor did they understand that the triumph of the October Revolution signalled a decline of the system of international relations based on the oppression of the weak states by the strong ones, on the exploitation and plundering of the enslaved nations. This was clearly realized and foreseen by Lenin who elaborated a teaching on socialism's foreign policy. He had worked out a whole number of its theses even before the revolution took place.

The need to ensure favourable external conditions for consolidating revolutionary gains, and for establishing normal, friendly relationships with other states and peoples became an urgent task of Soviet Russia since its emergence. Lenin emphasized on this score: ". . . from the very beginning of the October Revolution, foreign policy and international relations have been the main questions facing us" (*Collected Works*, Vol. 28, p. 151).

Lenin carried out tremendous work on the definition and scientific substantiation of the main goals, basic principles and directions of the international activities of the Communist Party and the Soviet state. Directing these activities in the course of several years, he combined for the first time ever the theory of scientific communism with the foreign policy practice of a socialist state. This fruitful combination gave birth to the hitherto unprecedented foreign policy which became a reliable support for the peoples in their struggle for peace, freedom, independence and socialism.

One cannot speak without admiration about Lenin's fundamental contribution to the development of Soviet foreign policy and diplomatic service. It includes, among other things, the elaboration of the strategy and tactics of this policy, scientifically-based prevision of the course of revolutionary and liberation struggle, the use of inter-imperialist contradictions, and a masterly application of the whole variety of forms and methods of socialist diplomacy. Lenin's foreign policy activities were and remain the brightest and fully valid example of commitment to Party principles, highly principled attitudes, an ability to form a correct estimate of social, economic, and political processes and phenomena in inseparable and controversial interrelation, and to respond promptly to changes in the international situation.

". . . Politics is a science and an art that does not fall from the skies or come gratis, and that, if it wants to overcome the bourgeoisie, the proletariat must train its *own* proletarian 'class politicians', of a kind in no way inferior to bourgeois politicians" (*Collected Works*, Vol. 41, p. 65). It would be appropriate to note in this context Lenin's outstanding role in the training of a whole generation of diplomats of a new type—Soviet diplomats who were defending on the international arena not the exploiter classes, but the interests of the working people, of the advanced, socialist system. They were learning from Lenin the skills of diplomatic art—to keep the initiative and launch diplomatic offensive, but also to be able to hold the line, and to manoeuvre when this is required by the interests of the Soviet state. The CPSU follows this Leninist approach to the Soviet diplomatic service today, too, proceeding from the premiss that the implementation of Soviet foreign policy is a complicated and responsible undertaking, and that it requires a high level of theoretical schooling and professional qualification of diplomatic workers.

Lenin was directly engaged in all—big and small—questions of Soviet foreign policy and diplomatic service. He concerned himself even with such problems of current interest as, for example, instructions on organizing the diplomatic messenger service or the time schedule of work at the People's Commissariat for Foreign Affairs. The People's Commissar for Foreign Affairs, G. V. Chicherin, who worked under Lenin's direct leadership, wrote subsequently that he had quite often discussed with Lenin all details of more or less important routine diplomatic affairs. According to him, "immediately grasping the gist of every question, and instantly giving to it a very extensive political coverage, Vladimir Ilyich invariably made a brilliant analysis of the diplomatic situation in his conversations, and his advice (quite often he gave it right away), and the very text of an answer to another government could serve as models of diplomatic art and flexibility" (G. V. Chicherin, *Articles and Speeches on Questions of International Politics*, Moscow, 1961, p. 277).

Lenin wrote hundreds of documents on the questions of foreign policy—from the Decree on Peace, the first foreign policy act of the Soviet state, to directives for Soviet delegations at international conferences, notes and instructions to ambassadors. These documents are distinguished by deep thought, and meaningful, always extremely accurate and expressive form.

Lenin often had to handle the state's diplomatic affairs. He was sending messages to heads of state and government, supervizing talks and conducting them himself, meeting and talking with many foreign representatives, diplomats, public figures, journalists and writers.

Lenin taught us a realistic, sober approach to the versatile reality of international relations. "His inimitable political realism," recalled G. V. Chicherin, "quite often saved us from mistakes which could be made by

other comrades who were more likely to be misled by their im-
pressionableness" (*ibid.*).

An ability to foresee the development of state-to-state relations for
moves ahead lay at the basis of Lenin's tactical flexibility which his
contemporaries found so striking. The line of action which he mapped
out, quite often caught unawares those who, continuing to think in the
categories of the past, failed to realize that the situation had changed.
These features of Lenin were manifest most vividly in the decisive
moments of history, such as the conclusion of the Brest–Litovsk peace
treaty, the Genoa conference, or the signing of a treaty with Germany at
Rapallo.

Lenin attached special importance to the need for a strictly scientific
approach to the phenomena of international life and foreign policy, an
approach which is incompatible with voluntaristic attitudes, opportun-
istic considerations, superficial improvization, and scholastic speculation. He wrote: "Marxism requires of us a strictly exact and
objectively verifiable analysis of the relations of classes and of the
concrete features peculiar to each historical situation. We Bolsheviks have
always tried to meet this requirement, which is absolutely essential for
giving a scientific foundation to policy" (*Collected Works*, Vol. 24, p. 43).

Underscoring the idea that politics must rely on a solid scientific
foundation, Lenin noted: ". . . Anybody who tackles partial problems
without having previously settled general problems, will inevitably and
at every step 'come up against' those general problems without himself
realizing it. To come up against them blindly in every individual case
means to doom one's politics to the worst vacillation and lack of
principle" (*Collected Works*, Vol. 12, p. 489).

In their entire activities on the world scene the CPSU and the Soviet
state are invariably loyal to Lenin's behests: to correctly determine the
leading trend in social development by giving a scientifically-sound
definition of the character of the modern epoch. Lenin noted: "We
cannot know how rapidly and how successfully the various historical
movements in a given epoch will develop, but we can and do know *which
class* stands at the hub of one epoch or another, determining its main
content, the main direction of its development, the main characteristics
of the historical situation in that epoch, etc. Only on that basis, i.e. by
taking into account, in the first place, the fundamental distinctive

features of the various 'epochs' (and not single episodes in the history of individual countries), can we correctly evolve our tactics; only a knowledge of the basic features of a given epoch can serve as the foundation for an understanding of the specific features of one country or another" (*Collected Works*, Vol. 21, p. 145).

An essential feature of Lenin's approach to international affairs is an analysis of the problems of foreign and home policies as an integral whole which is determined by the fact that both policies are dialectically interrelated and have common roots, since the main content of both foreign and home policies of states is defined by their socio-economic systems. Lenin resolutely denounced the bourgeois concepts which "proved" the independence of home and foreign policies from each other and gave the priority to foreign policy. "It is fundamentally wrong, un-Marxist and unscientific, to single out 'foreign policy' from policy in general, let alone counterpose foreign policy to home policy" (*Collected Works*, Vol. 23, p. 43).

It is exactly the inseparable interrelation of foreign and home policies of a socialist state which stems from its social system that explains why socialism alone guarantees genuinely democratic principles of inter-national communication, full respect for the sovereignty and territorial integrity of all countries, and equitable state-to-state co-operation, and renders disinterested support to the peoples fighting for national liberation and social progress.

Lenin attached paramount importance to a strictly class analysis in assessing international events and tackling practical questions of foreign policy of the Soviet state. For every Communist, especially if the Party and the state entrusted him with implementing and upholding our line in foreign policy, it is a precept which he must strictly fulfil, mobilizing his intellectual abilities, energies, experience and knowledge.

In viewing the foreign policy of states as the expression of the interests of their dominant classes, and the essence of world politics as a class struggle between the opposite socio-economic systems, Lenin always skilfully revealed the class roots in any international issue, no matter how deep they were hidden. He wrote: "When it is not immediately apparent which political or social groups, forces or alignments advocate certain proposals, measures, etc., one should always ask: 'Who stands to gain?' . . . In politics it is not so important *who* directly advocates particular views. What is important is who *stands to gain* from these views, proposals, measures" (*Collected Works*, Vol. 19, p. 53).

Lenin emphasized that "the position of the socialist revolution in Russia must form the basis of any definition of the international tasks of our Soviet power" (*Collected Works*, Vol. 26, p. 443), that it was necessary to subordinate everything to the interests of defending and consolidating the socialist gains in our country. This was exactly what he was doing. One can cite the following episode as an example. In February 1918, Lenin happened to talk with a certain de Lubersac, a French officer and an advocate of German defeat. Lenin recalled that the monarchist views of his interlocutor did not prevent him from entering into an "agreement" with de Lubersac "concerning certain services that French army officers, experts in explosives, were ready to render us by blowing up railway lines in order to hinder the German invasion". Lenin called this "an example of an 'agreement' . . . in the interests of socialism" and noted: "The French monarchist and I shook hands . . . But for a time our interests coincided. Against the advancing rapacious Germans, *we*, in the interests of the Russian and the world socialist revolution, utilized the equally rapacious counterinterests of *other* imperialists" (*Collected Works*, Vol. 28, p. 67).

Lenin was waging uncompromising struggle against the so-called "Left" in our Party, people who believed it possible to sacrifice the already available revolutionary base as represented by the Soviet power for the sake of what they called precipitation of world revolution. At the same time he exposed the right-wing defeatists who did not believe in the triumph of socialist transformation in our country surrounded by a hostile capitalist world.

Our Party has always proceeded from the assumption that a tendency to yield to imperialist threats and a propensity for ultra-revolutionary phraseology have one and the same roots. They both stem from the underestimation of the power and variety of potentialities which the working class and the socialist states have in carrying out their historic mission in the world arena.

So, defence of the vital interests of the Soviet people, and ensuring, together with other socialist states, of favourable international conditions for the building of socialism and communism is the main idea of Lenin's behests for today.

The status of our country in the world and the international situation have drastically changed since the time when Lenin stood at the head of the Soviet state. Our country has immeasurably increased its economic, defence, scientific, technical, and cultural potential. As a result of the historic victory scored by the Soviet people in the Great Patriotic War, the USSR was unreservedly recognized as a great power on the world scene, a country without which not a single more or less big problem can be solved. This is borne out, among other things, by the Yalta and Potsdam agreements. This is reflected in the Charter of the United Nations, which entrusts the Soviet Union as a permanent member of the Security Council with special responsibility for maintaining international peace and security.

Just as in the matter of building communism as a whole, our country is faced with ever new tasks in the field of international policy. But today, too, in such a sophisticated sphere as relations among peoples and states, where various economic, political, military, national and even psychological factors interact, intertwine and clash, and where the total outcome of forces acting from different directions is not at all easy to determine in advance, the Communist Party of the Soviet Union has a correct and reliable guide—the Leninist teaching on foreign policy of the socialist state, and the Leninist practice of its implementation.

Born of the socialist revolution, Soviet foreign policy was and remains at the service of the revolutionary transformation in our country. This foreign policy is internationalist in character, since the interests of the Soviet people coincide with those of the working people in all countries of the world. It is permeated by the spirit of solidarity with all revolutionary and progressive forces of our time. Soviet foreign policy is distinguished by its profoundly and genuinely democratic character, by a *de facto* recognition of the equality of all states, of all races and nationalities. Soviet foreign policy is essentially humanist for it is a consistent policy of peace. Socialism knows of no other goals than concern for the interests of people, which primarily implies tireless work to prevent war.

The class, socialist character and content of Soviet foreign policy are reflected in its fundamental principles—proletarian internationalism and peaceful coexistence of states with differing social systems, the principles which were put forward by Lenin.

Explaining the essence of proletarian internationalism, Lenin wrote that "capital is an international force. To vanquish it, an international workers' alliance, an international workers' brotherhood, is needed. We are opposed to national enmity and discord, to national exclusiveness. We are internationalists" (*Collected Works*, Vol. 30, p. 293).

Having emerged at the dawn of the international communist movement, proletarian internationalism has become one of the main principles of ideology and policy of the working class and its party. It is an expression of solidarity of working people in different countries in the struggle against capitalism, for their social and national liberation, for the building of socialism and communism and for a peaceful life of the peoples.

With the victory of the October revolution proletarian internationalism became the cornerstone of Soviet foreign policy and found its expression in the consistent support for the revolutionary and liberation movement of the working masses and oppressed peoples. The ideas of proletarian internationalism were first put into practice during the building of socialism in the USSR where the nationalities issue was solved, a multiethnic state of equal nations was created and international relations without class and national antagonisms took shape.

The principle of proletarian internationalism found its qualitatively new expression with the emergence of the world socialist system (it was the most important event after the October revolution), which Lenin brilliantly predicted as individual countries or groups of countries would break away from the capitalist system. He also foresaw the main features of future relations between the socialist countries. The resolution of the All-Russian Central Executive Committee of November 13, 1918, on the abrogation of the Brest–Litovsk peace treaty (the resolution was signed by Lenin) said that such relations "can rest only upon the principles which correspond to the fraternal relations between the working people of all countries and nations (. . .), the relations between nations built on these principles (. . .) will be not only peaceful relations. That will be an alliance of the working masses of all nations in their struggle to create and strengthen the socialist system on the wreckage of the system of militarism, imperialism and economic slavery."

As applied to relations between the socialist states, proletarian internationalism achieves its highest form—socialist internationalism, which implies not only unity of actions of the national groups of the victorious working class and their Marxist–Leninist vanguard, but also all-round solidarity and co-operation between the fraternal countries. Socialist internationalism is a legitimate stage of development of international solidarity of the working class under the historical conditions when it became the ruling class and its Marxist–Leninist parties became the ruling parties and when they began to put into practice the tasks of building socialism and communism, developing and strengthening interstate relations of the socialist type, consolidating the international positions of the world socialist system and ensuring collective defence of the socialist acquisitions.

To implement these tasks means to do what is maximally possible in each country to ensure the growth of the might and cohesion of all the socialist states and do everything to ensure the implementation of the principle of socialist internationalism in their relations. The policy of the socialist countries must organically combine the national interests of each country and the common internationalist interests of the socialist community. It is clear that the establishment of the socialist system in a number of countries does not automatically solve all the problems of building new relations between them. All this requires, above all, active, conscious and purposeful work of the ruling communist parties. That is what the CPSU and the other fraternal parties did and are doing.

At the present stage the socialist community is a group of countries characterized by co-operation between the ruling communist parties, state organs and mass organizations on the principles of Marxism–Leninism and socialist internationalism, rapid development of economic integration and unprecedented expansion of co-operation in all spheres of life, including effective co-ordination of activities in the international arena. The relationships between these countries, which are international relations of a new type, are characterized, besides genuine equality, non-interference in the internal affairs of one another and mutual respect for independence, sovereignty and territorial integrity, by fraternal friendship and comradely assistance, which constitute, as a whole, the essence of socialist internationalism.

Close co-operation between the socialist states, united by similar political, social and economic systems, an identical world outlook and common aims and ideals in the struggle for peace and socialism, has now grown into a fraternal alliance embodied in the Warsaw Treaty Organization and the Council for Mutual Economic Assistance and a system of bilateral treaties of friendship, co-operation and mutual assistance which link these countries. This alliance finds its expression in the process of all-round drawing together of the socialist states, a process which keeps growing deeper and manifests itself as an objective law. Through harmonious combination of national and international interests this process leads to their further cohesion, to closer merger of their economies, mutual appreciation of cultures and the pooling of efforts, expertise and resources for jointly tackling the key problems of building socialism and communism and strengthening the positions of socialism in the world.

In their development the socialist countries face some problems which are rather serious sometimes. For this development goes along an untrodden path, through the struggle of the new with the old, the settlement of internal contradictions and the overcoming of illusions and mistakes. Lenin wrote that the proletariat "will not become holy and immune from errors and weaknesses" just because it has carried out a social revolution (*Collected Works*, Vol. 22, p. 353).

The international situation also does not always facilitate the development of the socialist community. The socialist countries exist under the conditions of a fierce class confrontation between the two systems and are subjected to strong pressure by imperialism.

Life confirms the fact that the socialist community is capable of coping with all the problems that hinder its advancement. Let no one doubt the common determination of the fraternal states to safeguard their interests, ensure the strength of all the elements of the community and defend the socialist acquisitions.

"Assessing the present situation in our countries, we can say with satisfaction that the socialist community is a mighty and healthy organism which plays a great and favourable role in the modern world," Yuri Andropov said.

This role manifests itself to the full extent in the Leninist foreign policy pursued by the Soviet Union and based on the Peace Programme formulated by the 24th, 25th and 26th congresses of the CPSU and in the activities of all the fraternal countries in the international arena. There is reason to speak today about a common foreign-policy strategy of the socialist community, which constitutes a potent instrument of favourable influence on the course of world developments and is an effective and consistent means of promoting peace, international co-operation, freedom and independence of the peoples. The importance of this policy of the socialist states is especially great in the current international situation which has seriously deteriorated as a result of the aggressive actions of imperialist circles, especially in the United States.

The effectiveness of socialism's foreign policy and its success depend a great deal on co-ordination and cohesion of actions and efforts of the socialist countries in international affairs. Co-ordination of these actions and efforts rests upon a solid contractual basis. It is envisaged by the Warsaw Treaty and also by the bilateral treaties of friendship, co-operation and mutual assistance.

The socialist states have accumulated vast and positive experience of co-operation in the field of foreign policy. The forms of such co-operation include consultations on major international problems, mutual and constantly growing exchange of information, the formu-lation and implementation of a common co-ordinated policy and close co-operation in carrying out practical actions in the international arena.

There is an effective mechanism of co-ordination of foreign policies of the socialist countries. The exchange of views on crucial international issues and the elaboration of a joint line of foreign policy are a constant topic of negotiations between the leaders of the fraternal parties and countries during their regular bilateral and multilateral meetings, including the meetings held within the Warsaw Treaty Political Consultative Committee. At the sessions of the Political Consultative Committee the socialist countries worked out major proposals on the crucial issues of European and international politics. Many of these proposals were laid at the base of debate at the United Nations and other international forums or were incorporated in a number of major treaties and agreements concluded with the participation of countries with different social systems. New far-reaching initiatives are for-mulated in the Political Declaration adopted by the Political Consultative Committee in Prague last January. The Committee of Warsaw Treaty Foreign Ministers also makes its contribution to the co-ordination of foreign-policy initiatives of the socialist countries.

Co-ordinated actions of the socialist countries in the international arena made it possible successfully to solve many important and complex problems for whose solution they had been working for a long time. These actions had a decisive role to play in undermining the imperialist blockade of Cuba, ensuring international recognition of the German Democratic Republic, bringing about the conclusion of the treaties between the USSR, the GDR, Poland and Czechoslovakia and the Federal Republic of Germany and the Quadripartite Agreement on West Berlin, ensuring the successful completion of the European conference, safeguarding the glorious victory of the Vietnamese people over the American aggressors and also bringing about the conclusion of a number of arms control agreements.

Lenin predicted that socialism, once it had grown from a national force into an international one, would be "capable of exercising a decisive influence upon world politics as a whole (*Collected Works*, Vol. 31, p. 148). His prediction is coming true. At the present time the socialist community is the chief obstacle to the adventurous policy of imperialism, the powerful bulwark of all forces fighting for their national and social liberation and a potent factor of the world's development today.

Being well aware of their historic responsibility for the future of peace and socialism, the socialist countries always seek further to close their ranks. The cause of friendship and co-operation with the fraternal countries always occupied and will occupy a special, priority place in the foreign policy of the CPSU and the Soviet government.

Lenin's teachings serve as a lodestar for the policy of the CPSU and the Soviet government to the countries which have thrown off the yoke of colonial oppression and to the national liberation movement.

On the basis of an analysis of social development in the epoch of imperialism and socialist revolutions Lenin formulated the thesis that "the socialist revolution will not be solely, or chiefly, a struggle of the revolutionary proletarians in each country against their bourgeoisie" but "it will be a struggle of all the imperialist-oppressed colonies and countries, of all dependent countries, against international imperialism" (*Collected Works*, Vol. 30, p. 159). He showed that the countries and peoples that were in colonial or semi-colonial dependence inevitably turned from a reserve and deep rear of imperialism into an active anti-imperialist force and an ally of the socialist revolution. Attaching paramount importance to the close international alliance of the revolution in Russia with the liberation movement of the peoples of colonial and dependent states, Lenin wrote this even before the victory of the October Revolution: "We shall exert every effort to foster association and merger with the Mongolians, Persians, Indians, Egyptians. We believe it is our duty and *in our interest* to do this, for otherwise socialism in Europe will *not be secure*" (*Collected Works*, Vol. 23, p. 67).

The political significance of Lenin's thesis about the close ties between the social emancipation of the working class in the parent countries and the struggle for independence in their colonial possessions is obvious. It concerns the historical destiny of the majority of the world's population and the alignment of forces on a worldwide scale. Lenin formulated the main laws of the development of the national liberation movement, predicted the inevitable collapse of the colonial system, substantiated the idea of non-capitalist development and elaborated the problem of building a new society in economically under-developed countries.

Lenin said that in developing co-operation with the countries seeking to throw off the fetters of colonialism, strengthen independence and ensure national and social progress, the socialist states should be guided by the objective identity of their fundamental interests and the fundamental interests of these countries in the struggle against imperialism. They should therefore be guided in such co-operation not only by the principle of peaceful coexistence governing relations between states with different social systems, but also the principle of internationalism which regulates the relations between the socialist countries and the forces related to them by their class interests and all the anti-imperialist forces. Such an approach takes into account the real position of the states which are an object of imperialist exploitation even when their policies are determined by governments which represent bourgeois and sometimes even feudal circles.

Guided by these considerations, Lenin outlined the specific tasks of the policy and diplomacy of the socialist countries with regard to these countries: support for their efforts to strengthen national independence and assistance to all progressive undertakings, help in overcoming economic and cultural backwardness, strict observance of the principle of equality and non-interference in internal affairs, appreciation of and respect for national and historical traditions, assistance to effective participation in tackling international problems, and solidarity with the struggle against the imperialist forces. This new, socialist policy laid the groundwork for an international anti-imperialist front.

The Great October Socialist Revolution united in a single effort the struggle waged by the proletariat for socialism and the peoples' movement against colonial oppression and provoked an unprecedented rise of this movement which has achieved spectacular successes since then.

The principles of equality and sovereignty of the peoples, the renunciation of all national and national-religious privileges and restrictions and the principle of free development of the national minorities and ethnic groups, which were formulated in the first foreign-policy documents adopted by the Soviet Republic, facilitated the solution of the nationalities problem in the USSR on the basis of justice and socialism. The proclamation and implementation of these principles eliminated the causes of the national strife of the past and earned the Russian working class trust of the peoples of the non-Russian provinces, which threw off the fetters of exploitation and united with the Russian people into a multinational socialist state.

Lenin's appeal "To All the Toiling Moslems of Russia and the East", which was adopted on November 20 (December 3), 1917, was of great importance for the establishment of friendly relations with the countries of the East. "It is not from Russia and her revolutionary government that your enslavement is to be expected, but from the European imperialist robbers (. . .), from those who have transformed your fatherland into a plundered and despoiled 'colony'," it said in the part addressed to the working people of the East. "You yourselves must be the masters of your country! You yourselves must arrange your lives in your own way. That is your right, for your destiny is in your own hands."

The appeal proclaimed the secret treaties directed against the interests of the peoples of the East, especially the treaties on the division of Turkey and Iran, null and void. The unfair treaties with China were terminated later.

At the same time, Soviet Russia urged the countries of the East to establish good-neighbourly relations on a genuinely volunteer basis and on the principles of equality and mutual respect. During the first few years of the existence of our state it established diplomatic relations and began to arrange friendly co-operation with China, Mongolia, Turkey, Iran, Afghanistan, Saudi Arabia and Yemen. The treaties concluded at that time with Mongolia, Iran, Turkey and Afghanistan and the selfless support which Soviet Russia gave them enabled those countries to safeguard and consolidate their national independence.

Continuing the cause started when Lenin was alive, the Soviet Union exerted great efforts in the field of foreign policy to shatter the colonial system and ensure the victory of the liberation struggle waged by the peoples of Asia, Africa and Latin America. The routing with decisive participation of the USSR of the most reactionary and aggressive forces of imperialism in the second world war and the emergence of the world socialist system removed the curbs that hindered the impetuous growth of the national liberation movement.

It should be recalled that the Soviet Union insisted on the inclusion in the UN Charter of the clause on equality and self-determination of the peoples, thus creating conditions for the subsequent actions taken by the United Nations in support of the liberation struggle. It is a well known fact that the Declaration on the Granting of Independence to Colonial Countries and Peoples, which the United Nations adopted at Soviet initiative in 1960, was a great impetus for those who were to fight against the colonialists.

Dozens of peoples came to freedom and independence as a result of the collapse of the shameful system of colonialism. The possibility of relying on the Soviet Union and the other socialist countries was and is of vital importance for many of them. Many a time the Soviet Union's vigorous moves in support of the victims of aggression and its material support helped newly-independent countries repel imperialist inter-ference in their internal affairs.

It is quite understandable that temporary failures and setbacks are inevitable in a matter of such dimension as the process of the national liberation of countries and peoples and the efforts to strengthen independence of developing nations. The ultimate outcome of their struggle is indisputable.

The Soviet Union still remains committed to the Leninist traditions of friendship and co-operation with the peoples of Asia, Africa and Latin America. Our country gives them wide-ranging political, economic and other support. A series of treaties of friendship and co-operation concluded between the USSR and India, Syria, Angola, Ethiopia, Mozambique, Afghanistan, the People's Democratic Republic of Yemen and other states testify to the high level of the development of relations between the Soviet Union and these countries. These are treaties between equal, independent and peaceloving countries.

The Soviet Union is on the side of those who still have to fight for freedom and independence, for the very existence of their peoples, those who are compelled to fight back the aggressive forces of imperialism or are threatened with aggression on their part. The USSR firmly supports the just struggle of the Arab peoples against the Washington-encouraged Israeli aggressors. It is rendering the necessary assistance to the Afghan people who are defending from outside encroachments their inalienable right to arrange their life the way they see fit. The Soviet people are in full sympathy with the people of Nicaragua, who are rebuffing the brutal imperialist pressure, and with the courageous patriots of El Salvador, fighting against the rotten anti-popular regime being propped up by Washington patrons. Our country expresses solidarity with the struggle of the people of Namibia who are certain to win their freedom and independence.

The USSR treats with respect the non-aligned movement whose strength lies in its stand against imperialism and colonialism, against war and aggression. It is this stand that provides the key to a further enhancement of the non-aligned movement's role in world politics. The results of the 7th Conference of Heads of State and Government of Non-Aligned Countries, held in March in New Delhi, are very positive in this respect.

The CPSU and the Soviet state will as before pursue consistently, as was stressed by the 26th Congress of our Party, a course towards the development of co-operation with the newly free countries, towards strengthening the alliance between world socialism and the national liberation movement.

Lenin had theoretically prepared our Party for the situation which took shape with the victory of the socialist revolution in Russia. Having discovered the law of uneven development of capitalism in the stage of imperialism, he came to the conclusion that socialism would not be able to triumph simultaneously in all countries and, consequently, coexistence of countries belonging to two opposed social systems—the socialist and the capitalist—was inevitable.

Struggle between these systems constitutes the main content of the historical epoch in which we are living. But Lenin rejected the view that this struggle would inevitably develop into ceaseless wars between the capitalist and the socialist countries.

The question of relations between countries of the different systems was raised by Lenin as a practical matter in the works he wrote on the eve of the October Revolution, in particular his "Letters from Afar", where he examined measures to be taken by a newly installed workers' and peasants' government. Time and again he spoke on that question in conversations and interviews with foreign correspondents when the Soviet Republic worked for withdrawal from the war and for the conclusion of the Brest peace.

Lenin's Decree on Peace proclaimed peaceful coexistence between countries with different social systems one of the fundamental principles of the foreign policy of a socialist state.

Now we should turn to the events connected with the Genoa Conference of sixty years ago—the first international forum to which the Soviet state was admitted. Some comrades suggested that Lenin, who was appointed chairman of our delegation to that conference, should use its rostrum for sharp and accusatory speeches. But Lenin, who directed the Soviet delegation's preparations for the Genoa conference, saw the task in a different light. He set for it directives that proceeded from the need to have normal business relations with the capitalist countries. It needed a far-seeing mind of brilliant prevision, in conditions of enormous social upheavals that were rocking the world, to chart a long-term general line for relations between the Land of the Soviets and the capitalist world.

In his amendments and remarks to the draft declaration of the delegation, Lenin, proceeding from the principle of peaceful coexistence, proposed that "all mention of 'inevitable forcible revolution and the use of sanguinary struggle' must definitely be thrown out"; that "the words about our historic conception being definitely based on the inevitability of new world wars should be definitely deleted". "Under no circumstances," he went on, "should such frightful words be used, as this would mean playing into the hands of our opponents" (*Collected Works*, Vol. 42, p. 410).

It is common knowledge that Lenin did not go to Genoa, obeying a special resolution of the Central Committee of the R.C.P. (B), since the working people of our country firmly decided that his life should not be exposed to risk. G. V. Chircherin, deputy chairman of the Soviet delegation at the Genoa conference, was the man who delivered there the speech which was to have been made by Lenin. That speech opened with a policy-making statement: "While adhering to the communist principles, the Russian delegation admits that in the present historical epoch, which makes possible the parallel existence of the old and newly arising social systems, economic co-operation between countries representing these two systems of property is imperative for the general economic restoration" (*Documents of Foreign Policy*, Vol. 5, Moscow, 1961, pp. 191, 192. In Russian).

Lenin more than once discussed the principle of peaceful coexistence in his works, presenting its different aspects and explaining it. Sometimes he would use the term "peaceful cohabitation" of the systems, sometimes his wording would be different, but the sense always remained the same—there were objective possibilities for peaceful relations between the Soviet state and the surrounding capitalist world.

During Lenin's lifetime, in June 1920, when the foreign policy of Soviet Russia was debated at a meeting of the All-Russia Central Executive Committee, G. V. Chicherin said: "We want no one to prevent us from developing the way we wish, building our new socialist society in peace. We are not bringing our system and our power at bayonet point, this is known to everyone, and still ever new enemies are being set on us. Our policy is a policy of peace, but it is not a policy of surrender." And further: "Our slogan was and remains the same: peaceful coexistence with other governments, whatever they may be" (*Documents of Foreign Policy of the USSR*, Vol. 2, Moscow, 1958, pp. 638, 639. In Russian).

Reviewing the results of the socialist revolution and the civil war in Russia, in November 1920 Lenin emphasized that the Soviet state had entered a long period during which it would exist "in the network of capitalist states". ". . . We," he said, "are in a position of having won

conditions enabling us to exist side by side with capitalist powers . . ."
(*Collected Works*, Vol. 31, p. 412).

It took decades of persistent struggle against imperialist attempts in
one way or another to liquidate the socialist system and to strangle the
Soviet state before the West learned to pronounce correctly the words
"peaceful coexistence". Started on the fronts of the civil war and
struggle against foreign intervention and continued in the clash with
Hitler's Germany and its allies, the dispute between socialism and
capitalism on the possibility or impossibility of peaceful coexistence
between states regardless of their social system has been settled by
history. Settled in favour of recognizing socialism and its foreign policy
mapped out by Lenin.

Peaceful coexistence is a specific form of class struggle between
socialism and capitalism. Such a struggle goes on and will continue to go
on in economics, politics and, unquestionably, in ideology, since the
world outlooks and class goals of the two social systems are opposed
and irreconcilable. But this historically inevitable confrontation must be
conducted in forms that would not create armed conflicts or, moreover,
jeopardize the very existence of mankind.

In the present-day conditions the strict observance of the principle of
peaceful coexistence has acquired special significance, for peaceful
coexistence between the socialist and the capitalist states is the only
reasonable alternative to nuclear catastrophe.

The foreign policy of socialism, pursuing as it does a restructuring of
international relations on the basis of the principle of peaceful
coexistence, does not regard that as an end in itself, but as a major
component element in the solution of the most burning problem of our
time—exclusion of war from the life of human society and assertion on
the Earth of a lasting, just and democratic peace. Working for that has
nothing in common with concessions to the militarist circles of
imperialism, and combines consistent peaceableness with a firm rebuff
to aggression.

The incorporation of the principle of peaceful coexistence in relations
between socialist and capitalist states is directly and immediately linked
with the growing might of socialism as a social system. The increased
might and cohesion and active peaceloving policy of world socialism, its
increasingly strong alliance with all progressive and anti-war forces, as

well as the dawning awareness on the part of sober-minded leaders of the bourgeois world of untenability of the calculations to resolve the historical dispute between capitalism and socialism by force of arms— all these created prerequisites for the beginning in the 'seventies of a turn in the development of international relations from the cold war and confrontation to *détente* and mutually advantageous co-operation. The principles of peaceful coexistence began increasingly to assert themselves as a norm of relations between states with different social systems.

That period saw the solution of some previously seemingly insoluble problems which had for a long time been poisoning the international atmosphere. Political contacts, including summit-level ones, became a practice in relations between countries belonging to different social and economic systems. Dozens of important agreements and treaties were concluded between these countries, and ties were expanded in the commercial, economic, scientific, technical, cultural and other spheres.

The principle of peaceful coexistence, which thereby entered the fabric of European and world politics, was confirmed in major bilateral and multilateral agreements. Thus, the 1972 document on the basic principles of relations between the USSR and the USA stated the two sides' intention to act in the common belief that there was no alternative except peaceful coexistence to maintaining relations between them in the nuclear age. That principle was made the underlying concept of the Final Act of the Conference on Security and Co-operation in Europe.

"We are deeply convinced that the 'seventies, characterized by *détente*, were not—as is usually asserted today by certain imperialist leaders—a chance episode in the difficult history of mankind," Y. V. Andropov noted at the November 1982 Plenary Meeting of the CPSU Central Committee. "No, the policy of *détente* is by no means a past stage. The future belongs to this policy. All are equally interested in preserving peace and *détente*."

Lenin's principle of peaceful coexistence of states with different social systems, which is consistently upheld by the foreign policy of socialism, accords with the character, basic laws and requirements of the present-day epoch and, for this reason, possesses a great life-asserting force.

"The central direction in the foreign policy of our Party and Government is, as it has always been, to lessen the danger of war and to curb the arms race," says the Report of the CPSU Central Committee to the 26th Party Congress.

Lenin clearly saw that the destinies of the revolution in Russia and of the whole liberation struggle of the peoples largely depended on correct resolution of the problem of war and peace. Marxism–Leninism bared the aggressive nature of capitalism and of its highest stage, imperialism, which, while being a historically doomed social system, professes the cult of force and banks on militarism. Lenin stressed that militarism has two forms—internal and external, and that in both of its forms it is "the 'vital expression' of capitalism—as a military force used by the capitalist states in their external conflicts . . . and as a weapon in the hands of the ruling classes for suppressing every kind of movement, economic and political, of the proletariat . . ." (*Collected Works*, Vol. 15, p. 192).

On the contrary, in socialist society there are no classes or social groups, interested in war. The striving for peace is inherent in this society because the interests of building socialism and communism require peaceful conditions. "An end to wars, peace among the nations, the cessation of pillaging and violence—such is our ideal . . ." (*Collected Works*, Vol. 21, p. 293).

At the height of the First World War Lenin pointed out that only a workers' and peasants' state is "*capable* of successfully carrying out the extremely difficult and absolutely urgent *chief* task of the moment, namely: to achieve *peace*, not an imperialist peace, not a deal between the imperialist powers concerning the division of the booty by the capitalists and their governments, but a really lasting and democratic peace . . ." (*Collected Works*, Vol. 23, p. 340).

Under Lenin's slogan of ending the imperialist war and establishing peace, the Party of Bolsheviks led the masses of people to accomplish a revolution. On the following day the Soviet government published a Decree on Peace which condemned imperialist wars as "the greatest of crimes against humanity" and advanced a proposal to put an end to the world war and to conclude a just, democratic peace.

Lenin attached particular importance to the role of the masses of people in the struggle for peace. In the Decree on Peace the Soviet state called upon the class-conscious workers of the foremost nations to help bring about the success of the cause of peace by their comprehensive, determined, and supremely energetic action. Substantiating the necessity of appealing to the broad masses of working people, Lenin said in the report on peace made at the Second Congress of Soviets: "Our appeal must be addressed both to the governments and to the peoples . . . We must . . . help the peoples to intervene in questions of war and peace" (*Collected Works*, Vol. 26, p. 252).

Lenin's pronouncements to the effect that "socialists have always condemned wars between nations as barbarous and brutal" (*Collected Works*, Vol. 21, p. 299) and that "we know only too well the incredible misfortunes that war brings to the workers and peasants" (*Collected Works*, Vol. 33, p. 149) remain topical. But Lenin was far from cheap pacifism.

Placing the interests of the toiling classes, i.e. of the majority of the Earth's population, above any other considerations, he advanced the thesis of just wars—wars which are waged with the aim of liberating the masses of working people from social and national oppression, defending the people against external aggression, and defending a socialist state from an attack from outside.

Lenin uncompromisingly stigmatized various imperialist coalitions, "ententes" and other combinations, behind which there stood the predatory interests of the big imperialist powers that set the peoples against each other in order to divide and redivide the world, in order to engage in pillaging and exploitation. What immense efforts the Soviet Union made to prevent the Second World War! Using every opportunity, including the League of Nations in Geneva, the Soviet foreign policy did its best to paralyze the forces of aggression and to counterpose a collective front of peace champions to the coming war. And when the most aggressive forces of imperialism, first of all Hitler's Germany, unleashed the war, the Soviet people made the decisive contribution to the rout of Nazism.

Also in the present-day conditions, when the imperialist circles, first of all those of the United States, continue rattling the sabre and make attempts to gain military superiority over the world of socialism, the Soviet Union has to care for maintaining its security and the security of its allies on the proper level. At the same time, the CPSU and the Soviet state continue to work actively for peace in the international arena, acting in line with Lenin's ideas—"a minimum of general assurances, solemn promises and grandiloquent formulas, and the greatest possible number of the simplest and most obvious decisions and measures that would certainly lead to peace, if not to the complete elimination of the war danger" (*Collected Works*, Vol. 33, p. 386). The entire policy of our Party and of our state is aimed at implementing Lenin's behest: ". . . we promise the workers and peasants to do all we can for peace. This we shall do" (*Collected Works*, Vol. 27, p. 379).

The Soviet Union has always been a peace champion and an opponent of predatory wars. It was and is now an advocate of disarmament, international *détente*, and solution of disputable questions by peaceful means. The peaceable character of the Soviet foreign policy is reflected and formalized in the resolutions of the Congresses of the Party and of the Plenary Meetings of its Central Committee, in the decisions of the Soviet government, and in the appeals by the USSR Supreme Soviet. The policy of peace and friendship among the nations is a concentrated expression of the will of all Soviet people in international affairs.

"A comprehensive history of our epoch will obviously be written some day," Y. V. Andropov stresses. "We can rest assured that the following indisputable fact will be written down in that history in golden letters: without the firm peace-loving policy of the Soviet Union our planet not only would have been a much more dangerous place to live on but also, which is very probable, would have encountered an irreparable catastrophe. If it has been averted, if we have been living in the conditions of peace for almost forty years now, and if we are confidently looking into the future, this has been largely due to the foreign policy of the Soviet Union, its struggle against the threat of a nuclear catastrophe, for life and for the preservation and prosperity of mankind."

A characteristic feature of our foreign policy in the form in which it shaped up under Lenin's direct influence is the bringing of problems concerning the fundamental interests of the peoples to the foreground of international life and the ability to make the governments and world public opinion rivet their attention exactly on these problems. A concrete expression of this is the struggle for curbing the arms race and for disarmament.

This problem was raised by our country long ago, at the Genoa conference. At its first plenary session the delegation of Soviet Russia submitted, on Lenin's instructions, a proposal to carry out a universal reduction of armaments and armies of all states and to ban the barbarous forms of warfare—toxic gases and means of destruction aimed against civilians.

The Soviet Union firmly retains the initiative in the questions of disarmament. It can be said in no uncertain terms that no other state in the world has made such a big contribution to the formulation and analysis of this problem as the USSR has made and continues to make.

It goes without saying that today, just as at the time of the Genoa conference, we are well aware of the difficulties in the way of resolving these questions, and of the obstacles which are raised by the militarist circles of the West. And still, as a result of the persistent and indefatigable struggle of the CPSU and the Soviet state, there have been attained results which to a certain extent curb the arms race in some directions.

These are the treaty banning nuclear weapon tests in the atmosphere, in outer space and under water, the treaty on principles governing the activities of states in the exploration and use of outer space including the Moon and other celestial bodies, the treaty on the non-proliferation of nuclear weapons, the convention on the prohibition of the development, production and stockpiling of bacteriological (biological) and toxin weapons and their destruction, the convention on the prohibition of military or any other hostile use of environmental modification techniques, and some other agreements. The bilateral Soviet–US agreements—the treaty on the limitation of anti-missile defence systems and the SALT I treaty—served to realize the same objective. An effective contribution to the cause of peace could be made also by the SALT II treaty which was signed in 1979 but has not come into effect through the fault of the USA.

The historic decision of the USSR to assume a unilateral obligation not to make first use of nuclear weapons, and the other proposals which it tabled at the Second Special Session of the UN General Assembly on Disarmament, held last year, clearly testify to its striving to avert the threat of nuclear catastrophe and to attain real results in the sphere of disarmament. At present the Soviet Union is actively working to achieve mutually acceptable accords at the Soviet–US talks on the limitation of nuclear armaments in Europe and on the limitation and reduction of strategic armaments, which are being held in Geneva. At the Vienna negotiations on reducing the armed forces and armaments in Central Europe the socialist countries have recently submitted new proposals which provide a realistic opportunity for reaching concrete agreements.

The proposal to conclude a treaty on mutual non-use of military force and on maintaining relations of peace between the Warsaw Treaty countries and the countries—members of NATO, which was advanced in the Political Declaration of the recent conference of the Political Consultative Committee of the Warsaw Treaty member states, is a large-scale initiative.

Advancing constructive and far-reaching initiatives in the sphere of the limitation of the arms race and disarmament, the Soviet Union expects the Western countries to deal with them in a businesslike manner and with due responsibility.

Lenin attached great importance to the use of economic instruments in the foreign policy of the Soviet state. "There is a force more powerful than the wishes, the will and the decisions of any of the governments or classes that are hostile to us. That force is world general economic relations, which compel them to make contact with us" (*Collected Works*, Vol. 33, p. 155).

A champion of equitable and mutually beneficial economic relations with the capitalist countries, Lenin clearly saw the aims that could be achieved through their development: on the one hand, Soviet Russia's participation in the international division of labour would promote its rapid economic growth and help it forge broad economic links with other nations, and, on the other, such co-operation would provide the material foundation for peaceful coexistence between states belonging to different social systems.

However, Lenin emphatically rejected any attempts of the imperialist forces to impose their economic terms on our country, all their efforts to damage our economic development. Nowadays, too, the Soviet Union firmly rebuffs, together with other fraternal countries, the imperialist forces eager to unleash a trade, financial and economic war against the countries of the socialist community.

The economic might of the USSR, and the successes the Soviet people achieved in carrying out the CPSU's socio-economic plans constitute the reliable basis of Soviet foreign policy. "Steady economic growth and rises in public wellbeing," Y. V. Andropov said, "are both our duty to Soviet people and our internationalist duty. Interpreting this question as it does, the Party proceeds from Lenin's far-sighted words to the effect that we exert our main influence on the world revolutionary process through our economic policy."

Lenin said that Soviet foreign policy should not fail to exploit contradictions among the imperialists. He showed us how to do this on the example of the Brest peace treaty which gave our country a respite it desperately needed and which allowed it to use one imperialist vulture as a shield to protect itself, for the time being, from the others.

But for the ability we legated from Lenin to play on trends and nuances in the bourgeois quarters and the differences and clashes of the interests of imperialist states, there would have been no anti-Hitler coalition that included the Soviet Union, the United States, Britain and France. Although, as we know, the coalition did see frictions and disagreements, it went down in history, and is remembered by the peoples, as an example of the co-operation of states, belonging to different social systems, in the struggle against a common enemy.

Following undeviatingly Lenin's guidelines, the Soviet Union conducts an honest and open policy in international affairs.

In order to promote its interests the bourgeoisie, Lenin wrote, vigorously exploits the fact that "popular ignorance of a foreign policy is incomparably greater than of home policy". He stressed that "the 'secrecy' of diplomatic relations is sacredly observed in the freest of capitalist countries, in the most democratic republics" and that "popular deception has become a real art in foreign 'affairs'" (*Collected Works*, Vol. 25, p. 85).

The publication of tsarist Russia's secret treaties was one of Lenin's first instructions carried out by the People's Commissariat for Foreign Affairs, just established at that time. A rupture with secret diplomacy has nothing in common, of course, with the way this question is sometimes interpreted by the man in the street. It would be absurd to remove all confidentiality from relations between states and not to make top secret of questions relating, say, to the shaping of our foreign policy and its co-ordination with socialist countries, or some aspects of our relations with friendly states, the divulgence of which could damage our cause. Whenever necessary, the Soviet government holds consultations behind closed doors also with capitalist states, and the results of such exchanges of opinion are made public later.

Non-acceptance of secret diplomacy means that in foreign policy the USSR's words are not at variance with its deeds and that our country pursues the aims it proclaims for all to hear. It can be said with confidence that statements issued by the capitals of imperialist powers speak about peace, freedom, democracy, independence and the rights of nations as frequently as our documents on foreign policy. However, the genuine aim of such statements is to hush up the anti-popular aggressive character of imperialist policy.

The ideologists of capitalism are going out of their way to beautify capitalism. They fabricate all kinds of theories, if this word can be applied to ideological poverty, to make capitalism look noble. However, there can be no doubt that, as has been the case until hitherto, they will not succeed in concealing, let alone neutralizing, the exploiter nature of the capitalist system, of imperialism, through the fault of which over 70 million people were killed in the two world wars alone and many more were mutilated. For all its glitter, the gold of all capitalist banks would not cover up the crimes which imperialism has perpetrated or perpetrates.

Ideological emptiness, cultural decay and the mental maiming of the youth constitute a product of capitalist society, which has been built up in the course of more than three centuries and the historical doom of which was pointed out and substantiated by Marx, Engels and Lenin.

As for socialism, in the 65 years since its emergence it has radically transformed our country, which is a great power nowadays, and also a number of other countries which embarked on the construction of socialism and communism. All this has not come by itself. The achievements of our home and foreign policy are a result of the CPSU's farsighted course of principle and the efficient work of the Soviet people engaged in building a communist society.

Marxism–Leninism has irrefutably shown from the positions of science that the transition from capitalism to socialism and communism is an objective and inexorable process in the history of mankind. This is convincingly confirmed by the steady and confident advance of real socialism. Real socialism does not need to resort to force to confirm the correctness of its cause, the justice of its aims or its supremacy as a social system.

Hence our historical optimism which permeates, among other things, also the foreign policy of socialism.

Under the impact of Lenin's revolutionary ideas that transform our life, the world continues to experience profound political and social changes. It is not accidental therefore that the ideological opponents of Leninism mount fierce attacks against it. Unable to counter Lenin's teaching with anything but importunate allegations about the "communist danger" and the "Soviet military threat", calls for an anti-communist crusade, and the inhumane and criminal laudation of militarism and war, they not infrequently engage in the brazen falsification of facts and deceit.

In the world stage, the CPSU and the Soviet state use the priceless gift they received from Lenin—the ability to draw proper conclusions from the past, take precise bearings in the present, and see a grounded revolutionary prospect of the future.

The Leninist strategy of socialism's foreign policy, which the leadership of our Party and state follow undeviatingly, meets with understanding and support on the part of the fraternal socialist countries, all peace-loving nations, liberation movements, all honest people in the world. This strategy opens up boundless opportunities to work for a safer peace and to protect the right of the peoples to independence and social progress. Our country will continue doing what it can to implement this strategy and bring about the triumph of the cause of socialism and a peaceful future for this generation and those that will come after us.

The International Situation and Soviet Foreign Policy

Speech at the Eighth Session of the USSR Supreme Soviet, 16 June 1983

Dear Comrade Andropov,
Pleace accept my congratulations upon your being unanimously elected to the post of Chairman of the Presidium of the USSR Supreme Soviet and allow me to wish you success in your honourable and responsible activities for the good of the Communist Party, the Soviet people and our great motherland. The CPSU and the supreme body of state power of the USSR have entrusted this post to you, being fully convinced that as a Party leader and statesman enjoying deep respect and high prestige in our country and abroad you will cope with the new duties which have been placed upon you by the decision that was adopted today.

Comrade Deputies,
Questions of the international situation and the foreign policy of the Soviet Union are in the centre of attention of our Communist Party, the Supreme Soviet of the USSR and the Soviet government. Soviet people have always been and are deeply interested in the question of what external conditions they live and work in.

The pithy formula—"everything for the sake of man, everything for the benefit of man"—manifests itself also in the aims to the attainment of which our foreign policy is oriented. This is, above all, the elimination of the war danger and the consolidation of peace.

Consistent, tireless struggle for peace has been the heart of Soviet foreign policy since the time of Lenin's Decree on Peace.

Our people, perhaps like no other people, know the price of peace. They not only treasure peaceful life as the most valuable boon but by hard daily work are strengthening their country, the bulwark of international peace.

Expressing the will of the Soviet people, General Secretary of the CPSU Central Committee, Chairman of the Presidium of the USSR Supreme Soviet Yuri Andropov stresses "The Soviet Union will do everything it can to secure a tranquil, peaceful future for the present and coming generations. That is the aim of our policy, and we shall not depart from it."

The most important directions of Soviet foreign policy are inscribed in truly golden letters in the Constitution of the USSR. They are:

Safeguarding the state interests of the Soviet Union and consolidating the positions of world socialism;

Supporting the struggle of peoples for national liberation and social progress; and

Preventing wars of aggression, achieving universal and complete disarmament and consistently implementing the principle of the peaceful coexistence of states with different social systems.

All this is being embodied in the concrete steps being taken by the Soviet state in the world arena.

Permit me, Comrade Deputies, to report to you how the CPSU Central Committee and the Soviet government assess the main trends in the present international situation, what are the most pressing foreign policy problems which we have to solve at the present stage.

We are living in what you might say is not a simple time, in a stormy time. The pace of international life has drastically intensified. Never before have so many states participated in world politics. There are more than a hundred and fifty of them in the world now. Every day one has to deal with an avalanche of problems, and they range from the seabed to outer space.

Today's world presents a varied and complex picture. But we have a tested and reliable instrument enabling us to see beyond the multitude of facts and events the essence of what is happening, to identify the springs of the policy of particular states.

This instrument is the Marxist–Leninist teaching. Soviet foreign policy rests on its granite foundation.

If we are to single out the crux of the matter, the course of international events is determined by the confrontation of two lines: one is directed at the preservation and strengthening of peace, the other, the opposite line, is directed at undermining its mainstays. The Soviet Union, the other socialist countries, the overwhelming majority of states, including those that belong to a different social system, unequivocally come out in favour of peace.

The banner of peace which our Party and our people raised with the victory of the Great October Revolution is in strong hands and they have never dropped it. Three mighty revolutionary streams of our time—world socialism, the international workers' movement and the national liberation forces—have rallied under this banner, which is treasured by all peoples.

Many a time the world has welcomed the Soviet Union's acts and proposals which clearly breathe the spirit of peace.

It is Soviet foreign policy initiatives that have given life to a whole number of major international treaties and agreements—on the non-proliferation of nuclear weapons, on the prohibition of nuclear weapon tests in three environments, on the prohibition of stationing weapons of mass annihilation on the seabed and the ocean floor, on the prohibition of bacteriological weapons, and so on. Concluded in the 'sixties and 'seventies, they are fulfilling their designation to this day.

The special importance of the Soviet–American accords in the field of strategic arms, which were reached before the coming to power of the present Administration in the United States, should be stressed. Operative to this day is the treaty on the limitation of anti-ballistic missile systems and the agreement on the limitation of strategic arms (SALT I). As for the SALT II Treaty, on which abuse is being heaped today in Washington by its opponents, it also could have become a serious accomplishment both for the Soviet Union and for the United States and for the whole world.

On the basis of Soviet proposals documents highly charged with positive impact on the overall situation in the world are being adopted in the United Nations year after year. Among them mention should be made, above all, of the declaration on the strengthening of international security and the declaration on the prevention of nuclear war.

The fact that our proposals invariably get extensive support in the United Nations, where the majority of the world's states vote for them, shows that they are of a topical nature for the solution of pressing problems of concern to all peoples.

The outstanding role of the Soviet Union and other socialist countries in the success of the Conference on Security and Co-operation in Europe is known. We adhere to the cause of continuing the all-European process. It is exactly from this position that the USSR speaks at the Madrid meeting as well, pressing for it to conclude with an agreement on convening a conference on confidence-building measures, security and disarmament in Europe.

The signing by the Soviet Union, the German Democratic Republic, Poland and Czechoslovakia of treaties with the Federal Republic of Germany, and also the conclusion of the quadripartite agreement on West Berlin became an inseparable part of the process of *détente* in the continent of Europe.

Today the countries of the East and West of Europe are bound by a series of treaties and agreements embracing very diverse spheres of relations. Among them mention must be made of the long-term programmes for economic, scientific and technical co-operation signed by the Soviet Union with the Federal Republic of Germany, France, Italy, Greece, Finland and some other countries.

At the Vienna talks on the reduction of armed forces and armaments in Central Europe the USSR together with other socialist countries has recently submitted new proposals that make it possible to overcome the barriers artificially erected by Western states and to find a practical solution to that problem.

Associated with the name of our country is the adoption by the United Nations of the Declaration on the Granting of Independence to Colonial Countries and Peoples, which gave a mighty impetus to the worldwide movement to liquidate the colonial system of imperialism. The policy of the USSR, which proposed the adoption of this decision, dealt an immensely powerful blow at this system of oppression hated by the peoples, this system for the enslavement of more than half mankind by a small group of states.

In the overall complex of efforts made by the Soviet Union in the interests of peace a big place is taken by actions to remove seats of tension and war danger, to achieve a peaceful settlement of disputes and conflicts arising between states.

All this constitutes the impressive credit side of Soviet foreign policy and nobody will succeed in belittling this asset of our policy. The international policy of the USSR, its diplomacy will continue to remain equal to the tasks facing it.

The cause of fraternal friendship and co-operation with countries of socialism always has held and will hold a special place of priority in the policy of the CPSU and the Soviet state.

The Soviet Union is tirelessly strengthening close all-round ties with these countries on the basis of the principle of socialist internationalism, and is actively participating in economic integration and in the international socialist division of labour.

The countries of the socialist community are fruitfully co-operating in all fields of life. Their fraternal alliance finds its embodiment in the Warsaw Treaty Organization, the Council for Mutual Economic Assistance, in the system of bilateral treaties on friendship, co-operation and mutual assistance.

The ties and contacts between our countries are manifesting themselves in a many-sided way. Bilateral and multilateral meetings at a summit level are being held regularly. Very important questions of relations between socialist states are studied and resolved during these meetings, and topical problems of international politics are also discussed. The results of the Meeting of the Political Consultative Committee of the Warsaw Treaty countries, held in Prague, are in this sense characteristic.

In-depth consultations on questions relating to the field of foreign policy are conducted at the Committee of Foreign Ministers. The Committee of Defence Ministers is acting vigorously in the interests of ensuring the security of Warsaw Treaty countries.

Economic plans are being successfully co-ordinated and the practice of jointly working out solutions to key tasks of economic development is being expanded. Preparations are in hand for holding a summit economic conference of CMEA member states.

Along with Warsaw Treaty countries our relations of fraternal co-operation are developing with Mongolia, Cuba, Vietnam, Laos and Kampuchea.

Our ties with Yugoslavia continue to strengthen. We firmly support the struggle of the Democratic People's Republic of Korea for the peaceful, democratic, unification of the homeland.

The CPSU and the Soviet state sincerely wish the development and strengthening of relations with all socialist countries.

As before, the Soviet Union is for the normalization of relations with the People's Republic of China on the basis of reciprocity, for seeking possibilities of gradually expanding bilateral ties and contacts. We stand for continuing the Soviet–Chinese political consultations that have begun and would like them to lead to positive results. We are confident that normalization and improvement of mutual relations accords with the cardinal interests of the peoples of both countries.

The class enemy is putting the emphasis on weakening and, if possible, splitting the socialist community. And although this invariably ends in fiasco for him, he does not cease his importunate attempts to achieve his aim.

Hostile actions of a political and economic nature are being taken against the countries of socialism, ideological subversion is being carried out against them, and resort is made to subversive actions and other methods that are impermissible in the practice of inter-state relations. This is seen with particular clarity in the policy of the West in respect of the Polish People's Republic.

Poland, as is stressed by its leadership, and this has been repeatedly stated also on behalf of its allies, the Warsaw Treaty countries, has been and will be an inalienable part of the socialist community. Only those who have become hopelessly ossified in their hostility to socialism can fail to understand this. This hostility impairs their sight and obscures the real state of affairs from them.

In words and in deeds the socialist community has proved more than once that it is capable of coping successfully with everything that impedes its advance. All attempts to inflict damage on the lawful interests of this community and to test its strength have been smashed to smithereens.

Let nobody have any doubt about our common resolve to uphold the inviolability of our borders, to ensure the reliability of all the links comprising the community, to defend our socialist gains. The fraternal countries are guarding their unity as the apple of their eyes and will guard it in every way, and there is no force capable of disrupting it.

"As we assess the present day of our countries, we can say with satisfaction," Yuri Andropov noted, "that . . . the socialist community is a powerful and healthy organism which is playing an enormous and beneficial role in the world of today."

Our country, our allies have one course in international affairs, the course for peace and friendship among peoples, the course for ensuring that when outstanding issues arise countries will strive not to cross swords but to solve them by peaceful means, at the negotiating table.

It was precisely such an approach that was confirmed in the Declaration adopted by the Prague meeting of the Political Consultative Committee of the Warsaw Treaty states.

The socialist community is increasingly asserting itself as the leading factor in exerting a positive influence on world development. It firmly holds the initiative in the search for solutions to pressing international problems.

Our resolute course for peace, for ensuring international security is opposed by the policy of aggressive imperialist forces. That policy is the source of the serious worsening of the international situation in recent years, in which tension at times reaches dangerous limits.

This is happening because representatives of circles with sharply expressed imperial ambitions, preaching the cult of force in international relations and claiming to remake the world according to their own standards have now appeared at the helm of Washington's foreign policy. The turn in US policy towards the attainment of military superiority is precisely a consequence of this.

The inspirers of this policy are pouring out torrents of slander in their attempt to prove that the threat to peace allegedly comes from the Soviet Union while the West is only reacting to that challenge.

If cause and effect changed places in their contentions about who is creating the threat to peace, that would be exactly in accordance with the real state of affairs.

Generally speaking, deceiving people as to the foreign policy course of the United States and Soviet foreign policy has long—and, it can be said, tenaciously—been resorted to by Washington. There is every sign that it has no intention of discarding it, hoping to continue to confuse a part of public opinion in the West and to implement its militarist programmes.

Resort is also made to deception in interpreting the events of today as well as events that have become part of history. But real facts, for instance, the facts of the post-war period, convincingly show the origin of the danger to the peaceful life of peoples.

Let us recall that the United States started laying the foundations of its hegemonist global policy directed above all against the USSR at a time when the flames of the Second World War had not yet died out everywhere. From the very outset our country condemned that policy, noting that it flagrantly contradicted the bonds of alliance linking the states of the anti-Hitler coalition and their commitments under Allied agreements on post-war organization.

Hundreds of military bases were scattered throughout the world, mostly close to Soviet borders. The creation of military blocs also began. Thus came into being the North Atlantic Alliance which has sworn loyalty to the positions of strength policy worshipped to this day by the leaders of the NATO bloc as the supreme deity.

From the very first post-war years, resorting to political pressure, diplomacy and bags of money, the United States set out to impose an arms race upon the world. This was at a time when the states who had won the war faced the tasks of arms reductions and disarmament. Since that time, year after year the US has continuously striven to increase the scale of arms production, especially the production of mass annihilation weapons.

Some public figures in the West strive to rewrite history, to put the facts upside down in a bid to whitewash Washington's policy on questions of the arms race. They resort to this means, above all when it comes to nuclear weapons. But those who were the first to use them against people will indelibly remain in mankind's memory. No rhetoric, even the most lavish dose of it, will be able to wash away the strain on those who perpetrated this crime.

A different, contrary stand was taken by our country on matters of disarmament as a whole, and on questions pertaining to nuclear weapons. Peoples well remember that no sooner had the curtain fallen over the tragedy just experienced by mankind that the Soviet Union was the first to raise its mighty voice against these weapons.

Already at that time the Soviet state declared that the use of atomic energy for military purposes was incompatible with the conscience of mankind.

It came out with a proposal on concluding an international convention to ban the military uses of atomic energy for all time, switching it over to peaceful purposes only.

This demand met with wide support from all honest people on earth, including such outstanding scientists in the West as Einstein, Oppenheimer and Joliot-Curie.

The position adopted in this connection by the United States is well-known. It was not at all part of the intentions of those who determined its policy to give up atomic weapons or to prohibit them. The temptation of dominating the world by threatening to use these weapons proved more compelling than the realization of the need to ban them.

Attempts are now being made to whitewash such a policy by alleging that the American side never harboured evil intentions as far as nuclear weapons are concerned. It is stated, sometimes at the highest level, that, at one time possessing a monopoly of the atomic bomb, the United States could, if it wished, have dictated its conditions to others, including the USSR, but that it decided against such a course out of lofty moral considerations.

There is not a grain of truth in this argument. And one should never have portrayed virtue where none has existed.

People using the above argument would be well advised to take a look at the developments from another angle.

What could the Soviet Union have done when fascist Germany had already been routed, and what frontiers could have been reached by the mighty wave of the Soviet armies who had just ground the Hitler military machine to smithereens, if the USSR had not been true to its Alliance obligations?

So why do the leaders deciding US foreign policy today need to pass off falsehood is presented in elegant packaging—and with references to some noble motives?

Despite the stubborn desire of the imperialist circles throughout the post-war period to achieve military superiority over the countries of socialism, a balance of forces was achieved between the Warsaw Treaty Organization and NATO. It is this military-strategic parity that has served and must serve as a reliable guarantee of international stability.

The Soviet Union is in favour of proceeding, starting from the existing parity, along the road of arms limitation and reduction so that at any given moment the balance is preserved but at an increasingly lower level. This would mean using for the purposes of peace—and not letting it slip—the truly historic opportunity offered by the existing parity.

Our country is doing and will continue to do everything to retain such parity. This has once again been clearly stated by Yuri Andropov at the plenary meeting of the CPSU Central Committee, which has just ended. This position is a realistic, politically and scientifically substantiated one and promoted the interests of both sides and the cause of peace throughout the world.

It would seem that all those who bear the main responsibility for resolving the acute problems facing mankind should adhere to a similar position. In Washington, however, they think not in terms of parity, but in terms of superiority. There they are banking on changing the strategic alignment of forces in their favour.

This is the principal objective of US policy in international affairs. It is aimed, above all, against the Soviet Union and the other socialist countries. But it is also aimed against the world as a whole.

For this, programmes are being implemented at an accelerated rate to build up all types of armaments, above all, nuclear ones. They have also launched a five-year project for "rearming America", and they are going to earmark over 1,500,000 million dollars for it. In the five years it is planned to spend on weapons of destruction a sum equal to that spent in the previous twenty years.

They are not only arming themselves. They are spurring on their allies to do the same, demanding that they keep increasing their military budgets. In order to upset strategic parity, they are ready to go to any length to get new nuclear missiles to Western Europe and to deploy them there.

Monstrous as it sounds, people in Washington do not rule out the possibility of being the first to use nuclear weapons.

What a variety of doctrines has been spawned by the inflamed imagination of some strategists—including "limited nuclear war", a "protracted nuclear conflict" and "first nuclear strike"—in the vain aim of gaining the upper hand in a nuclear clash.

People in Washington ought to know that there will be no winners in a nuclear war—this is the opinion of scientists, of serious politicians and of all those who, without concealing the truth, take a realistic approach to assessing the formidable danger of a nuclear conflict.

Today a militarist intoxication, one may say, pervades the political atmosphere in the United States. Nuclear war is pronounced to be permissible and even expedient. They are trying to impress it on people that such a war is not so horrifying.

And this is being done in a sort of frenzied state by politicians of the highest rank, and by generals, by even minor officials, to say nothing about candidates for such posts.

So, what is being pursued is shameless war propaganda. No account is taken of the fact that it was prohibited by a special United Nations decision which, incidentally, the United States also voted for. That decision was adopted on the Soviet Union's initiative.

If one takes only the attitudes of the United States and of the USSR to the propaganda of nuclear war, will it not be clear whose position on this question is inhuman, and whose is humane, meeting the aspirations of all peoples?

The question arises: in some of the Western capitals are they aware that nuclear war is the gravest crime against humanity?

This political course is causing alarm among sober-minded leaders in the United States itself, and in other countries of the West. Their voices at times do not come through clear enough because of the din of the militarist drums, but the voices are there, and they are growing increasingly stronger, and they reflect sentiments widespread among the influential public segments of these states.

The wave of the anti-nuclear and anti-war movement that has arisen in the West is a kind of a popular referendum. The movement's participants do not hesitate on the question of war and peace. They declare themselves for peace, against the plans of war preparations and the continuance of the lunatic arms race.

Attempts are being made to claim that this movement is obeying the "hand of Moscow". To us, naturally, it is flattering that peace actions should be associated with the policy of the Soviet Union. But the "hand of Moscow" has nothing to do with all this. Broad circles of the public in their anti-war actions are spontaneously reflecting the people's desire to defend their right to life.

Yes, precisely the right to life. It is well known what shameless use is made of the question of human rights in some countries, how it is drowned in demagogy. And when actual human rights are at issue, above all, the right to life, these rights go unheeded.

The Soviet Union rejects the very idea of nuclear war as reckless and calls for it—as criminal. We proceed from the assumption that everything must be done so nuclear weapons are never used. This is the deep belief of the Soviet leadership, of the whole of our Party and of the whole of the Soviet people.

One may say with a clear conscience that the Soviet Union puts all the authority of its foreign policy and the whole of its immense peaceable potential on the balance in favour of peace and the prevention of a nuclear catastrophe.

Committing itself unilaterally not to be the first to use nuclear weapons, the USSR has once again confirmed that concern for removing the war threat remains the chief element of its policy. The world applauds the courage and the noble nature of our action.

The Soviet Union has a right to expect a similar step to be taken by other nuclear powers which have failed to assume a similar commitment. No reasons or excuses can be stronger than the need to prevent nuclear war.

The NATO countries are trying to call into question the commitment we have assumed and to belittle its significance. They are adducing the argument that the USSR allegedly reserves freedom of action for itself in the use of conventional weapons in which it is alleged to possess a superiority. This argument is designed to mislead people.

The Soviet Union and its friends refute such assertions in a most convincing manner. In the Political Declaration, adopted by the Warsaw Treaty member countries in Prague, they proposed than an agreement be concluded between the states members of that treaty and those of NATO, which would contain a reciprocal commitment not to resort to the use of any weapons—either nuclear or conventional. In other words, not to use force at all in relations between them.

No small a period of time has elapsed already since the proposal was put on the table of our Western partners. And if anything in it is not clear to anyone, we and our allies are ready to provide the necessary explanation. We are prepared to embark on negotiations forthwith, and we once again call on the NATO countries to consider our initiative seriously.

Their reaction, contained in the communiqué of the June session of the NATO Council, is quite incomprehensible, to put it frankly. It indicates that, in all probability, they are still unable or reluctant to admit how radically the situation in Europe and all over the world would turn towards improvement if it proved possible to agree on the non-use of force between the two groups of countries.

Long ago Lenin said that "disarmament is the ideal of socialism". And we take pride in the fact that for over sixty years our country has been consistently advancing proposals designed to end the arms race and to achieve disarmament.

Today Soviet initiatives and proposals comprise an all-embracing programme of measures—from individual steps in the field of arms limitation to general and complete disarmament, including a total ban on nuclear weapons, and their destruction.

We hear allegations—and this is said precisely by those who are clearly showing a deficit as regards their own initiatives—that our proposals are not radical enough. But the world knows that not a single country has done so much as our socialist state has done to have the sword of war buried in the ground.

The fact is that it was the USSR that proposed the most radical of possible solutions—general and complete disarmament. What can be more radical? In the West they do not like to recall it frequently. But the proposal is there, and it remains in force.

They also say that in tackling the disarmament issues, be that general and complete disarmament or partial disarmament, the principal stumbling block is the question of control. It is well known, however, that the Soviet Union has submitted a proposal on universal and comprehensive control. This proposal also remains in force. Verification to us has never been an obstacle to fulfilling agreements.

They also say: general and complete disarmament combined with universal and comprehensive control—is not too much to propose since this cannot be achieved at one. The Soviet Union's reply is: it agrees to a stage-by-stage approach, and we have already put forward a relevant proposal.

The fact of the matter is, however, that neither the first, nor the second, nor the third has been accepted.

Thousands of speeches and statements have been made, all designed to hide what is obvious, but they have failed to achieve their end. World public opinion regards the Soviet Union as a resolute champion of disarmament.

And what is the record of the United States today in this respect?

It has derailed the SALT II Treaty, broken off a whole series of negotiations which were gathering momentum or were close to achieving practical results.

It refuses to resume talks on the complete and universal prohibition of nuclear weapons tests, on limiting the shipments and sales to other countries of conventional weapons, on limiting military activity in the Indian Ocean and on a number of other problems.

It refuses to engage in negotiations. And it says precisely this: I just do not want to and that's that! This alone speaks for itself.

From what has been said about the difficulties encountered in the struggle to end the arms race and to achieve disarmament, it does not at all follow that this struggle must be relaxed. On the contrary, it must be pursued with still greater energy and persistence; we and our allies have both. The problems that remain unsolved and the existence of a big threat to peace oblige us to do this.

The USSR has repeatedly stated and states once again that in the present situation it would be senseless for anyone to count on attaining military superiority. The USSR has never striven and does not strive for this. And we do not recognize any other's right to military superiority. Our country has all the necessary resources—material and intellectual— to prevent this from happening. And the Soviet Union shall prevent it.

For responsible leaders, the more so for those standing at the helm of the policy of states, it should be clear that the only reasonable road is to seek and find mutually acceptable solutions. This is the only reliable road.

The main thing is to conduct honest talks, not to try to outwit the partner, not to try to present deceit for truth and vice versa. Agreements must be based on the principle of equality and equal security. The Soviet Union will not retreat from this principle. And it would be good if Washington realized this.

It is impossible to overestimate the importance of resolving the problems of limiting and reducing strategic arms, and also limiting nuclear arms in Europe. The US Administration is pursuing an obstructionistic line at the Soviet–American talks on these questions that are now going on in Geneva. In contrast to our position of achieving far-reaching mutual reductions of delivery vehicles and warheads to agreed-upon levels, they propose to the Soviet Union something which is unacceptable—the Soviet Union's unilateral disarmament.

Steeped in the same spirit is the face-lifted position on strategic arms announced recently by the American President who tried to present it as an expression of US flexibility at the talks. This position is fully tailored to suit the current further expansion of American military programmes.

Washington's approach remains unchanged: to subject to limitations only specific components of strategic forces suiting the American side, while leaving other components outside the framework of agreement, simply turning a blind eye to them. In effect, the United States would like to destroy the existing structure of the Soviet strategic potential, while retaining a free hand to build up its own corresponding armaments.

So flexibility here is purely for show. The American position does not offer a way leading towards mutually acceptable agreements. Judging by everything, no such aim is set. The intention is to lull or, to be precise, to deceive public opion, to neutralize the mounting opposition to Washington's militaristic preparations.

Neither can the proposals on confidence-building measures advertised by Washington conceal the unconstructive and lopsided nature of the line pursued by the United States. The point is that the American proposals, unlike the much more far-reaching proposals made by us, do not limit the military activity of the sides in any way and actually amount to an exchange of information between them on some types of such activity.

Besides, the American side hushes up the fact that it rejects the USSR's proposals providing for the prevention of crisis situations and for the strengthening of trust.

In short, the Soviet Union stands for preventing dangers and crisis situations, while the United States proposes a mere exchange of information on this.

It is becoming increasingly clear that the present American Administration is pursuing a course not of reaching agreements but of fulfilling its programmes of building up strategic arms and deploying new medium-range missiles in Western Europe.

This course is clearly seen also in the statement adopted late in May at the meeting in Williamsburg and in the communiqué of the session of the NATO Council that has just ended. They contain quite a few pompous words about the West's striving for talks with the Soviet Union, for "arms reduction" and for "lessening the danger of war". But these words do not change the militaristic, aggressive essence of the course steered by the United States and NATO.

The security interests of the USSR and its allies compel us, as the Soviet government warned in its May 28 statement, to take counter-measures to strengthen our defence capability.

These measures, however, are forced upon us. Their sole aim is to prevent an upsetting of the existing balance of forces. While issuing this warning the Soviet Union at the same time reaffirms the invariableness of its principled approach both to the limitation and reduction of strategic arms and to the limitation of medium-range nuclear arms in Europe.

It is not yet too late to stop the dangerous development of the international situation if the United States and its NATO allies respond to the constructive proposals of the USSR. We like to hope that common sense will prevail among our partners.

As a first step, it would be reasonable to reach agreement at least on halting the future stockpiling of nuclear arms by putting a quantitative and qualitative freeze on the nuclear arsenals of the sides. Such a step, which is on the whole easy to carry out and also effective, would create more favourable conditions for the conduct of talks as well.

Many politicians in the West are aware of the need for implementing such a measure. The idea of a freeze is supported by broad sections of the public in the United States and in Western Europe.

A complete and universal ban on the tests of nuclear weapons would help considerably to block the possibilities for the development of new types of such weapons and strengthen the regime of their non-proliferation. The Soviet Union considers that the tripartite talks with the United States and Great Britain on the elaboration of a respective treaty should be resumed.

It is worth noting in this connection the Soviet–US treaties on limiting underground nuclear weapons tests and on nuclear explosions for peaceful purposes, which have not so far entered into force. The US Administration refuses to have them ratified. We again express the hope that it will modify its attitude to these two important agreements, and that they will enter into force.

The problem of maintaining military-strategic stability at lower levels involves a complex set of questions. Many of them are closely interconnected. Such is the state of correlation between offensive and defensive strategic arms.

The US Administration took a step toward severing this interconnection by deciding to start the development of a large-scale ABM system. This was done not at all for defensive purposes, but as part of a vast militaristic programme.

The Soviet Union believes that measures must be taken to prevent the arms race from developing in new directions. We proposed the following to the US government: let Soviet and American scientists, specialists in the field, get together and discuss the possible implications of establishing a large-scale ABM system. So far we have received no answer from the US Administration.

It would be a tragedy for mankind if outer space became a sphere of contention between states, and, worse still, a sphere of their military clashes. Only with a total lack of understanding of the grave responsibility involved and with extreme recklessness can one steer a course that would make the space above mankind pose a threat to its existence.

The priority task in this connection is to conclude an international treaty on the non-deployment of weapons of any type in outer space, which has been proposed by the Soviet Union. We are prepared to go even further—to agree on banning in general the use of force both in space and from space with respect to the Earth. We are prepared to enter into talks on this subject without a moment's delay.

Facing the world in all its magnitude is the problem of the earliest prohibition and liquidation of chemical weapons, one of the most barbarous means of the annihilation of people.

It is known to all that not so long ago Washington did not hesitate to use such weapons in the war against the Vietnamese people, and this shameful page cannot be torn out of the history book. Chemical weapons continue to be actively stockpiled in the US, and their increasingly lethal types are being developed.

Consistently calling for the removal of chemical weapons from the arsenals of states, the USSR has put forward concrete proposals. We hope that the states—our partners in negotiations—will agree, and this is what we are urging them to do, to elaborate an international convention on banning and destroying these weapons.

It would be useful to take parallel steps, leading to the same objective, within the European continent. The Warsaw Treaty member countries propose that Europe be made totally free of chemical weapons.

The realities of the present international situation call for the exercise of special restraint not only in the field of arms and military policy, but in all spheres of relations between states, above all when the interests of countries with different social systems are involved.

Neither group of states, nor the world as a whole for that matter, stand to gain from a situation in which antagonism in relations between them is artificially stirred up, different kinds of provocations and unseemly methods are resorted to, mistrust and suspicion are sown, and in which not even a minimal amount of courtesy in inter-state relations is observed.

This atmosphere makes it all the more difficult to solve not only questions of ensuring international security, but also such global problems as energy, food, environmental protection, and the exploration of oceans and outer space for peaceful purposes, in which all peoples and countries, regardless of their social system, are interested.

Regrettably, certain political leaders still cannot or do not want to understand this even if they claim that they are pursuing a policy pleasing to God himself.

What is the main creed of their policy? They often formulate it with a flourish. It is open advocacy of the rolling back of socialism as a socio-political system. And when they are carried away, they even voice the hope for eliminating it altogether.

In the past there had also been figures who went so far as to predict the impending doom of socialism. Each of them tried to prove that it was he who saw everything with an eagle's eye. Today there are places in the West where statements to this effect have become all but a fad.

Such figures invent whatever you like. Today they say that it is necessary to stop trade with socialism, tomorrow—that it would be a good thing to block its access to science, and the day after tomorrow they are ready to launch a campaign—more than that, a crusade—against it. There is a lot of fantasy in all this but it does not get off the ground.

One may say without the risk of exaggeration that politicians who allow themselves with such ease and even frivolity to make such statements are caricaturing their own hostility towards socialism. These crystal gazers fully deserve to be painted by our famed Kukryniksy cartoonists.

Those who lay claim to the laurels of theorists have rather vague ideas about the laws of development of human society, to say the least. If they want to show in this way their unwillingness to know these laws we, naturally, cannot be much troubled by that. Socialism is gaining and will continue to gain strength. The world is developing according to the objective laws discovered by Marxism–Leninism.

There is, however, another aspect of this: differences in the social systems of states and ideological divergencies are being turned into a basis on which foreign policy is formulated and questions of war and peace decided.

Many high-sounding words are pronounced in Washington in extolling this policy. They go so far as to proclaim its being highly moral. They believe that one only has to declare one's actions on the international scene to be the utmost in morality and no other arguments are called for.

But who will believe in the morality of a policy that is aimed at preparing for war and at the first use of nuclear weapons?

And is it moral to continue speeding up the production of weapons intended for the mass annihilation of people at a time when mountains of weaponry have already been piled up in the world.

Is it moral to resort to deliberate deception by saying that the threat to peace is posed by those who are working tirelessly for peace and for preventing war?

And is it moral to toy with the lives of one's own people by basing one's policy on the admissibility of nuclear war while knowing perfectly well what such a war would mean for that people?

Is it moral to claim as all but its hunting grounds foreign lands lying hundreds and thousands of kilometres away from the US and to declare whole regions of the world to be spheres of its "vital interests", arrogating to itself the right to interfere in the internal affairs of other peoples up to the point of military intervention?

Today Washington is at odds with morality in its foreign policy. It has no room for it there.

The policy pursued by the US Administration is fraught with consequences that are dangerous for all mankind. It is posing a grave threat to peace. The peoples are growing increasingly aware of this.

Concern for peace must now be placed above everything else. This is the duty of all those who are involved in major political decision-making. The world expects the US leaders to show greater responsibility and common sense. The solution of acute international problems can only be achieved through halting the arms race and improving the political climate in the world, through a relaxation of tension.

Attempts to insist on approaches which would meet only the interests of the US and the NATO bloc and which would prejudice the legitimate interests of the USSR and its allies are hopeless.

The Soviet Union consistently calls for normal and stable relations with capitalist countries. These relations benefit both those countries and us.

We want to keep our relations with the United States on an even keel, being aware that this is important for preventing war. It is our belief that the United States of America should also proceed from the objective need to maintain normal relations with the USSR. The common interests of both countries would be promoted by eliminating the threat of nuclear catastrophe. All the peoples, the states of all continents have a vital interest in this.

We appreciate the relations that have emerged between the Soviet Union and Canada, which is not so far away from us. We express the hope for reciprocity, for we want these relations to be maintained and to continue to develop.

The West European countries are a large and influential group of states. We have fairly developed relations of co-operation with almost all of them, more with some, less with others.

A keen and quite understandable awareness of the danger posed by the existing international situation has become widespread in that region of the world. The Soviet Union expresses the hope that the West

European countries will not allow themselves to be dragged into plans posing a grave threat to peace.

A new government came to power in Federal Germany at the end of the last year, and it is introducing its own nuances, as they say, into the policy of that country. We are for maintaining relations with Federal Germany in the same key in which they have been built throughout the past few years, in particular, for widening economic co-operation.

But the most important field, of course, concerns questions of security. The Soviet Union will give priority attention to them in its contacts with the present government of Federal Germany, in particular, during the forthcoming talks in the course of an official visit by Chancellor Helmut Kohl to the USSR.

Our country is for maintaining good relations and fruitful co-operation with France, jointly with which a good deal has been done on a reciprocal basis to promote the interests of peace and co-operation among European states, and also with Italy, Britain, Spain, and all the other West European countries, both large and those which are referred to as medium-sized and small. Naturally, these relations can develop if those states also want it.

We say with satisfaction that we are in favour of maintaining and deepening relations with our good neighbour, Finland. And the results of the recent visit by Finnish President Mauno Koivisto to the USSR, his meetings with Yuri Andropov and the extending of the Soviet–Finnish Treaty of Friendship, Co-operation and Mutual Assistance for another 20 years formalized during the visit, put relations between the two countries on an even firmer basis.

As before, we believe it important to maintain normal relations with our neighbour—Japan. The interests of the peoples of the two countries, the interests of peace and security in the Far East and in Asia as a whole would be promoted by good-neighbourly co-operation between the Soviet Union and Japan.

However, in the recent period its leadership has been tilting towards building up a military potential, revitalizing militarist tendencies in the country and joining in the global strategy of confrontation imposed by Washington. Obviously, there are still persons in Japan who are nostalgic for the past, a past that had often brought sufferings to the Japanese people.

If Tokyo makes a choice in favour of peace and good-neighbourliness, the USSR will be Japan's dependable partner in developing extensive mutual contacts in the political, economic and other fields.

However differently relations between the Soviet Union and capitalist countries may develop, we are following and will continue to follow consistently the line for ensuring that the principle of peaceful coexistence, the most important foundation of the Soviet foreign policy course, remain dominant in relations between countries having different social systems.

The peoples struggling for the assertion of their national independence and for social progress are coming out ever more resolutely to the forefront of world politics. They, and they alone, decide which road of development to follow. Outside intervention in the internal affairs of sovereign states is impermissible. This is an inviolable provision of the UN Charter and it must be respected.

However, Washington is still quite bad at telling its own affairs from those of others. The Soviet Union, like all states cherishing their sovereignty, independence and freedom, resolutely rejects this policy and practice.

The attempts to impose anti-Arab deals and to advance plans for a Middle East settlement which ignore the legitimate interests of the Palestinian people are causing the growing opposition of the Arabs. This policy has brought about the situation in which Lebanon is being torn apart before everyone's eyes and in which it has been forced at gunpoint into capitulatory agreements with Israel.

Syria, which is strengthening its defences and pursuing a principled policy with regard to the affairs in the Middle East, is now being made a target of pressure and open threats.

The role of the Soviet Union in that region, adjacent to our borders, is not merely the role of a passive onlooker. Our country has formulated just principles for a political settlement, including a proposal to convene an international conference on the Middle East. They are known to the whole world.

Washington and Tel Aviv are putting obstacles in the way of a Middle East settlement. Peace can be brought to the Middle East by such a settlement which, instead of imperialist arbitrariness and actions carried out by Israel with impunity, backed by expansionistic ambitions, will lead to the liberation of all the occupied Arab lands and ensure the establishment of an independent Arab Palestinian state. Much depends on the Arab countries themselves, on their cohesion in the struggle against the forces of aggression.

The conflict between Iran and Iraq is a senseless one. Whoever may oppose an end to the war, takes an unreasonable stand. The continuation of the conflict only plays into the hands of the imperialist forces who are interested in weakening of both states.

We are linked by relations of friendship with Iraq. We are for maintaining normal relations of friendship with Iran as well. The Soviet Union would like to see Iran remain an independent state and has always worked for relations of good-neighbourliness with it. Regrettably, actions like those recently taken by the Iranian side with regard to a group of employees of Soviet organizations in Iran do not at all contribute to the development of such contacts between our countries. In short, the USSR will act with account taken of whether Iran wishes to respond on a reciprocal basis and maintain normal relations with us or whether it has different intentions.

The Soviet Union fully supports the programme for a political settlement put forth by the Democratic Republic of Afghanistan. On its basis it is possible to reach agreement on a solution of questions related to the external aspect of the Afghan problem. And precisely to the external aspect since internal matters must be solved only by the Afghans themselves.

We hope that the contacts established between Afghanistan and Pakistan through the representative of the United Nations Secretary-General will bring positive results.

Our country is and will continue to be a good friend of Afghanistan — an independent, non-aligned state.

An easing of tension in Southeast Asia is being obstructed by interference by external forces into the affairs of that region. The USSR expresses full solidarity with the proposals of the countries of Indo-China aimed at normalizing the situation in Southeast Asia and turning it into a zone of peace, good-neighbourliness and co-operation.

The United States is developing on an increasing scale a campaign of threats and crude pressure against sovereign states and national liberation movements in the region of Central America and the Caribbean. Demonstrated here before the whole world is the oppressive imperialist policy of interference aimed at keeping anti-popular juntas, bloody puppet régimes in power in some countries.

To justify these actions recourse is made to utter lies. Once again the usual invention about "intrigues" by Moscow and Havana is trotted out.

Without batting an eyelid some people also hold forth on the subject of democracy and human rights. In El Salvador these are being introduced by force of arms.

There is also the desire to "teach democracy" to sovereign Nicaragua by arming bands of mercenaries which intrude into its territory. The whole world resolutely condemns the aggressive policy and terrorist activity of the United States against Nicaragua. Aggression against that country has actually been organized by the United States of America, and it bears full responsibility for it.

One can say with confidence that such a policy cannot crush the irrepressible striving of the peoples of Latin America for independence and freedom. The Soviet Union thinks that the Central American and Caribbean countries should be left in peace and that outside interference in their internal affairs must cease.

We regard with understanding the efforts undertaken by Mexico and some other Latin American states in the interests of a political settlement of the situation in that region and of safeguarding the sovereign rights of its peoples and states.

A tense situation still remains in the South of Africa. The interests of peace demand that the Republic of South Africa stop its aggression against neighbouring states and withdraw its troops from the territory of the People's Republic of Angola, that the decisions of the United Nations Organization on granting independence to the people of Namibia be fulfilled and that an end be put to such shameful phenomena as racism and the system of apartheid.

There are more than fifty states on the African continent and our country has normal diplomatic relations with almost all of them. It is not from textbooks but from the history of arduous struggle for independence, against the yoke of colonialism that the peoples of these countries come to know well the Soviet Union's contribution to this struggle that mightily flared up under the impact of the Great October Revolution.

Today too, we regard support for the liberation movements of the peoples of Asia, Africa and Latin America, the struggle for the strengthening of the independence and sovereignty of the countries of these regions of the world as our internationalist duty.

The Soviet Union welcomes the fact that an increasing role in international affairs is being played by states belonging to the non-aligned movement which is coming out ever more actively from anti-imperialist and anti-war positions, and this is confirmed by the results of the recent forum of these countries in New Delhi.

We express solidarity with the struggle of the developing countries for a just international economic order. Not all of them have liberated themselves from exploitation by some states, by their monopoly capital.

Relations of friendship link us with such a large country as India, co-operation with which promotes stability in Asia and universal peace. Soviet–Indian relations rest on the fruitful basis of the Treaty of Peace, Friendship and Co-operation. These relations have withstood a good test and both sides value this. The Soviet Union is for the strengthening of friendship with India.

We have concluded treaties on friendship and co-operation with quite a number of non-aligned states, which is an indicator of the high level of development of our relations with them. Among the non-aligned countries with which the USSR has established good relations mention should be made of Syria, Algeria, South Yemen, Libya, Angola, Ethiopia, Mozambique and the People's Republic of the Congo.

The Soviet Union's international ties with states of a broad political spectrum indicate a recognition of our state's high prestige.

They indicate an understanding of the fact that without its participation not a single major question of world politics can be solved and in practice is not solved. That is how it should be.

Comrade deputies,

The CPSU Central Committee and the Soviet government regard the international situation of our state as strong.

It is strong in the sense that we have the ability to protect our achievements in building communist society. The Soviet people have always had enough stamina at any turn of history, however sharp.

It is strong in the sense that Soviet foreign policy is efficient in upholding peace because it expresses the innermost aspirations of peoples.

The strong impact of Soviet foreign policy is inseparably linked with our achievements in fulfilling national economic development plans, increasing the productivity of social labour, enhancing order and discipline, improving the people's welfare, developing socialist democracy, and strengthening the defence of the country, which is a constant concern of the Party and the state.

The Communist Party of the Soviet Union and its headquarters, the Central Committee, are strong not only because of the lofty goals and ideals for the attainment of which the Soviet people are working but also because of their unity and their unflagging will to lead the country along the road charted by Lenin's genius.

The effectiveness of our policy both in domestic and in foreign affairs is fortified by the heroic work of the Soviet people, by every ton of metal and oil produced, by every kernel of grain grown, by every kilowatt-hour of electricity generated and by every machine tool and grain harvester manufactured, by every discovery made by our scientists.

As Yuri Andropov said, the immutable goals of our foreign policy are to ensure a lasting peace and to protect the right of peoples to independence and social progress. In striving for these goals, the leadership of the Party and the state will act in a principled, consistent and well-balanced way.

We have been living in conditions of peace for almost 40 years now. This is a great achievement of the international activity of our Party and country and their Leninist foreign policy.

The CPSU and the Soviet state will continue to do everything in their power to safeguard world peace. And all those who are championing this great and noble cause will always find alongside them the Soviet Union, the Soviet people.

Speech at the Final Stage of the Madrid Review Conference of States Party to the Conference on Security and Co-operation in Europe, 7 September 1983

Esteemed Mr. Chairman,

The Madrid Meeting has come close to its completion. Its weighty results are reflected in the final document.

We regard this document as a balanced and substantive one. It firmly relies on the principles and provisions of the Helsinki Final Act.

The document provides for broadening the range of possibilities for the mutually advantageous co-operation of the states-participants in the meeting in most diverse fields, for their efforts in the interests of strengthening European and universal peace.

In approving this document, the Soviet Union declares that, for its part, it will consistently implement the agreements reached. And this, of course, is what we expect from other participants.

The positive outcome of the Madrid Meeting is a notable achievement of that line in international affairs which aims at dialogue and mutual understanding, at settling problems at the negotiating table.

A "healthy and encouraging sign"—that was how Yuri Andropov described the choice made in Madrid in favour of finding mutually acceptable solutions.

There is no need to go over all the peripetias experienced by the Madrid Meeting in the course of its work.

The main thing is that its participants have been able, by overcoming differences, to achieve an agreement. The realization that attempts to turn away from the road paved in Helsinki lead to blind alleys of confrontation has gained the upper hand. With respect to the results of

293

the Madrid Meeting the following conclusion suggests itself: it is necessary to continue firmly keeping to the road indicated.

This requires, in the first place, a consistent observance of the principles of respect for the sovereignty of states non-interference in their internal affairs, inviolability of their frontiers—in a word, of all the known principles by which the countries represented here have undertaken, under the Final Act, to abide in international affairs.

And one of the important measures contributing to this would be to reflect the above principles, as is provided for in the final document of the meeting, in the legislation of each country—in a manner consistent with its practice and procedures. Now, as before, the Soviet Union is true to these principles. They are reflected in our Constitution—the Fundamental Law of the Soviet State.

Our country is consistently against spreading ideological differences to relations between states. Regrettably, this sort of practice has been resorted to on a large scale, especially of late.

This was not avoided also in Madrid where representatives of certain countries of the West embarked on the path of "psychological war", for it is difficult to describe in any other way the known attempts to turn the meeting into a forum of confrontation rather than talks. And, of course, matters were complicated at such moments, threatening to jeopardize the meeting and the opportunity as such for carrying on the all-European process.

The course and results of the Madrid Meeting have demonstrated with utter clarity once again that attempts at pressure on socialist countries and interference in their internal affairs are hopeless.

On the other hand, the experience accumulated in Madrid confirms that, despite all the differences in their policies and despite all the differences in their assessments of the causes of the present state of international affairs, despite all the tension of the present-day situation in Europe and the world, states with different social systems can reach mutually acceptable accords which benefit all nations and help to clear the skies of European and world politics. And this conclusion ought to be borne in mind for the present and for the future.

The participation of foreign ministers in the final stage of the Madrid Meeting underlines not only the political significance of the achieved results but also the responsible nature of the moment.

The results of the Madrid Meeting are a further confirmation that the reserves of the policy of *détente* are far from being exhausted. The specific steps co-ordinated in Madrid can facilitate its dynamic continuation and development.

This refers, first of all, to the holding of a conference on confidence-building measures and disarmament in Europe, which is to become an important factor of strengthening European and international security. This also includes the decision to mark in a fitting way the 10th anniversary of the signing of the Final Act, another all-European meeting in Vienna in 1986, and a number of other conferences and forums at working levels.

The intention, confirmed in Madrid by the participating countries, to undertake further efforts towards reducing or gradually removing all manner of impediments to the development of trade and to widen economic, scientific and technological links may only be hailed.

On the principled basis defined by the Final Act, measures have also been charted, pertaining to exchanges in the field of culture and education, the spread of information, contacts between people, institutions and organizations, the tackling of humanitarian issues.

One would wish to hope that the success of the Madrid Meeting would provide an example of how, on the basis of taking into account reciprocal interests and showing good will, it is possible to untie complex political knots.

But what has been agreed in Madrid, however, is not sealed off by a hermetic wall from other events in the world and in Europe. And in the first place this, of course, is the planned deployment of new US missiles in a number of European NATO member-countries.

What constitutes now the essence of the problem of safeguarding European and international security?

In the most concise manner it can be expressed like this: this is maintaining the rough military-strategic balance between the Warsaw Treaty and NATO, that has evolved in Europe and on the global scale.

Throughout the recent decades this balance has objectively contributed to preserving peace. Reluctance to take this reality into account, and the desire for military superiority to assure a dominant position in the world leads to whipping up the arms race and to a growing threat of nuclear catastrophe.

The Warsaw Treaty states have repeatedly stated that they do not strive for military superiority themselves but neither will they permit others to break the existing military-strategic parity.

At the same time the Soviet Union, the countries of the Warsaw Treaty do not in any way change their approach of principle: no chance lost, no opportunity unused when it comes to moving away from and preventing the threat of catastrophe for Europe, for the world as a whole. Again and again, they pronounce themselves in favour of a substantial reduction in the nuclear confrontation.

It is still possible to come to an agreement at the talks between the USSR and the USA on nuclear arms limitations in Europe. Without repeating here the well-known Soviet proposals tabled in the course of those negotiations, one ought to lay a special stress on the position recently presented by Yuri Andropov in his answers to questions from the newspaper *Pravda* which received a wide response in the world.

We hope that in Washington they will take a sober view of the situation. A lop-sided approach to talks affecting the security interests of states, calculations built on the desire to obtain a unilateral disarmament from the partner—are unacceptable. Realization of this would also largely contribute to putting the Soviet–American talks on strategic arms limitations and reductions on a constructive track.

The Soviet Union's appeal for an immediate freeze of the nuclear arsenals of all nuclear states, and above all those of the USSR and the USA, fully preserves its topicality. This would create more favourable preconditions for a turn toward a radical improvement of the political atmosphere in the world, and serve as a point of departure for the stopping of the build-up of nuclear arms, their subsequent reduction and eventually complete liquidation.

The Soviet Union has committed itself to not being the first to use nuclear weapons. How the degree of trust between states possessing such weapons would increase if those of them that have not yet done so assumed a similar commitment.

Lately, there has been much talk in the West that reciprocal trust ought to be strengthened. They keep discussing and discussing but they build their military policy on doctrines which do not at all exclude being the first to deal a nuclear strike.

This kind of doctrine, and any concept based on the admissibility of the first use of nuclear weapons, unleashing a nuclear war—in particular the allegedly "limited" one, i.e. in Europe—ought to be subjected to universal condemnation. Nuclear war itself must be condemned unconditionally and for all time as the gravest of crimes that can be perpetrated against mankind.

Militarization of space poses a real threat to peace. Implementation of the new Soviet initiative—the proposal to conclude a treaty banning the use of force in space and from space with respect to Earth—would facilitate the task of preventing this threat.

The Warsaw Treaty countries proposed that the member-states of the North Atlantic alliance and the Warsaw Treaty states conclude a treaty on the non-use of military force and maintaining the relations of peace, a treaty in which all European and other countries of the world could take part. Would it not be a major confidence-building measure in the broadest sense of the word? Would it not meet the aims of the Final Act? This proposal is moving with increasing clarity to the forefront of European and world politics.

Long overdue is the question of making progress toward an agreement at the Vienna talks on mutual armed force and arms reductions in Central Europe. A possibility for this is offered by a draft treaty presented by the socialist countries, which accommodates the legitimate interests of the sides participating in the talks. Success in Vienna depends on whether the Western partners will display the desire to agree on a realistic and mutually acceptable basis.

On our side, there is no lack of readiness for agreements also on other issues of arms limitations and disarmament, requiring solutions.

All these problems and tasks directly affect each of the states—participants in the conference on security and co-operation in Europe, regardless of their size, geographic position, social system, or of whether they possess nuclear weapons or not, are part of a particular military-political grouping or not, are non-aligned or neutral.

And the Final Act points with complete justification to the "interest of all of them in the efforts aimed at reducing military confrontation and facilitating disarmament", to "the need for adopting effective measures in these fields". To contribute, not in word but in deed, to reducing tensions, strengthening the security and developing co-operation in

Europe, to strengthening universal peace—is the duty of all states represented here.

Among the decisions adopted at the Madrid meeting, of special significance, in the general admission, is the agreement to convene a conference on measures to enhance trust and security, and disarmament in Europe. The holding of this conference, including its preparatory meeting to open in October in Helsinki, ought to be approached with all the high degree of responsibility it warrants.

The aim of this conference has been outlined. Its first stage will be devoted to discussing and adopting confidence-building and security measures that will embrace the whole of Europe and the adjoining sea and ocean regions as well as the air space over them. The confidence-building measures already being implemented under the Helsinki Act, have proved their usefulness. Now it is necessary to get down to elaborating such measures in this field that would permit a reduction in the threat of military confrontation in Europe.

It is important that from the very beginning the conference be held in a businesslike manner and fit in with the efforts aimed at erecting a barrier in the way of the arms race in Europe. The conference's success would require contributions by all the participating states.

The Soviet Union has been and remains a resolute champion of respect and protection of human rights. The Great October Socialist Revolution was carried out in the name of freedom of the peoples, in the name of human rights and above all of those of the working people. We take pride in the fact that our country was the first country in the world to assert in its territory genuine equality of people, and human and civil rights which have not only been proclaimed but are actually guaranteed.

In the years of the Second World War the Soviet people displayed heroism unparalleled in history and sustained exceptionally heavy losses to defend its independence, freedom and rights, to save mankind from the threat of fascist enslavement, from the darkness of rightlessness and oppression. The peoples of Europe and of the whole world know and will never forget this.

At the present stage we are tackling big and complex tasks in the process of the improvement of our society, expanding and deepening socialist democracy, and guaranteeing our citizens all socio-economic, political and individual rights and freedoms.

The Soviet people feel legitimate indignation at attempts to slander their way of life and the socialist system. They reject unasked-for advice as to how they should go about their business and what procedures must be established in their own home.

Neither the UN Charter, nor the Final Act or any other recognized international instrument do or can authorize anyone to pose as a kind of an umpire in these questions. Those prepared to co-operate with us on relevant issues on a genuinely humane and honest basis will, as before, find in us a responsive partner.

If, however, they raise their hand against our moral, social and civil values, if in their hostility toward socialism they intentionally engage in fuelling tensions in the world, then these sort of actions have met and will continue to meet with a due rebuff.

Pronouncements are being made from this rostrum about the incident with the South Korean aircraft. The incident—and this is well known—is being deliberately exploited by certain circles in the United States to exacerbate the international situation. They have loosed a wave of slander and shameless insinuations against the USSR and the socialist countries.

We reject all this resolutely and indignantly. The basic question arises: Has anyone the right to violate with impunity foreign borders, the sovereignty of another state? Nobody has such a right. This major provision has been enshrined in the most authoritative documents, in the Charter of the United Nations.

It is now absolutely clear that the South Korean aircraft was enjoying special treatment of the US authorities and their relevant services. It made an incursion of immense distance into Soviet airspace and remained there for a long period of time, overflying our critical strategic facilities.

Why and how did it come to be there? Even that legitimate question is the one that they are trying to evade.

We have already given clarifications about the factual side of the incident, including the statement by the Soviet government which was published yesterday. We have also given our assessment of the criminal actions of those who committed that act against our country.

Since the intruder plane did not obey the order to proceed to a Soviet airfield and attempted to evade, an air defence interceptor carried out the order of the command post to stop the flight. Such actions are in full conformity with the law on the USSR state border which was published. We have expressed regret over the loss of human lives.

We state: Soviet territory, the borders of the Soviet Union are sacred.

No matter who resorts to provocations of that kind, he should know that he will bear the full brunt of responsibility for it.

That criminal act will not be justified either by a dishonest juggling of facts or by false versions donned in the toga of concern for human rights—regardless of the level at which those versions are produced in Washington. Those who today are still giving credence to that falsehood will, no doubt, at long last understand the true aims of this major provocation used by its instigators in the interests of their militaristic policy and of the fuelling of military psychosis.

In the matter of peaceful co-operation our country, the states of the socialist community have given ample proof of good will. It would be worth recalling that the final document of the Madrid meeting represents a synthesis of different positions held by the participants. Some of its provisions have of necessity the nature of a compromise. This compromise, however, is one that does not prejudice anyone's state interests, but is rather the result of what has been possible in the international situation in which the Madrid meeting was held.

We pay tribute to the constructive efforts of other participants, and particularly of the neutral and non-aligned states who have worked hard in elaborating the draft final document.

Both here, in Madrid, and at other international forums and talks, in all the directions of world politics, the Soviet Union is actively working to stop the arms race, to achieve the return onto the road of *détente* and to strengthen peace.

"We strive," Yuri Andropov pointed out, "for a radical improvement of international relations, the strengthening and development of all the good beginnings in these relations."

Esteemed Mr. President!

We would wish to see the hopes generated by the results of the Madrid meeting justified. Our country, for its part, will do all it can to achieve this.

In conclusion, allow me to express appreciation to the people and the government of Spain for the good organization of the Madrid meeting and the hospitality extended to all of us.

INDEX